7/97

AT HOME IN THE LOOP

AT HOME IN

Southern Illinois University Press

Carbondale and Edwardsville

How
Clout and
Community
Built
Chicago's
Dearborn
Park

THE LOOP

LOIS WILLE

Library of Congress Cataloging-in-Publication Data

Wille, Lois.
At home in the loop : how clout and community built
Chicago's Dearborn Park / Lois Wille.
p.   cm.
Includes bibliographical references (p.   ) and index.
1. Dearborn Park (Chicago, Ill.)—History.
2. Chicago (Ill.)—History.   I. Title.
F548.65.D2W55   1997
977.3'11—dc21   96–53100
ISBN 0-8093-2126-2 (alk. paper)   CIP

The paper used in this publication meets the minimum
requirements of American National Standard for Information Sciences—Permanence of Paper for Printed Library
Materials, ANSI Z39.48-1984. ∞

For Wayne, for all the love and joy

CONTENTS

ILLUSTRATIONS

INTRODUCTION

DEARBORN STREET, RUNNING SOUTH FROM THE CHICAGO RIVER IN THE HEART OF THE city's downtown, is the most stunning architectural showcase in America. For a mile and a half it offers up one marvel after another. Rippling bays and curtains of bronze-tinted glass rise to the sky, but don't forget to look down at the sidewalk. There are sculptures by Picasso and Miró. A mosaic wall by Chagall. A flaming red stabile by Calder.

At the start of the promenade, by the river, is the fresh green granite geometry of the Leo Burnett Building. Look south from its coppery arcade, down 11 blocks lined with a century's worth of skyscrapers, and you'll see what appears to be an overgrown toy castle, rosy red with a crenelated clock tower. Once it was a railroad station, linking the 20th Century Limited out of New York with the Santa Fe Chief to California. It's still a conduit, but in a dramatic new role.

The walk to the little station is a visual feast. There's the ornamental Delaware Building, started just months after the Chicago Fire of 1871. The strong, rectangular russet steel of the Daley Civic Center with its matching russet steel Picasso. (A woman's head? An Afghan hound? A harp? It doesn't matter to the children sliding down its front.) The blue-green glass and stainless steel—naturally—of the Inland Steel Building.

The inward sweep of the First National Bank Building, rising 850 feet above its multilevel plazas, fountains, outdoor café, and Marc Chagall's witty mosaic tribute to a great city. The Xerox Centre, 40 elegant stories set back, rounded at the corner, and sheathed in glass to reflect the First National's curves. Ludwig Mies van der Rohe's stylish complex of three federal buildings around a central plaza, with Alexander Calder's red *Flamingo* in brilliant contrast to their dark steel ribs and walls of glass.

Then come a bevy of old beauties from the 1890s: the Marquette, a

National Historic Landmark with bronze reliefs and glittering mosaics depicting the Jesuit priest Jacques Marquette's 17th-century explorations of northern Illinois waterways; the bayed waves of the Monadnock, another landmark; the Gothic-style Fisher, enlivened by fanciful terra-cotta fish, eagles, and salamanders; the Manhattan, pioneer in steel-frame construction. And then, jumping ahead 100 years: the polished red granite Harold Washington Library Center, biggest city library building in the nation, with startling coppery green owls spreading their wings at each corner of the roof.

The path to the station ends with two blocks of eclectic facades known as Printers Row, once a national center of the graphic arts and printing industries. Here the character of the street changes.

There's a festive quality to the refurbished tile mosaics, the terra-cotta trim, the projecting bays. Young trees line the sidewalks. The storefronts tend to be small, lively, and informal: coffee shops, restaurants, a bookstore, dry cleaners, a pet supply store, a beauty salon, a gentrified tavern, a sit-down delicatessen. Three churches and a synagogue share a restored, spiffed-up commercial building.

In the windows above are clues that people live here as well as work here. Masses of houseplants and bookshelves rise under vaulted ceilings. Splashes of color decorate exposed-brick walls. A cat sits on a windowsill. A young couple emerges in running clothes. A woman sits under an umbrella in a small sidewalk café, sharing ice cream with the toddler on her lap.

Finally, here is Dearborn Station, only survivor of Chicago's 19th-century passenger terminals. Walk around the walls of red brick and pink granite; it isn't very big. Or go through it—there's an arcade of little shops and food stands, a scattering of tables with people dividing their attention between newspapers and cappuccino. Suddenly you are transported from the heart of a great city into a peaceful community of green parks and tree-lined walkways. Some of the leafy paths lead through clusters of creamy brick townhouses reminiscent of English mews. Others pass a pair of red-brick apartment towers with graceful bay windows, into courtyard gardens wrapped by terraced buildings with their backyards in the sky.

Ahead are a half dozen interpretations of how to fit good-sized family dwellings into small city spaces. Tall, narrow, brightly colored frame houses with high front porches echo 19th-century Chicago. Red-brick rowhouses look distinguished with their limestone trim and copper window bays. Another brick townhouse complex of warm earthen shades and varying heights has lively accents of teal. Flowers are massed on rooftop gardens and street-level patios. Stately homes with horizontal lines recall Frank Lloyd Wright's turn-of-the-century Prairie houses. Scattered here and there are playgrounds and tennis courts, abundant greenery and inviting benches. People of various shades and ages walk dogs, wash cars, push baby strollers, bring home groceries.

The city is a world away. But turn around: There's Sears Tower, the Board of Trade, First National Bank. Chicago's mighty Loop—its commercial and retail heart—rises close behind you.

This is Dearborn Park, one of the most successful urban renewal efforts in the country, home to a multiracial, multi-ethnic community of 3,500. Its residents talk as if they've discovered a secret village, their own private sanctuary that gives them special entrée to what is good and exhilarating about life in a big city, while shielding them from its dangers and disorder. They say they have created a genuine neighborhood, with a closeness and mutual concern rare today in suburb and city alike. Others—mostly they don't live there—say Dearborn Park is smug as well as snug, keeping the real city at bay with brick walls and wrought-iron fences and a street pattern like a maze. It mixes skin colors and ages and occupations, but income levels start at middle and go up from there.

Still, fans and critics alike agree that Dearborn Park is one of the nicest places to live in any American city, and certainly one of the most unusual. Its origins are equally extraordinary. Twenty-five years ago, this pretty little community at the foot of city skyscrapers was a sooty expanse of unused railroad tracks stretching behind a vacant, forlorn Dearborn Station. On the other side of the station, Printers Row was a dark lane of empty hulks. The bleakness and decay had begun to infect the entire southern portion of the Loop. A small group of business leaders, worried about their own real estate as well as the impact on the city if its central core crumbled, decided to build a neighborhood in that forsaken landscape.

They raised $14 million from Chicago corporations, used it to generate $250 million in housing, and seeded another $1.2 billion in residential and commercial growth in the vicinity. By 1997, the desolate South Loop of 1972 had blossomed into a thriving new town of 14,500. Along the way, the business group had to cope with a decade of upheaval in Chicago's City Hall and an economy ravaged by inflation. Dearborn Park had barely broken ground when the interest rate on construction loans surged to 20 percent and mortgage rates topped 16 percent. Several times, the project was on the verge of going under. "We went through the Perils of Pauline," said Thomas G. Ayers, the utilities executive who headed the effort from its inception to its completion.

Dearborn Park left a formula that other cities can use to turn fallow land into vibrant communities, and without big subsidies. It involves shared investment and shared risk on the part of local businesses and local government. It tempers political and social ideology with practicality and marketability. And it requires the grit and guts and civic spirit that built Dearborn Park.

This is the story of how those elements worked together to build a neighborhood in Chicago's Loop.

AT HOME IN THE LOOP

1

"It Is the Borderland of Hell"

First National Bank Building usually spent a few minutes admiring the lake-front panorama. Water endless as an ocean. Parks left and right as far as eyes could see. A stately cluster of museums. A grand boulevard.

On this March morning in 1970, though, his two guests weren't interested in blue Lake Michigan. It was the blackened landscape below that riveted them.

To the north, Chicago's central business district segued gracefully into old stone mansions and new high-rise apartments. To the west, it was leapfrogging the Chicago River with glass-and-steel office towers. Michigan Avenue and Grant Park had long been a beautiful eastern border. But the men were looking south, where the city's mighty financial center ended in a sorry string of sleazy bars, vacant storefronts, and 600 acres of mostly unused rail yards.

Ayers recalled later that one of them said, "What the hell should we do with those tracks down there? They look so awful."

The pronoun is significant: What should "we" do with them, not "they." The three men in Ayers's office could muster the power and the influence to push Chicago in just about any direction they wanted, so long as they didn't collide with the wishes of the "Man on Five," Richard J. Daley.

After nearly 15 years as mayor of Chicago, Daley controlled every facet of local government from his fifth-floor office in City Hall. He was the single most important influence on state government and on the Illinois delegation 1 in Congress. Senators, judges, Cook County Board members, garbage truck loaders, city Health Department physicians, school janitors, police captains, building inspectors—all got their jobs through routes that led to and from his office. He was more comfortable with labor leaders and politicians than with business chiefs, but he had a cordial and mutually beneficial relationship with them, too. They were in awe of his ability to get things done in a setting foreign to them, and he felt the same way about their accomplishments.

If he also judged them loyal to Chicago, a mystical quality that he valued above all others, then they truly had his respect and his ear. The three men in Ayers's office filled that bill.

Gordon M. Metcalf, 62, was chairman of the board and chief executive officer of Sears, Roebuck and Company, the world's biggest retailer. In the spring of 1970 he was deep into plans for erecting nine tubes sheathed in black aluminum and tinted glass that, bundled together in assorted setbacks, would soar 110 stories into the sky and give Chicago the world's tallest building.

Donald M. Graham, 57, was chairman of the board and chief executive officer of Continental Illinois National Bank and Trust Company of Chicago, the biggest bank in the Midwest, the biggest employer in downtown Chicago, and City Hall's biggest single creditor. It had 6,500 workers and more on the way. Instead of moving its heavy-duty computer and check-processing operations to an island in the Caribbean Sea—the current fad among businesses such as Continental—it was buying an old General Electric Company building in the southwest corner of the downtown area and planned to transform it into a technical center employing about 2,000.

Thomas G. Ayers, 55, was president-on-the-path-to-chairman of Commonwealth Edison Company, the biggest power company in the Midwest and the nation's leading producer of nuclear energy.

All three were star members of the tightly knit Chicago business establishment, about two dozen men who served on each other's corporate boards and sat together on the boards of the city's cultural, educational, and charitable institutions. Most of them lived in the suburbs, but their hearts as well as their wallets had deep roots in Chicago. No other city in the country, they liked to say, could match Chicago in the civic devotion of its executive corps. Daley recognized that and always had a few of them on every city commission and blue-ribbon panel. John H. Perkins, second in command to Graham at Continental Bank, recalled countless 6 A.M. trips downtown from his North Shore suburban home for what his wife called "another of those save-the-city breakfasts."

None of the business leaders worked harder in this civic role than Tom Ayers. His cherubic round face, rosy cheeks, and perpetually cheerful manner were deceptive. Ayers was also tough and driven. The "poor boy from Detroit," as he described himself, was raised by parents who expected all of their five children to help families who were even poorer. He worked his way through the University of Michigan, saved enough to buy his first suit when he was 20, and got a job at Packard Motors when he graduated in 1937. When hard times forced a shutdown at Packard in 1938, Ayers took a bus to Chicago. He found a cheap room in a YMCA hotel a few blocks from the South Loop rail yards and a job with the power company that became Commonwealth Edison. He began by digging ditches and laying pipes, and 26 years later was president of the company.

Ayers sat on a half dozen of the city's most prestigious boards—Sears, for one, and First National Bank of Chicago. He was past president of the Chicago Association of Commerce and Industry, chairman of the board of trustees of Northwestern University, and a powerhouse on the Chicago Symphony Orchestra board. In 1969 he had helped form Chicago United, an interracial alliance of black and white executives looking for ways to improve race relations. Three years before that he had mediated a nasty confrontation over housing discrimination among Dr. Martin Luther King Jr.'s Chicago organization, local political leaders, and the Chicago Real Estate Board. The agreement he forged cracked the area's segregated housing patterns and created the Leadership Council for Metropolitan Open Communities, a watchdog group of investigators and lawyers that became a model for the nation. He still chaired it and considered it his proudest achievement. "You saved the city," Daley told him.

Thomas G. Ayers, leader of Chicago's business and civic establishment. Photo by Austen Field.

Ayers, like his two guests, had a house in the suburbs. But he and his wife, Mary, kept a city apartment just north of the Loop and spent a great deal of time there. He liked to call himself a Chicagoan.

The three, along with other executives, had met that morning to discuss the fall Crusade of Mercy, a fund-raising effort for Chicago-area charitable agencies. Their colleagues already had left when the trio focused on the rail yards. It wasn't just the ugliness so close to their offices that bothered them. They were worried about recent changes in the downtown area, and in the city as a whole.

New data from Commonwealth Edison's research department and the U.S. Bureau of the Census indicated that Chicago's population had fallen from nearly 3.6 million to just over 3.3 million during the 1960s, while the suburban area had exploded with 1 million new residents, to 3.6 million. Like many other big cities, Chicago had experienced a pronounced racial shift: Its black population had grown by 300,000, to about 1.1 million, while the white population had dropped by 570,000. And the city was getting poorer. In 1960, about 1 in 10 received some form of welfare assistance; by 1970, it was close to 1 in 5.

For years Chicago had been losing white middle-class families to the suburbs. New studies showed that black middle-class families also were starting to move out. They didn't have much choice, considering that construction of family-type homes in Chicago had virtually ceased. There was nothing, for example, to match what developer Philip M. Klutznick was doing on the outskirts of the metropolitan area: building entire new towns of affordable houses, such as Park Forest to the south and the four now on his planning boards that would be coordinated with his new regional shopping centers.

Even the famous Loop was exhibiting symptoms that upset Ayers and his companions. The nickname came from the transit tracks built around Chicago's central business district in the 1880s, and it stuck as the district grew beyond the tracks. By 1970 "the Loop" meant an area from the Chicago River on the north to the rail yards on the south—about a mile and a half, or 12 blocks in Chicago's orderly grid street system—and from the lakefront's Grant Park on the east to the river's south branch on the west, about three-fourths of a mile. The Loop had an elegant offshoot sprouting from its northeast corner: the Magnificent Mile, a shopping and commercial strip along North Michigan Avenue that was getting more magnificent by the year.

Based on the construction dollars invested in the Loop in the previous 10 years, worrying about it seemed foolish. Daley, who loved huge building projects and had the clout in Washington to get them financed, had masterminded a new Civic Center, new federal buildings, three new expressways, a mammoth new lakefront convention center, and a new campus of the University of Illinois.

These helped generate a half dozen striking office towers, such as the First National Bank Building, and new residential high-rises for the well-paid young professionals working in the new offices. Two projects were especially notable. Architect Bertrand Goldberg's masterful Marina City opened in 1965—a tightly packed riverfront complex with twin 60-story towers resembling giant corncobs, a 16-story office building, an ice rink, bowling alleys, a food store, restaurants, a marina, spiraled parking garages, a health club, and movie theaters. Its 900 wedge-shaped apartments filled almost overnight. Architect Bruce J. Graham's tapered, muscular John Hancock Center, rising 100 stories above the Magnificent Mile, was finished in 1969. It had Bonwit Teller and other fine shops on its lower levels, offices in the middle, and expensive condominium apartments on top.

Now construction was about to begin on one of the world's biggest mixed-use developments, Illinois Center. Over the next 20 to 30 years, its investors would erect office buildings, apartment buildings, hotels, and a vast underground shopping mall on 83 acres of former Illinois Central Railroad tracks near the river mouth and Lake Michigan at the northeast edge of the Loop.

No American city could match the boom in downtown Chicago in the 1960s, in style or in substance. The unofficial motto of those years seemed to be working: "Don't let Chicago become another Detroit" (or Cleveland, or Philadelphia, or Baltimore, or Atlanta, or whatever city was being pitied at the moment because of its ailing downtown). Daley seethed at the news media and civil rights groups for harping on such embarrassments as the city's bloody riots of 1968 and its massive, increasingly violent, racially isolated public housing projects instead of touting its achievements.

The three men in Ayers's office fully appreciated the good things happening in the Loop. But they knew that much of it had developed a split personality: lively during office hours, deserted after the commuter trains pulled out. The new buildings were part of the problem. They had gobbled up small stores and restaurants and replaced them with stark, granite-and-marble lobbies. Concert goers leaving Orchestra Hall on Michigan Avenue for the commuter stations a mile west passed nothing but empty, dark towers, iron gates over shop doors, and shuttered, lunch-hour-only restaurants.

Jack Cornelius, executive director of the Chicago Central Area Committee, told the *Chicago Daily News* that "our biggest concern is that this will become a five-day-a-week, 10-hour-a-day downtown." When the Central Area Committee worried, Chicago's business establishment worried. The committee was created in 1956 by downtown corporations to enhance the area's physical and cultural environment. True, people had started to move into the downtown area during the 1960s, but they were concentrated on the Loop's northeast fringe—along the river and near the lakefront. There weren't enough of them to have a real impact. And in these smart new high-rise apartments, school-age children were as rare as lawn mowers.

The only residents of the South Loop lived in tiny cubicles in the flophouses and cheap hotels near those empty railroad tracks. Some of them, in fact, lived *on* the empty railroad tracks.

There was another matter. "I'll tell you what's wrong with the Loop," the enormously successful and famously outspoken real estate developer Arthur Rubloff told the *Chicago Daily News*. "It's people's conception of it. And the conception they have about it is one word—black. B-L-A-C-K. Black. We have a racial problem we haven't been able to solve. The ghetto areas have nothing but rotten slum buildings, nothing at all, and businessmen are afraid to move in, so the blacks come downtown for stores and restaurants."

Urbanologists might have explained it more delicately, but Rubloff had a point. Black and Hispanic neighborhoods to the south and west had lost their commercial strips to expressways and urban renewal, and to crime. Increasingly, residents relied on the Loop for shopping and entertainment. The big downtown movie palaces, concentrated in the North Loop near Marshall Field Company's great State Street store, responded with cynicism and stupidity. They stopped booking the best of first-run movies and switched to the violent black exploitation films of the late '60s and early '70s.

Whites began to fade from State Street when the sun went down. Good restaurants folded and big retailers trembled. Young black men in four-inch heels, coats of checkerboard fur and silver lamé, huge Aussie hats and enormous berets with flopping pompons—the Super Fly outfits of the era—promenaded along the sidewalks.

The truth was, they weren't hurting anyone. The worst that happened was noise and litter in the movie houses and paper cups blowing around the sidewalk when morning came. Even so, police cars stepped up their patrols; the crime rate, always low in the Loop, fell further. But, as Jack Cornelius of the Central Area Committee observed, try convincing those white suburbanites of that. This was 1970; the fires and riots following Dr. King's murder were still fresh in people's minds, and in heavily segregated Chicago the presence of exuberant young blacks in the North Loop was unnerving to whites.

The South Loop was different. Nearly everyone felt uncomfortable there in the evenings, blacks as well as whites. In the blocks close to the rail yards, daytime wasn't much better. There, hard-core porn arcades and bookshops, rough bars and sleazy hotels were about the only flourishing businesses. Under the elevated transit tracks a block south of the Board of Trade, muggings and purse snatchings and assorted assaults were on the rise. They weren't nearly as commonplace as the rumors about them, but the impact was the same. People were afraid of the South Loop. Continental Bank, biggest property owner in the area, was nervous about security around the building it had bought for its new technical center; most employees would be women, and most would work at night. Some people thought Sears was crazy to put its new tower, and 5,000 employees, in the South Loop.

Anything bad that was happening in the South Loop was magnified by an old image problem. In Chicago, "North Side" and "South Side" conjured up embedded stereotypes, and not just "white" and "black," though that certainly was part of it. The South Side had political power and blue-collar Catholics and fiercely cohesive communities of ethnic Europeans in miles and miles of bungalows. Mayor Daley was a lifelong resident of Bridgeport on the Southwest Side, as were a scandalously high percentage of the public workers who owed their jobs to his Cook County Democratic Party. The North Side had money and prestige and Protestant professionals and the despised (in City Hall) "lakefront liberals," led by that portion of the affluent Jewish community who did not live in the city's other liberal enclave, Hyde Park and its University of Chicago.

The South Side had Robert Taylor Homes, the nation's biggest public housing development, 4,300 apartments in 28 buildings lined up for two dismal miles along South State Street. The North Side had the nation's biggest lakefront park, beautiful Lincoln. The political and business interests, led by the *Chicago Tribune*, that had plunked the McCormick Place convention center on the South Side lakefront would never have dared commit that desecration on the North Side lakefront.

The South Side had festering slums and crime and drugs and warring gangs, and the North Side did not—or at least that was the perception in 1970. These were gross generalizations and exaggerations, but much of the Chicago area believed them—especially North Siders and suburbanites, who now outnumbered city dwellers.

Yet the South Side, at least the part close to the lakefront, had some of the world's finest museums and illustrious institutions, including the University of Chicago, the Illinois Institute of Technology, the Field Museum of Natural History, the John G. Shedd Aquarium, the Adler Planetarium, the Museum of Science and Industry, Michael Reese Hospital, and Mercy Hospital.

In the 1870s, the city's elite built imposing mansions along Prairie Avenue on the Near South Side. The original Marshall Field was a South Sider, as were George M. Pullman of Pullman railcars and Philip D. Armour of the meatpacking empire. By the early 1900s, 40 of the 60 members of the exclusive Commercial Club lived in a five-block area along Prairie and adjoining Calumet Avenue. A small community of affluent blacks lived nearby. The rich whites began to leave in the 1920s, when rooming houses sprouted to accommodate waves of European immigrants. Before long, nearly every residence had been carved up into tiny flats. And then carved up again in the 1940s, when the great influx of southern blacks who moved to Chicago to work in its factories and steel mills and stockyards were barred from living in other parts of the city. By the end of World War II, much of the Near South Side was dilapidated tenements.

Just 20 years later, the area had undergone one of the most dramatic transformations in any American city. The driving force behind it was a Chicago real estate developer, manager, and mortgage banker who had been born on Prairie Avenue and had an abiding love for the South Side: Ferdinand Kramer.

In the late 1940s, Chicago's new Land Clearance Commission, prodded by Michael Reese Hospital and the Illinois Institute of Technology, used its federal money to demolish a vast tract of the slums. Kramer persuaded New York Life Insurance Company to develop a major portion of it, 70 acres near the lakefront. The city sold the land for $3.4 million, about one-fifth of its acquisition and clearance costs. Beginning in 1950, New York Life built 10 high-rise apartment buildings with 2,033 units, all rental, and a small shopping center. The concept followed recommendations of a planning team hired by Michael Reese and inspired by the Swiss-born French architect Le Corbusier and his towers-in-a-park model cities. The pristine buildings, widely spaced in expanses of greenery, covered only 9 percent of the land. The city's familiar street grid was abandoned.

The new Lake Meadows apartments were efficient and affordable, with magnificent lake views. They filled as fast as New York Life could put them up and Ferd Kramer could lease them. But, to his great disappointment, the early tenants were overwhelmingly black. He wanted a permanently integrated community, not the traditional Chicago version, in which "integration" was that brief period between the arrival of the first blacks and the flight of the last whites.

With Lake Meadows well under way, Kramer formed a new corporation to build his own renewal project on an adjacent tract of the cleared land to the north. His five Prairie Shores buildings, begun in 1958 and completed in 1962, added 1,677 rental apartments. This time, using aggressive marketing targeted to whites and tenant-acceptance policies that favored whites, Kramer was able to make Prairie Shores largely white. The area as a whole came close to a 50–50 breakdown, and Kramer believed he had achieved his goal: a beautiful, clean, livable neighborhood that would remain racially integrated. Eventually, he hoped, the new South Side would spread and be knitted to the Loop just as seamlessly as the North Side.

But how to overcome that colossal dead end of railroad tracks and switching yards?

Actually, it had once been a neighborhood of sorts. German and Irish immigrants who came to the infant city in the 1830s and 1840s to dig a shipping canal built a shantytown of wood cottages there. Italian immigrants followed. Next, freed and escaped slaves joined this early version of ethnic and racial diversity. But by the late 1850s, the little community looked so disreputable that Chicago's 6-foot 6-inch, 300-pound, terrible-tempered Mayor "Long John" Wentworth threatened to tear down these "dirtiest, vilest, most-rickety, one-sided, leaning forward, propped up, tumbled-down, sinking fast, low-roofed and most miserable shanties."

He was soon distracted by a more evil settlement north of the river mouth, where, the *Chicago Tribune* reported, "beastly sensuality" reigned. Mayor Wentworth smashed that one instead. Even the great Chicago Fire of 1871 spared the shantytown, though the blaze started just across the river from it and leveled almost 17,500 buildings to the north. The reprieve didn't last long. Three years later a smaller fire destroyed the shanties.

Throughout the late 1800s, one new railroad line after another steamed into the rapidly growing city. Businessmen didn't want them to disrupt their newly rebuilt downtown, so the depots lined up on the outskirts. Four were built on the Loop's south edge within less than a mile of each other: Dearborn Station in 1885, Grand Central in 1890, Central Station east of Michigan Avenue in 1893, and LaSalle in 1903. The cluster of stations brought thousands of jobs to the area, but, as historians Perry R. Duis and Glen E. Holt wrote in *Chicago* magazine, the heavy passenger traffic also "attracted houses of prostitution, gambling rooms and saloons. Of all Chicago's vice districts, the largest was . . . at the front door of the terminals and within walking distance of the major hotels."

By the early 1900s, the district had outgrown its quarters and moved south of the stations. "Vice has thrown off its masks and flaunts its hideousness in our faces," wrote one 1912 observer, cited by Duis and Holt. "It is the borderland of hell."

What bothered the city's business leaders more than vice being flaunted in their faces was that the rail yards blocked expansion of the Loop to the south. In 1913 the City Council recommended consolidation of the stations, the first of about 30 such plans offered by government and civic groups over the next 50 years. The railroads dismissed them all as frivolous or too expensive.

Early in his second term, Mayor Richard J. Daley sought to build a University of Illinois campus on the rail yards to replace the cramped, two-year branch on Chicago's Navy Pier. But he grew impatient with the railroads' haggling over prices and red tape, and ripped up part of an old Italian and Greek neighborhood about a mile and a half southwest of the Loop for the new campus. It was a convenient location for students and spurred vigorous growth in the remaining neighborhood, but the cries of betrayal from the dislocated families haunted the mayor. Thirty years later, his son Richard M. Daley, the new Man on Five, said it was the toughest decision of his father's long political career.

After the collapse of plans to put a university in the South Loop, executives from the Chicago Board of Trade and Continental Bank tried to enlist city support for clearing out the decay and replacing it with new office, residential, and entertainment towers. They were afraid, one of them said, that the "flophouses, taverns, stumbling drunks, and panhandlers" would topple Chicago's financial strongholds. But in the absence of a city-approved plan for the central area and broad corporate interest, their proposals stagnated.

By the late 1960s, the plunge in passenger rail travel and the growth of transcontinental trucking accomplished what decades of civic efforts could not. In 1969, Grand Central and LaSalle stations closed. By 1970, Dearborn and Central stations were winding down, with only months to go.

The decline of the rail industry hurt the businesses that had grown up around it. In the South Loop, the chief casualty was the printing industry concentrated around Dearborn Station. The location had been ideal; paper and other supplies arrived through the terminal, and finished publications left from it. Skilled German, Italian, and Polish immigrants got off the trains from New York and walked a few steps up Dearborn Street into jobs as typesetters, engravers, mapmakers, and bookbinders. As the industry thrived, owners commissioned new buildings from the talented architects who had settled in Chicago to help rebuild it after the 1871 fire. The district became a showcase for a city already famous for its architecture.

The collapse of the rail industry during the 1950s and 1960s coincided with the introduction of technologies that made the printing establishments obsolete. They moved to new plants elsewhere, and the great Dearborn Street buildings emptied out. So, in addition to the vast stretches of abandoned rail yards and the porn-and-sleaze strip slithering toward the financial district, the South Loop by 1970 was burdened with blocks of vacant and vandalized buildings.

Tom Ayers, Donald Graham, and Gordon Metcalf knew it was high time to remove the blackened carcass of rail yards from the South Loop, and they knew downtown Chicago needed an infusion of around-the-clock life and the added sense of security that would go with it.

How best to put the two together?

Who owned all this land? Was it for sale? At what price?

How could they generate development there? And what should that development be? Before they left Ayers's office that morning, they resolved to seek the answers from another member of their circle, James C. Downs Jr. He was chairman of the Chicago-based Real Estate Research Corporation, one of the nation's leading real estate consulting firms. He was a leader of the Chicago Central Area Committee, on the ladder to becoming its president. And he enjoyed another invaluable asset: the trust of Richard J. Daley.

They didn't expect Jim Downs to undertake this assignment for nothing, so they agreed to split his charges three ways.

Nine months later they got a bill for $5,546.39, and many of the answers they sought.

2

"The First Step . . . a Meeting with the Mayor"

JIM DOWNS WAS POSITIVELY ECSTATIC ABOUT THE POTENTIAL OF THE SOUTH LOOP RAIL yards. "The huge scale and unique location . . . provide development opportunities without parallel in Chicago or most anywhere else," he wrote in his report. If the vacant fields and largely empty commercial buildings around the yards were included, the area was as big as the entire existing central business district.

The aerial photographs and maps he attached showed a thick band of tracks, about three-fourths of a mile wide, converging on the South Loop railroad stations from Cermak Road, two miles to the south. A branch of the Chicago River flowed through the western portion of the site. South State Street, just two blocks from the lakefront's Grant Park, formed the eastern border.

The riverbanks were littered with rubble and trash, but, as Downs noted, they had great recreational possibilities. Lake Michigan and the wonderful cluster of museums in Grant Park were within an easy walk of much of the site. So were the Loop's financial district and the big State Street stores. Access to all of the city's expressways and its rapid transit system was excellent.

The site was suitable for housing, retail and commercial buildings, hotels, or light industry, he said—maybe all of the above. But the development would require "tremendous cooperative effort by numerous participants over many years," Downs wrote. They would have to be "of the highest caliber," able to "commit substantial resources in manpower, money and influence." First, though, a catalyst was needed, a leadership core that could muster

those resources from government as well as the private sector, that could mo-
tivate everyone involved and keep them on track. Downs suggested an ideal
catalytic entity: the threesome who had commissioned his report, and the
powerful corporations they headed.

Tom Ayers, Donald Graham, and Gordon Metcalf were prepared to take
on major roles in getting something started, but they had no intention of running a mammoth development project by themselves. They had demanding
jobs. The concept of a business-led South Loop development effort appealed
to them, but only if they could add a dozen or so executives like themselves to
their ranks. Property acquisition clearly was going to be a headache. Downs
had determined that 13 railroad companies owned pieces of the land, singly
or in combination with each other. Most of it was no longer in use, but commuter trains from southern suburbs still ran on choice parcels near the river.
The city had used urban renewal powers to acquire the property for Ferd
Kramer's big South Side renewal projects, but it had no legal right to do that
with railroad land—used or unused.

And which of all the possible uses Jim Downs listed should have top
priority?

Donald Graham preferred light industry, to compete with the parklike
suburban settings that were siphoning off so many of the city's manufac-
turing jobs. All three thought the riverfront was the prime property, perhaps
for resort hotels and apartment buildings with marinas, restaurants, and a
promenade.

Jim Downs had a preference of his own. He reminded the three that "the
economic and social vitality of the Loop" was critical to their corporations,
"both from the standpoint of financial commitments as well as concern in the
public interest. . . .

"While Chicago's Loop is still strong and continues to grow as a center
of office employment, danger signs are appearing. Most Loop streets are deserted after 6 P.M., and there is growing fear of walking them at night." On
three sides the downtown was expanding with healthy development. "It is,
therefore, only on the southern flank where the Loop needs protection."

The best way to secure that protection, he said, was to build a neighborhood, beginning on the land closest to the Loop from State Street to the river.
He proposed that his firm prepare a housing development plan, employing
traffic consultants, site planners, market analysts, and other specialists, and
draw up financial models. Meanwhile, his three clients should create a deci-
sion-making structure, develop a relationship with city officials, and gain control of key land parcels. His suggested fee was $8,000 to $10,000 a month, plus
expenses, to continue through the implementation.

The three executives didn't want to make that kind of commitment; not yet. But now they had their focus. Housing was what the South Loop needed. And the more they talked about it, the more enthusiastic they got about creating a different kind of urban renewal project, one conceived and directed by corporate committee. As Downs said, it would be in the interests of their companies as well as a contribution to the health of the entire city.

It was premature, though, to start fund-raising in the business community. First, they needed a set of goals and concepts to present in corporate boardrooms. And they wanted to formulate it among themselves rather than spend money to have Downs's staff do it.

The first order of business was to expand their little group. They sent the Downs report to two other Chicago executives they knew well, men with superb credentials in housing development. One was Ferd Kramer, 69, mastermind of Lake Meadows and Prairie Shores and head of Draper & Kramer, one of the nation's leading real estate brokerage and mortgage-financing firms. Two years earlier Draper & Kramer had bought Lake Meadows from New York Life. It now owned and managed both of the big South Side renewal efforts, as well as residential and office buildings in other parts of Chicago and throughout the country.

The other was Phil Klutznick, who would turn 65 in a year and was getting ready to retire as chairman of Urban Investment and Development Company. A man of prodigious energies and intellect, he had built some of America's first suburban shopping centers in between his years as U.S. ambassador to the United Nations Economic and Social Council and president of B'nai B'rith International. He was on the path to becoming president of the World Jewish Congress, deeply immersed in Middle Eastern affairs, yet still working with his son Thomas on the development of new towns around their shopping centers. He had recently sold Urban to Aetna Life and Casualty Company, but he retained control. The deal was arranged by his old friend Ferd Kramer, who had secured Klutznick's first shopping-center development contract and arranged financing for most of them.

Klutznick plunged into the Downs report with his customary zeal, drafting a four-page, single-spaced memorandum on South Loop development for Ayers to circulate among his group.

Downs was absolutely right, he said. The only way the business districts of America's major cities could be saved was by inducing people to live nearby. "They not only provide consuming power which downtown stores can use," he wrote, "but they also provide personnel for the many offices and they increase the security."

Klutznick wanted the housing to be primarily for families, racially integrated, and tailored to a broad income range. The new apartment towers at the north end of the Loop didn't fit any of these criteria, though they had a sprinkling of well-off blacks. Tom Ayers already had made integration a top priority. He was meeting every few weeks with the new, interracial Chicago United group to seek advice on fostering stable, harmonious integration. Two eminent scholars from the University of Chicago frequently attended: the black historian John Hope Franklin and the white sociologist Morris Janowitz. So did Edwin "Bill" Berry, director of the Chicago Urban League, and two other blacks trusted and respected by white corporate leaders: George E. Johnson, president of Johnson Products Company, manufacturer of grooming and beauty aids, and Ernest T. Collins, president of Seaway National Bank of Chicago. The young crop of black civil rights leaders, such as the Rev. Jesse L. Jackson, occasionally were invited to address the group, but, unlike the black CEOs, they were not part of the club.

Chicago United was enthusiastic about the prospect of a model integrated community in this city of vast one-race neighborhoods. Three principles emerged: Good public schools were essential; so was a sense of security; and beware of the "tipping point," the percentage of blacks that must not be exceeded in order to keep whites in the neighborhood. No one knew exactly what this was; perhaps 20 percent black, surely no more than 40 percent. But there was general agreement that such a figure did exist, and that Chicago's South and West sides had plenty of living, rancorous proof.

Another factor was not so clear-cut. Phil Klutznick, who had a long background in federal public housing programs, thought the group needed every available federal, state, and local subsidy; the only way to attract families to the seedy South Loop was to offer the best buy in the metropolitan area. Ferd Kramer also had a long background in government housing programs, but he came away with the opposite view. He agreed that government should pay for streets and sewers and other basic infrastructure, but he was wary of housing subsidies. They came with too many restrictions and delays.

But those decisions were still far in the future. For now, in one of his many memos to Ayers and the others, Klutznick volunteered the services of his planning staff at Urban "to bring the project to a definitive stage where it would justify major investment."

And if we are really serious about doing this, he wrote, we've got to begin where any big Chicago undertaking must begin: "The first step would be a meeting with the Mayor."

Donald Graham set up the appointment. He, Tom Ayers, and Gordon Metcalf were ushered into Daley's office the afternoon of January 31, 1972. It was just an informal chat, as Tom Ayers recalled it. "We had commissioned this little study, now we had it, and we thought we had a good idea. We thought we could get the business community to put up some money. It was important that he hear about it from us first—who was backing it, what we were looking at. We told him we hadn't any more than just the idea at this point, but we proposed to pursue it. And he encouraged the hell out of it."

No wonder. This was not a happy time for the mayor. Ten months earlier he had won an unprecedented fifth term, coasting to an easy victory over Richard Friedman, a liberal young Democrat-turned-Republican. But the years of civil rights protests, the stirrings of independence among the usually docile black faction of his Cook County Democratic Party, and the constant scoldings of white liberals were taking a toll. His political lieutenants were telling him that his candidates for governor and Cook County prosecutor were going to lose in the March Democratic primary. That would be devastating. He was furious about the national media attention on accusations of brutal treatment of blacks by his police department. And even more furious at a federal court order directing the Chicago Housing Authority to put public housing in white neighborhoods instead of stuffing all of it into black communities. Public housing in Chicago would be built only where the people of Chicago want it to be built, the mayor replied.

Now three of his city's most distinguished citizens were in his office with an idea that sounded heaven-sent. They wanted to be a catalyst for a new community on the barren rail yards south of the Loop. They wanted to halt the deterioration of the downtown area, strengthen its property values, and add to the city's tax base. They wanted the new community to be, as Donald Graham told him, "completely integrated, both economically and racially, from the subsidized level to the semi-luxury level." No families would have to be relocated to clear the land; there would be no painful uprising of a loyal, Democratic, blue-collar community, as when he tore up the Near West Side for the University of Illinois.

At the moment, the three told him, they wanted only one thing from him. Donald Graham repeated it in a follow-up letter: "Such an endeavor is totally impossible without the full and complete participation of the public institutions that are concerned. . . . We believe that the greatest help we could secure at this time is to have your personal intercession with the railroad companies involved so they may understand the business interests concerned are prepared to do everything within reason provided that the land itself may be secured at reasonable prices."

Daley told them he thought their idea was wonderful. He would help; he would talk to the railroad people. But first they should prepare more specific plans and make a presentation to him and his commissioner of development and planning, Lewis G. Hill.

Donald Graham provided space and clerical help in the Continental Bank Building, and the work began. Tom Ayers had emerged as the leading figure, the face and voice of the effort to the city's business and civic establishment. Graham faded out as an active participant and sent John Perkins, his designated successor at Continental. Perkins had a community-service résumé that almost rivaled Ayers's. They sat together on the boards of Northwestern University and the Chicago Symphony Orchestra. Perkins brought along Charles F. Willson, the director of area development for Continental, a position that had enabled him to develop excellent relationships in City Hall. Gordon Metcalf, chairman of Sears, also named a substitute: Warren G. Skoning, his vice president for real estate and president of Sears's Homart Development Company. Phil Klutznick and Ferd Kramer were regulars at the planning sessions.

Klutznick assumed the role of conceptualizer. With the help of his staff at Urban, he laid out a plan to give the mayor and Lew Hill:

■ The city or a state agency should sell tax-free revenue bonds to finance the purchase of the railroad land east of the river, or at least about half of it—perhaps 300 acres. He estimated an average price of $6 a square foot, a total of almost $80 million. The government entity would then lease the land to a corporation formed by the business leaders. Rental and sales income from the new housing would pay the debt on the bonds; enough should be left over to repay some of the city's expenses for streets, sewers, and other infrastructure.

■ The mayor should assign a task force of all the relevant city officials to work with the business executives and Klutznick's planning team from Urban. The mayor should also involve the Chicago Park District and the Chicago Board of Education. Under Illinois law these were separate taxing bodies independent of City Hall, but in practice the mayor controlled them. Good public schools were absolutely essential to attracting middle-income families.

■ The mayor should secure a written commitment from the Chicago City Council, the Park District, and the Board of Education assuring that they would provide infrastructure and public amenities.

■ The business group and the mayor should seek maximum state and federal aid to limit the cost to the city and to private investors and to keep housing prices down.

■ Once there was assurance that the city or a state agency would buy the land and install the necessary infrastructure, the business group would form a limited-dividend corporation that would raise capital and develop a portion of the land. This would stimulate participation by other developers. A corporation restricting investors to earnings of 6 or 6.5 percent was preferable to a nonprofit corporation, which would smack of charity to the business community. It was also preferable to unlimited earnings, which often came to 20 percent or more in the development industry and would provoke howls about rich insiders using tax money to fatten their fortunes.

Klutznick's agenda was efficient and logical, but his request for a commitment in writing was not the way Daley did business. In his City Hall, deals were sealed with a shake of his hand. Even wage settlements with city workers were finalized with a mayoral handshake, not a union contract. Over the years, this handshake had proved at least as reliable as any ordinance or written agreement. It also gave the mayor a flexible time span, if he needed it, and opportunities to apply a little pressure here and there for any modifications he might want.

The mayor assembled his key department heads for a presentation by Tom Ayers and Phil Klutznick on May 23, 1972. He listened politely to their plan and said again that middle-class families living in the downtown area was a wonderful idea, wonderful for the city. But he promised nothing, except that at some point he would talk to the railroads. It would be preferable, though, if Ayers and company made the initial contacts and gave the railroads some preliminary plans to look at. "I had the feeling," Tom Ayers recalled, "that the mayor had no stomach for the city owning the land."

Nor did Daley commit himself to paying for the infrastructure.

The next day, Phil Klutznick wrote to Lew Hill, urging him to meet with the business group "to determine a workable basis for the sharing of costs between the developer and public authorities." A miscalculation. Lew Hill was a shrewd and effective commissioner of development and planning, close to Daley; but he never would have carried on such negotiations without Daley's explicit instructions, nor would he even propose them to the mayor.

Klutznick tried another route to city action on land acquisition. He invited Alderman Thomas E. Keane, Daley's most powerful political ally and his floor leader in the City Council, to lunch. "As you know, he is generally conversant with all of the land acquisition activities and some of the problems that have emerged from the city involvements," Klutznick wrote in a memo the next day. (That was putting it delicately. A year later Keane was indicted and eventually convicted and sentenced to five years in prison on federal conspiracy charges. He was accused of using his City Council powers to grab title to tax-delinquent property that he sold at huge profits.)

The South Loop project was realistic only if the city acquired the land and leased it to a corporation he and his colleagues would form, Klutznick told Keane. Keane saw the possibilities immediately. The city, with its top-of-the-line credit rating, could sell 40-year revenue bonds at a rate of 6.5 percent or so, he said, buy the land, lease some of it for 8 percent to the new corporation, and sell the rest to the Board of Education for a school, the Park District for parks, and private interests for commercial or industrial development.

Klutznick reported that Keane told him "it would be an attractive transaction for the city." But even the wily Tom Keane, second-most-powerful person in City Hall, treated the mayor with extreme caution. He said he would not bring up the subject with Daley, but if Daley happened to ask his opinion, he would tell him he liked the idea.

That left up in the air the matters of land acquisition and who would pay for what infrastructure. Some progress was made, though, that spring of 1972. Jim Downs had become president of the Chicago Central Area Committee, the organization of influential downtown businesses. For months he had been talking to senior partners at Skidmore, Owings & Merrill, the nation's largest architectural firm and a major force in the Chicago establishment, about replicating what the Commercial Club of Chicago had done 60 years earlier when it sponsored architect Daniel Burnham's famed plan that laid out the city's lakefront parks, boulevards, even the double-deck Wacker Drive along the river. Over the past decade, City Hall planners had produced a series of development plans for Chicago neighborhoods but had not done anything with the downtown. Downs wanted the Central Area Committee to fill that gap. A new town in the South Loop would, of course, be a star feature of the plan, and he thought the resulting hoopla could be the ideal launching pad for a fund-raising drive among business leaders.

Downs had no trouble selling his idea. His fellow leaders of the Central Area Committee included his fellow South Loop planners Tom Ayers, John Perkins, and Warren Skoning. Downs talked to his old friend the mayor, who gave his blessing and offered the cooperation of Lew Hill and the city planning staff. For Daley and Hill, it was the solution to a sensitive problem. They would get an up-to-date downtown development plan, which they recognized Chicago needed. It would come with the built-in support of the business, civic, and architectural interests represented by the Central Area Committee. And they wouldn't have to pay for it. That was important. In the current mood, it would be a major political blunder for the city government to invest money and energy in downtown planning when there was so much to be done in low-income, minority neighborhoods.

The Central Area Committee raised $375,000 from its members and

hired Skidmore to prepare the plan. There never was any doubt about who
would get that contract. Skidmore had worked on all of the city's major planning efforts for 16 years, often at no fee; the payment frequently came later, of
course, when the city or private developers carried out some of the Skidmore
recommendations. Skidmore's senior partner, William E. Hartmann, sat on
the Central Area Committee's board and was its resident artist-intellectual, a
celebrity in Chicago's cultural circles as well as its business and political establishments. Six years earlier he had persuaded his friend Pablo Picasso to
design a sculpture for the plaza of Chicago's new Civic Center. Picasso gave
Hartmann a model and refused to take any money for it. That was astonishing enough, but then Hartmann accomplished something at least as remarkable. He persuaded another friend, Richard J. Daley, to accept the enigmatic
thing.

When United States Steel Corporation finished the 50-foot, 162-ton Picasso creation, Hartmann persuaded still other friends at Chicago foundations and charitable trusts to pick up the $300,000 bill. Now he was busy
gathering more treasures for the sculpture promenade shaping up along
Dearborn Street.

Another key Skidmore partner, Bruce Graham, was the lead architect of
the John Hancock Center and the forthcoming Sears Tower. He was Skid-

Bruce Graham,
Skidmore's chief
designer and pro-
moter. Photo by
Stuart-Rodgers-
Reilly, copyright
1988.

more's chief designer and most effective pro-
moter, responsible for securing many of the contracts that had made the firm the leading creator
of skyscrapers in Chicago and, increasingly, in
Europe and the Middle East. Skidmore had designed Ferd Kramer's Lake Meadows buildings
and the geometric concrete shapes that formed
the new campus of the University of Illinois at
Chicago.

Once the Skidmore architects and planners
had signed on to develop a plan for the Central
Area Committee, it was only natural that they
would also do the site plans and models for the
new town in the South Loop and become major
players on the South Loop team. To one Chicago
architect, however, Skidmore's new role was a
crushing disappointment.

Bertrand Goldberg, fresh from his Marina
City triumph on the North Loop riverfront, had
drawn plans for a much bigger development along

the south branch of the Chicago River. He called it River City. His hoped-for site was part of the very same railroad land that the business group wanted to acquire. Goldberg already had models in his Marina City office: triads of round, 70-story towers, each one with 1,000 apartments, joined at three levels and surrounded by pools and gardens. The towers would have their own schools, shops, offices, community rooms—even their own minigovernments. He wanted the complex to accommodate poor and rich and anyone in between and have "a kind of unspoken sense of democracy."

River City would be much more densely populated than anything Chicago had seen before, because Goldberg believed density was the key to a vibrant urban neighborhood. Only if people of mixed backgrounds and incomes lived in proximity could they all enjoy such blessings as good security, good schools, good transportation, and, above all, a sense of community. He planned on 15,000 apartments on 30 acres, or 500 units an acre. And that was just Phase One.

He had discussed his ideas often with J. Harris Ward, the chairman of Commonwealth Edison, who had grown close to him during the planning of the all-electric Marina City and had rented an apartment there. As Goldberg remembered those days, Ward was enthusiastic about another, bigger, all-electric development and talked about securing financial backing from Commonwealth Edison and other major Chicago corporations.

Goldberg had heard about the Ayers-Klutznick-Kramer plan. As he saw it, they were taking his idea—a new town in the South Loop—with his hoped-for benefactor, Commonwealth Edison, and hiring another architect. To him, Bill Hartmann and Bruce Graham and the entire Skidmore firm were elitist insiders, the pets of social Chicago. He was a lone, iconoclastic, and infinitely more creative outsider. It was too late to complain to Ward, however. The Edison chairman was ill and would soon retire, turning his job over to Tom Ayers.

Goldberg did talk to Ayers about River City, and he later recalled that "Tom was never anything other than polite and interested. But Tom was not a real estate developer, and Tom was not a real estate philosopher, and whatever else Tom was, he wanted to have some degree of financial security and development security, and I was not that image for Tom. So he went to Skidmore, and to Ferd Kramer and Phil Klutznick."

But Goldberg had no intention of shelving his models and his vision. He shopped around for financial partners and arranged talks with Chesapeake & Ohio Railroad, which through its subsidiary Baltimore & Ohio owned land along the east bank of the river.

Meanwhile, a joint planning team from Skidmore and from Klutznick's firm, Urban, prepared its own model to show to the mayor and his staff and, as the mayor had advised, to the railroads. Like the Goldberg plan, it was dramatic and futuristic. Ten superblocks, each with 9 to 16 acres and 2,000 to 3,000 dwellings, blanketed the northern portion of the rail yards. Half of the residences were stacked, stepped-back townhouses, with the roof of one forming the patio of another. Half were in soaring residential towers that sat on broad, eight-story bases containing parking garages, schools, transit stations, shops, glassed-in gardens, community rooms, and—at the fifth level—

Architects' model of a densely packed South Loop residential community, in foreground, shown to Mayor Richard J. Daley by business leaders in 1972. Courtesy Skidmore, Owings & Merrill.

enclosed walkways to the terraced townhouses. A little electric train and commuter riverboats ran back and forth into the Loop. Eventually, more superblocks would spread over the south half of the tracks.

In July, Tom Ayers, Ferd Kramer, and their architects Bill Hartmann and Bruce Graham made the first presentation to railroad executives. They met with John Hanifin and Jack Ford, representing Baltimore & Ohio and its parent, Chesapeake & Ohio. Hartmann and Graham showed their model. Ayers said they had the backing of the mayor and excellent access to financing and civic support. The railroad would be favorably disposed toward working with such a distinguished group, Hanifin told them, but they must understand that he was under pressure. He had been approached by developers who were ready to acquire portions of the property immediately, and he had responsibilities to his shareholders.

That must be Goldberg, the Chicagoans thought. They asked Hanifin to wait six months before selling, and he agreed.

They met next with Lee Champion, chairman of the Real Estate Reorganization Board of the bankrupt Penn Central, which had considerable land just west of the Baltimore & Ohio property. He liked their ideas and their credentials, he said, but he could accept nothing less than fair market value, which would be $10 a square foot. Could their project generate enough revenue to manage that? The Chicagoans were shaken. That was almost 70 percent higher than their estimates.

Before their next session with Daley and Lew Hill, Phil Klutznick's staff at Urban prepared a "South Loop Scenario" that, they hoped, would lay out clear and acceptable roles for the city and for private backers. The venture would be impossible, the report said, without government's authority and resources working in partnership with private entrepreneurial know-how and persistence.

The city's responsibilities, according to the scenario: Assure acquisition of land at a fair price. Create appropriate zoning regulations. Provide water, sewers, roads, transportation, schools, recreation, and public health services. Use available federal and state funds to help pay for these services.

The private responsibilities: Create a limited-dividend corporation with a 6.5 percent ceiling on any return to investors. Commonwealth Edison, Continental Bank, and Sears already were committed to investing, and others surely would join once "the degree and nature of [government] participation has been clarified."

The plan: Construct 25,000 dwelling units on 250 acres—dense, but much less so than the Goldberg plan. The city would sell $80 million in revenue bonds at 6 percent interest to buy 300 acres; it would then sell 50 of these acres for schools, recreation, limited light industry, and commercial ventures—making a profit on the industrial and commercial sales. The limited-dividend corporation would pay the city $6.25 million a year in rent for the land earmarked for housing, $2 million more than necessary to finance the city's debt on its bonds. To earn that $6.25 million, the corporation would sell the 25,000 units of housing for an average of $26,000 each, $3,000 more than construction and overhead costs; rentals would average $300 a month, about 10 percent over costs.

To swing this, the business group would raise $15 million to $17.5 million in capital and sell or rent 1,500 units a year.

The scenario was circulated among Ayers and his colleagues early in September. It was not well received. The densely packed superblocks didn't fit Ayers's idea of family housing, and Ferd Kramer thought they would be difficult to market. His sales staff at Draper & Kramer ridiculed one building that was 700 feet long. Who would want to live in that? Klutznick himself grumbled that some of the designs looked as if they had originated in Moscow.

There were other problems with the scenario. The units were too tiny, compared with the suburban homes that would be the competition. A townhouse or apartment of 1,000 square feet, for example, was supposed to hold three bedrooms. Annual sales and rentals of 1,500 were breathtakingly optimistic, considering that the site had such an unsavory reputation. And construction prices were creeping up; the projected $20 a square foot already was outdated.

Even so, Jim Downs, who had done the South Loop study for Ayers and his colleagues 20 months earlier, took the scenario to City Hall and reviewed it with Daley and Lew Hill. He reported that they were enthusiastic. But neither one, from what they told others, liked the density. As to the financial scenario, Daley told Downs there was just one little problem. His legal advisers thought Illinois law would not permit the city to lease land for private development.

Whoops. Daley threw this out almost as an aside. Klutznick didn't think it was a significant issue; the city should be able to do it, he said, with home-rule powers granted in the new 1970 Illinois Constitution. If not, Daley could get the law changed. But when Ayers heard about the remark he was convinced it confirmed what he already had sensed. "The mayor felt that this was putting too much of a burden on a roll of the dice," Ayers said later. "Maybe the whole thing collapses, and there's the city with all these bonds. Some of our people argued that the city would gain control of a deteriorating area, and so on. But [Daley] wouldn't buy that."

It dawned on Ayers and his group that they might have to buy the land themselves. Warren Skoning of Sears urged that they find the resources to acquire a site along the river as soon as possible. Jim Downs said they needed at least enough land for a demonstration project to have credibility when they started fund-raising in the business community. And that, they agreed, should coincide with the release of the central-area plan the Skidmore firm was preparing.

It already had a name: Chicago 21, for the 21st century. By late 1972, Bill Hartmann and his crew were showing models and drawings to selected business, civic, and professional groups around town. They met regularly with other prominent architects and planners, with bankers and developers, with top city officials. University of Chicago sociologist Morris Janowitz was hired as a consultant and discussed his theories on the "recentralization" of cities, led by transportation-weary suburban commuters and a young generation seeking urban lifestyles. "The question is how quickly it will happen, and under whose auspices," he told his fellow planners. "Will it be a collection of high-rise mausoleums or a series of vital communities fit for human habitation, human in their format?"

The planning team did not meet with residents from the inner-city neighborhoods that would be affected by the recommendations. That was the Chicago way; it was assumed that the professionals who would assemble the financing and do the building should also be the ones who did the planning. Nor did the planners consult with several celebrated architects who might be too abrasive in pitching their own ideas. One who was spurned was Bertrand Goldberg. He decided to appeal directly to Phil Klutznick, who, he thought, had a developer's dare, and thus was likely to be more receptive to his ideas than Tom Ayers. Goldberg had commissioned and narrated a 30-minute film on his River City and had been showing it around town to prospective investors and friends in the news media.

"We indicated the kinds of things that we were anticipating bringing into that area," Goldberg said later. "New educational systems, new management systems, sensitive governmental systems, which perhaps is what killed us. I showed the movie to Richard J. Daley in his office. I did the same thing for Phil Klutznick. And all Phil could say was, 'Well, you're a very good actor.'"

What neither of them realized at the time was that a third suitor of the rail yards had emerged. This one did not come from the world of real estate or architecture. He was the heart and soul of the city's beloved Bears.

3 Papa Bear Searches for a Den

ran the biggest utility company, yet by the end of 1972 it seemed as if they were spending half of their waking hours worrying about the price of railroad land.

The two of them, on behalf of the South Loop group, were working their way through meetings with all 13 owners and groups of owners of the rail yards. They weren't even close to getting a price low enough to make their housing plans feasible. "It was the most discouraging thing," Ayers recalled. "One of them wanted $50 a front foot for this land they could no longer use. I said to the fellow, 'That will be vacant for the next 100 years.' He said, 'Oh no, it's hot, it's near the Loop.' You would have thought the railroads were all cash rich, that they didn't need any money.

"So we went back to Daley and said we were having lots of trouble with this. And he said, 'Well, would you like me to be your purchasing agent?' We said, yes, we would. And he said, 'Let me think about it.'"

They hadn't yet heard from the mayor when John Perkins got a phone call on January 23, 1973, that unnerved him. It was from Sam T. Brown, president of the Chicago & Western Indiana Railroad and head of a partnership of three rail lines that jointly owned 51 acres behind the shuttered Dearborn Station. The three were negotiating to sell their parcel to Col. Henry Crown of Chicago for a sports stadium, he said. Would Perkins and his associates be interested in buying the land if the Crown sale did not work out?

Perkins couldn't believe what Brown had told him. Henry Crown was head of one of America's wealthiest families. He had worked as a teenager in a

26

Chicago brickyard, built a small concrete business into the giant Material Service Corporation, and then merged that company with the huge defense contractor General Dynamics Corporation. During World War II he had acquired the rank of colonel, as well as a chestful of medals from Allied governments, for procuring scarce materials while serving with the Army Corps of Engineers. His son Lester had succeeded him as executive vice president of General Dynamics, but the colonel was still on its board. Now, at age 76, was he really thinking of building a sports stadium?

Not directly, Sam Brown replied. The colonel was acting on behalf of George "Papa Bear" Halas, 77, founder, owner, and president of the Chicago Bears football club, a founder of the National Football League, and coach of the Bears off and on—he had fired and rehired himself several times—for half a century.

The Bears played in Soldier Field, the lakefront stadium owned by the Chicago Park District. It was well known that Halas was unhappy about the terms of the lease and even more unhappy about the condition of the poorly configured, 45-year-old structure, which looked like a European soccer field plunked down in a Greek theater. Only one-fourth of its seats were between the goal lines. Lakefront conservationists had long wanted to get rid of Soldier Field and its sprawling 41 acres of parking lots and use that prime shoreland for public recreation. In 1971 Mayor Daley had agreed to tear it down, but only if he could build another stadium south of it on the lake. His plan collapsed under an avalanche of civic protest, a rare defeat for him. He decided to improve Soldier Field instead. Halas, according to Sam Brown, wanted to get a new stadium under way somewhere other than the lakefront before Daley started remodeling Soldier Field.

Perkins promptly reported Sam Brown's message to Phil Klutznick and Jim Downs, who were horrified at the prospect of a stadium on that 51-acre site. It was long and narrow, beginning at the northern border of the yards, nearest the Loop, and running south for about a mile. It was only one-eighth of a mile from east to west, but those two borders were two of the Loop's most important streets—State and Clark. It was just a short walk to the lakefront parks and the big department stores. The red-brick-and-granite Dearborn Station with its charming tower sat on the site's northern edge, at the foot of Dearborn Street. A stadium there would kill hopes of creating a pleasant neighborhood anywhere in the rail yards.

The business group had to persuade Henry Crown to drop his arrangement with Halas, whatever it was. They didn't know the venerable colonel all that well, but they did know his son Lester. Jim Downs contacted him first. A few days later, in a letter to John Perkins, Downs said he told the younger

Crown that it was highly unlikely Mayor Daley would support plans for a South Loop stadium, if indeed that was what his father was up to. "I told him," Downs wrote, "that, first, the mayor is enthusiastic about Soldier Field and always has been; second, I do not believe that Chicago either can or should allocate the resources required to meet Halas's specifications."

Next, Phil Klutznick met with Lester Crown, who was on the board of Klutznick's Urban Investment and Development Company. In a memo to his fellow South Loop planners, Klutznick said he filled Crown in on what they had been doing for the past year or so, emphasizing "the communal aspect of our mutual thinking." In other words, housing in the South Loop will be marvelous for the city, the mayor likes the idea, the business establishment will line up solidly behind it—so don't let your dad spoil it.

The colonel himself was wintering in Florida. He returned to Chicago late in March for a meeting, but not with the business group. George Halas and Sam Rizzo, Halas's banker at Northern Trust Company, hosted a luncheon at the bank for the two richest men they knew: Henry Crown and another old Halas friend, Ray A. Kroc, a former Chicagoan and chairman of the McDonald's Corporation hamburger empire. Halas brought his son-in-law, Ed McCaskey, and Kroc brought his attorney, Donald G. Lubin, a partner in the firm of Sonnenschein Nath & Rosenthal. The plan, as outlined by Halas and Rizzo, was to acquire a site in the South Loop rail yards with private funds, donate it to the city, and raise $10 million toward construction of a multi-use stadium. That, they felt, would encourage the city to authorize tax-free revenue bonds for the stadium.

Crown already had told Halas he was interested in helping him. Ray Kroc said he was open to participating. He had been talking to Halas about buying the minority interest in the Bears that the Halas family had put on the market. But he didn't want it unless he could get controlling interest down the line. That, said Papa Bear, would never happen.

The meeting ended with an agreement to commission a study on the financial practicality of a stadium on the rail yards. The mayor surely would want an objective—and optimistic—analysis before putting city tax money at risk.

Within a few days, news reports of the luncheon and a possible South Loop stadium surfaced in the *Chicago Daily News* and *The Wall Street Journal*. George Halas could scarcely take out his garbage without making news in Chicago, let alone meet in a big bank with Henry Crown and Ray Kroc. Reporters speculated that Crown might provide the land for a stadium, but he denied this. Later, at a meeting arranged by his son Lester, he told Phil Klutznick the same thing: He had no plans to buy South Loop land for a stadium. All he had done was make a few phone calls and attend a few meetings with railroads in Halas's behalf.

Klutznick and the others were relieved. George Halas surely wouldn't go out and buy some railroad land on his own, would he? He was not a wealthy man. "And as my mother would put it, he was tight as the skin on a sausage," said Ayers. They could turn their attention to other matters; chief among these, at the moment, was the absence of anything happening in City Hall.

So far, Mayor Daley had followed through on only one item in the agenda Ayers and Klutznick had proposed to him about 10 months earlier: He had named a task force of city officials—top people in planning, zoning, traffic, transportation, streets, sewers, and water delivery—to work with the architects and planners from Skidmore and from Urban. But the city people had done little except pepper the others with questions about financial plans, design concepts, infrastructure requirements, marketing, and on and on. Allen Hartman, an assistant city attorney acting as liaison between the city task force and the South Loop group, "apologized profusely if we thought they were asking too many irrelevant questions," Klutznick wrote in a memo to Ayers and Perkins. "He asked me to convey the need for a little patience . . . and emphasized again and again that they wanted to be able to answer any questions the mayor might have."

Klutznick told the city attorney that he appreciated his position, but time might be running out for acquisition of prime railroad land. He repeated what had been his belief from the start: The project could not work financially unless the city used its bond powers to buy the land and then provided the necessary schools, parks, streets, and so forth.

In April, a few weeks after the Halas luncheon, John Perkins went to see Daley on another matter. The mayor surprised him by announcing that he had been meeting separately with the railroads. It was obvious their property was worth a great deal less than they thought, Daley told him. But, instead of negotiating lower prices, he had urged the railroads to join the business executives and be co-developers of the property. They had made a lot of money in Chicago, the mayor said; now it was time for them to give something back to the city. This would be a great thing for their public image.

It was quintessential Daley. The mayor ardently believed Chicago was the best place on earth to live and do business. Why shouldn't the railroads want to do something for this wonderful city that had made them so rich? The fact that a number of them were in receivership or close to it apparently did not faze him.

Daley also let Perkins know that he was getting fed up with prodding from the South Loop group about the use of city funds. "He has in mind somewhat critically that we have shifted from a private limited-dividend corporation to one that intends to operate by using the city's bonding power," Perkins wrote in a memo to Klutznick. Perkins thought he knew what was bothering Daley. "By 1973," he said later, "public money had gotten sensitive, race had gotten sensitive. It was my feeling that what he was most concerned about was the reaction from various interest groups if the city were to announce it was helping to finance a major housing program being developed by corporate interests. This would lead to all of the obvious problems with major social and emotional overtones."

The business executives had reason to be impatient. They wanted to get started on their fund-raising. Bill Hartmann and his architects and planners at Skidmore, Owings & Merrill, working with the city's own planning staff, had finished the Chicago 21 Plan commissioned by the Central Area Committee. They were showing it to influential business and civic groups around town for comment and suggestions. Months before the official announcement date, Chicago newspapers were publishing leaks of the plan's biggest news: a proposal for a new community in the South Loop, with "100,000 residents in futuristic superblocks," as the *Chicago Sun-Times* described it.

Jim Downs and Bill Hartmann formally presented the plan and an elaborate, 8-by-11-foot model of the new central area at a luncheon on June 14, 1973, on the top floor of the new John Hancock Center.

It "signals a renaissance" for the city, Daley said. "There is nothing this city can't do when it makes up its mind to do it."

Downs said the business community would "pledge the creation of a new private catalyst organization to initiate and sustain both public and private activities in support of this plan."

Downtown, said Hartmann, would become the best place in the entire Chicago area to live as well as work.

Press and television coverage was extensive and ecstatic. It "may well be the most far-reaching downtown plan ever for Chicago or any other city in the nation," said the *Chicago Daily News*. A lot of plans were gathering dust on City Hall shelves, it said in an editorial, but this one was different because it had the backing of a powerhouse lineup of corporations.

The plan's recommendations were thoughtful and constructive, designed to make the central city more attractive to businesses and residents in the entire metropolitan area. As happened with the Burnham plan of 1909, the proposals would be fixtures on civic agendas for decades. Nearly a quarter of a century later, an impressive number had been implemented: The barren, run-

Papa Bear
Searches for
a Den

down Navy Pier, a once-grand fixture on the lakefront, was rebuilt into a recreational attraction for families; Chinatown, the colorful, cramped community just south of the rail yards, was expanded and its tourist attractions enhanced; the roads along the downtown lakefront were realigned to straighten the notorious S curve on Lake Shore Drive; another portion of the drive was relocated to create a parklike setting for the city's celebrated lakefront museums; rapid transit service was extended from the downtown to O'Hare and Midway airports; tax incentives were enacted to encourage preservation of historic buildings; the Prairie Avenue section of the Near South Side became a historic district and architectural museum. One recommendation, to ban personal autos on State Street, widen the sidewalks, and create a mall-like effect, was implemented, judged a failure, and dismantled.

Other proposals, including some of the most important, were more elusive. They remained on the city's agenda, with progress distressingly slow and mired in controversy: Improve social and public services at the huge, miserable Cabrini-Green public housing development just northwest of the Loop, demolish some of its apartment towers, and replace them with low-rise units owned and managed by the occupants; create a continuous esplanade along the main branch and the two forks of the Chicago River; close Merrill C. Meigs Field, the little city-owned airstrip used chiefly by Illinois state officials and by operators of private aircraft, and transform the landfill island on which it sits into public parkland—as Daniel Burnham intended.

Despite all this, it was those "futuristic superblocks" for 100,000 that grabbed most of the attention. The South Loop business group had hoped to use that spotlight to raise capital, hire a staff, and jointly announce financial agreements and other plans with the city. But as the summer wore on, there were no assurances from the Daley administration that the city would provide the necessary parks, schools, streets, and sewers and help acquire the land.

Phil Klutznick explained the urgency to Allen Hartman, his City Hall liaison. "He told me [the task force of city officials] had made considerable progress in their thinking, but could not move beyond their present point until they had further instructions from the mayor," Klutznick wrote to Ayers and Perkins. "He found this difficult to obtain in light of certain other items requiring emergency attention. When I suggested that the South Loop had been put on the back burner, his response was that it had not been put on the back burner, but probably was moved to the side for the time being. . . .

"He needed nothing from us at this point but would be back to us as soon as he got his directions from the top man. My own judgment is that we are a long way from home if the present events do not change substantially."

The problem was, those "certain other items requiring emergency attention" in City Hall added up to the worst period of Daley's long tenure. He had been humiliated and infuriated the previous July at the Democratic National Convention when two young rebels, the Rev. Jesse Jackson and Chicago Alderman William Singer, led a revolt that unseated him and 58 other members of his Illinois delegation. A prominent black member of the Chicago congressional delegation, the former Olympic athlete Ralph H. Metcalfe, publicly broke with the mayor and joined civil rights activists who were accusing the Chicago Police Department of brutality against blacks. Daley's longtime friend, Cook County Clerk Edward J. Barrett, was convicted of taking $180,000 in kickbacks from a voting-machine company. Two aldermen, loyal Daley allies, also were convicted of corruption charges. A police captain and 23 officers, charged with taking payoffs from tavern owners, were on the verge of being convicted; another longtime friend, Police Superintendent James Conlisk, was getting ready to resign as a result. The mayor's closest friend, neighbor, and former patronage chief, Matthew J. Danaher, was indicted for conspiracy and tax evasion. His City Council floor leader, Thomas Keane, was about to go on trial on 17 counts of mail fraud.

The mayor was at war with Dan Walker, the new governor of Illinois and an independent Democrat; with Bernard Carey, the new Cook County prosecutor and a Republican; and with another Republican, James R. Thompson, the aggressive young U.S. attorney in Chicago who seemed determined to put Daley's entire political organization behind bars.

No wonder Daley's aides were reluctant to remind him that decisions had to be made on South Loop development.

The strain was getting to him. Not long before, a young Roman Catholic priest from a white, blue-collar neighborhood on the city's Southwest Side had led a delegation to City Hall to protest the city's authority to issue tax-free bonds without a referendum—the same authority the South Loop planners hoped would finance acquisition of their land. The mayor had always prided himself on his stony silence in the presence of noisy protesters. He pretended he couldn't see or hear them. But the Rev. Leonard Dubi in his clerical collar, a young man from a community very much like the mayor's own beloved Bridgeport, was too much. "What kind of priest are you?" Daley cried out. "I'm shocked at you."

His outburst had made all the evening television newscasts in Chicago, which escalated his anger. The protests—warnings, actually—from community groups about using city bonding powers for anything that might hint of private gain continued. They probably squelched any possibility that

Daley would sell bonds for residential development not tailored mainly for the poor.

Allen Hartman, the assistant city attorney dealing with Phil Klutznick, mentioned the concern in a letter to him. The City Hall task force was worried, he said, "that unthinking people would believe that the administration and some few major folks in the area had combined to create a bonanza."

In view of what was happening in City Hall, Klutznick would have been wise to refrain from contacting the mayor for a while. But he couldn't resist. Several newspaper articles had focused on deterioration in the theater and retail district of the North Loop, and on the possibility that the city would give tax incentives and other help to developers there. Klutznick wrote a long letter to "My dear Dick," exceedingly polite and tactful, suggesting that the North Loop eventually would revive on its own momentum. It probably did not need special help from the city. This was not true, he said, of the South Loop. He and his colleagues needed more than "the official encouragement of the City Administration to succeed." They needed city financial aid. Without it, this rare opportunity could well be lost, and "we will have a city which is alive only during working hours."

His colleagues were getting discouraged, Klutznick told the mayor. "There has been some concern about the role and the continued participation of such a group. . . . You will forgive me for burdening you with this at this time, but I do feel we are reaching a critical point."

He signed the letter "Phil."

Everything he wrote was valid and worded with Klutznick's considerable diplomatic skill. But he had enclosed a brochure about Detroit's Renaissance Center complex and the city's role in helping the business community develop it. Chicago's business community could collaborate with the city in the same manner, Klutznick wrote. "What they need, above all, is a signal from your administration."

With that, he had committed an unpardonable sin. He had praised another city at the expense of Chicago.

A few days later the mayor replied to the "My dear Dick" letter with a chilly "Dear Mr. Klutznick."

"It was gratifying to see the Detroit people using Chicago's example for both development activities and beautification of the Lakefront," he wrote.

"I think we all agree that the high goals set for the South Loop should be advanced with the strongest and broadest possible support from the city's business community. . . . I hope your letter does not suggest that such an important group is less serious than we have been led to believe."

He told Klutznick that the North Loop proposals were complementary to the South Loop plans, not competitive. But both needed further planning and definition. When he had all the necessary information, he would act.

The letter was signed "Richard J. Daley."

In September the Chicago 21 Plan was published in big, shining, silver-coated, 125-page books with a laudatory letter from the mayor. By this time its major recommendations were well known by business and civic groups and had been discussed in the press. Still, the details of the "South Loop New Town," as the plan called it, produced a new round of publicity, accompanied by drawings from Skidmore and the city planning staff.

The basics were unchanged from a year before, when Tom Ayers and his colleagues showed them to the mayor and to the railroads. The superblocks that Ayers, Ferd Kramer, and Phil Klutznick thought were unrealistic and

Skidmore, Owings & Merrill's sketch of typical South Loop New Town "superblock," published in Chicago 21 Plan in September 1973. Courtesy Skidmore, Owings & Merrill.

difficult to market were still the star features; the Skidmore architects loved the idea of creating a new kind of urban neighborhood, efficient and exciting and glamorous.

In 10 years, the Chicago 21 Plan predicted, the South Loop would be home to 60,000 people on 200 acres in the northern portion of the railroad district. A southern phase, less dense, would follow in the next decade and house another 60,000 on 400 acres.

The plan was vague about who would finance and develop this new town. The wording had been worked out carefully with the city Department of Development and Planning and the business leaders of the Central Area Committee: "To create the means to accomplish those elements of the plan, which due to financial, legal or organizational constraints are not now underway, it is recommended that a new limited-dividend corporation be formed to assemble land and initiate development which is beyond the capability of individual developers. To develop new sources of funding will require creative effort."

About the time the 21 Plan was officially released, another document was circulated among a few Chicago financiers—this one without publicity. The Stanford Research Institute of Menlo Park, California, had completed the feasibility study of a new sports stadium on South Loop rail yards commissioned by George Halas and his potential backers. Its conclusion: A domed stadium seating 78,000 could "produce acceptable operating profits and provide sufficient margins to cover market requirements for a 40-year municipal

South Loop New
Town's riverfront,
lined with 700-
foot-long build-
ings, as envisioned
in Chicago 21
Plan. Courtesy
Skidmore, Owings
& Merrill.

bond issue at an estimated rate of 7.5 percent. . . . Net operating revenues would be more than one and one-half times debt service requirements except during the initial years of operation."

The stadium, according to the study, would be suitable for football and other sports, musical and entertainment events, conventions, and trade shows. Revenues would come from rentals for these events, from private luxury suites and restaurants, and from parking that would be available for Loop-bound motorists every day.

Keith E. Duke, who prepared the study, wrote that a South Loop site was "appropriate and convenient," with excellent access by expressways and public transportation. He was familiar with the Chicago 21 Plan and its call for a vast new town on the rail yards. "The stadium complex could be included in the plan," he wrote, and "serve to stimulate . . . development of other elements of the plan."

Duke's financial projections included a figure destined to shape the future of South Loop development. The site would be acquired with private capital and donated to the city, he said. "A select group of interested citizens would also provide equity funds in the amount of $10 million, so that the City of Chicago would be in a position to authorize tax-free revenue bonds to construct the stadium." The cost of construction, plus amenities, was estimated at $66.3 million. Duke went on to report that a 51-acre site had been selected, and negotiations to acquire it "have progressed to the point of establishing a firm price for the land . . . of $7.3 million."

So George Halas, acting on his own, or with an assist here and there from Col. Henry Crown, had succeeded in getting a price from the railroad partnership headed by Chicago & Western Indiana of only $3.25 a square foot—less than half of the lowest price the South Loop group had heard in any of its many meetings with rail executives.

Once he had the feasibility study, Halas asked Ray Kroc's lawyer, Donald Lubin, to represent him in acquiring an option from the railroad partnership. Lubin brought in his partner Bernard Nath, a specialist in real estate law, to take over the negotiations. Both lawyers were amazed at the $3.25 price Halas had obtained. "Our people thought it was worth about $10 a square foot," Nath said later.

That fall of 1973, the South Loop business group was deep into plans for the coming year. The agenda was formidable: Create a limited-dividend corporation, raise capital, develop an executive structure, hire a staff, get some realistic housing plans, commission market analyses. They had heard about a stadium feasibility study that quoted a bargain land price, but their inquiries indicated that no option had yet been signed, so they weren't too worried. Yet.

They didn't know that Chicago developer Jerrold Wexler had been having long talks with Bertrand Goldberg about his ambitious River City and was enthusiastic about the possibilities. The two met with Robert C. McGowan, head of real estate for Chessie System, holding company of the Chesapeake & Ohio and Baltimore & Ohio railroads. McGowan was equally impressed by Goldberg's vision. More than a year had elapsed since Ayers and his South Loop delegation had asked McGowan's boss, John Hanifin, to wait six months before reaching an agreement with Goldberg. Now Goldberg had a deep-pockets investor in Jerrold Wexler. McGowan agreed that Chessie's riverfront land was ideal for River City. He and Hanifin offered an option at $10 a square foot, and Wexler was amenable.

Tom Ayers knew he couldn't wait for the land matter to be resolved before moving ahead. He had felt since the first time he talked with Daley about the South Loop that the mayor was sold on the idea of a middle-class neighborhood rising on the wasteland of the rail yards and would wind up solidly behind it, once the business community demonstrated its commitment. Daley appeared to be saying, through his oblique comments of recent months to John Perkins and Phil Klutznick, that he hadn't yet seen hard evidence of that commitment. It was time to put aside, for the moment, worries about land options and bond issues and infrastructure agreements and go out and sell the city's business leadership on the bright promise of a South Loop New Town.

4 | "A Small Town Establishment"

1980s with her husband, a prominent media executive, once joked that the big difference between the two cities could be explained by the clothes she wore to the farewell parties in Chicago and the welcome parties in New York. In Chicago, she said, the same people attended each event, so she needed something different each time. "In New York, I could wear the same outfit to every party; we hardly ever saw a person twice."

The phenomenon intrigued Andrew Neil, a political reporter for *The Economist*. "Behind the big-city facade is a small town establishment," he wrote in a report from Chicago in the March 29, 1980, issue of the British magazine. "It is still possible to meet almost everyone who is supposed to matter in Chicago at one cocktail party."

That quality got the South Loop project going—and kept it alive.

Tom Ayers, who surely would have been near the top of any guest list of people who mattered in Chicago, needed only to look around the room at the other guests to find the people he had targeted as likely investors. If he didn't want to do that at a party, he could see them at lunch in the Chicago Club. If not there, over breakfast at the Standard Club. And if not there, at a meeting of the trustees of the Chicago Symphony Orchestra or Northwestern University or the Chicago Central Area Committee.

One reason for the cohesiveness of Chicago's power structure was simple geography. Pastora San Juan Cafferty, a University of Chicago historian, analyzed the way things got done in the city for a study published in 1982 by the

Washington-based Committee for Economic Development. She noted that most major Chicago corporations had their offices in the compact, sharply defined rectangle that was the Loop. On one side was the lake; on two sides, the river; and on the fourth, the sooty wasteland of rail yards. Their executives were within an easy walk of each other and of the downtown clubs where, in those days, they met for lunch.

This physical togetherness was enhanced by an intense civic commitment. "I do not know of any other major city in the United States that has as great a degree of business leader involvement in the affairs of the city," Gaylord Freeman, the retired chairman of the First National Bank of Chicago, told Pastora Cafferty. Whether the executive lives in the city or in the suburbs, Freeman said, "if he works in Chicago, he is interested and likely to be active in its affairs. In New York, his identity is with his suburban community. New York City is run by the city officials." Freeman related an anecdote that he thought exemplified the difference. Two Chicago business leaders were lunching together when the chairman of a major New York company, visiting in Chicago, stopped at their table. One of the Chicagoans mentioned that the two were about to call on Mayor Daley to urge him to hire more blacks in the city Fire Department. The New Yorker, according to Freeman, was astonished. "Why would you be interested in that?" he asked. The Chicagoans were equally astonished that the New Yorker had to ask the question.

Ayers's plan for raising capital relied heavily on that corporate togetherness and civic concern. First, he would get a commitment from the city's most prominent companies for $1 million each. The South Loop group had decided this would be the maximum investment; with a cap, no single firm would have more influence than others—nor would it bear greater risk. The minimum investment would be $100,000. Individuals could not buy shares and donations would not be accepted; the group wanted this to be clearly a united business effort, run in a businesslike manner. They did not want some big developer to buy control. There were rumors that a few were interested, but none materialized. The area was that unattractive.

Investors were to provide 10 percent of their pledged amount immediately, with the remainder subject to call as needed.

Once the big boys were on board with $1 million each, Ayers hoped to use their stature to get additional financing from the second tier of corporations. Finally, he would secure the endorsement of a select group of individuals who were not part of the corporate clique, but whose names and influence would help promote the project to the community at large. Tied for first place on this list were John Cardinal Cody, the Roman Catholic archbishop of Chicago, and William A. Lee, president of the Chicago Federation of La-

bor and Industrial Union Council. Others were Louis Martin, an elder statesman in the civil rights movement and president of the black-owned Sengstacke Newspapers, publisher of 10 newspapers, including the *Chicago Defender*; the two University of Chicago scholars who had been advising Ayers
for months, John Hope Franklin and Morris Janowitz; and Edwin "Bill" Berry,
director of the Chicago Urban League. Martin advised Ayers to recruit one of
the city's younger, more fiery black leaders, and suggested Leon Finney Jr., a
disciple of community organizer Saul Alinsky.

No one had lived in the target area for a century. It was separated from
surrounding neighborhoods by the river and expressways, so Ayers and his
colleagues saw no reason to involve those communities in their planning.

The corporations represented by the three men who first conceived the
South Loop project were, naturally, down for $1 million each—Sears, Conti-
nental Bank, and Ayers's own Commonwealth Edison. Nevertheless, Ayers
made a presentation before their boards; it was a good trial run for his sales
pitch. He explained that the ailing area had been carefully studied by the
Real Estate Research Corporation—his audiences all knew its chief, Jim
Downs—and Downs had concluded that housing for middle-class families
would be the most productive use of the land.

"We always stressed that their corporate contribution might never be returned," Ayers said later. "And boy, we made a point of that. We promised to
make the area an integrated one. To do the project with private financing. To
have professional real estate and construction people in charge. And to make
the project the best housing value in the metropolitan area."

Even if they didn't get their money back, Ayers told them, they would get
a splendid return on their investment: protection for their holdings in the
Loop, a good source of housing for their employees, shoppers for their stores,
and a stimulus for redevelopment that would enrich the city's tax base—thus
easing their own tax burdens.

He left the Edison boardroom when it was time for a vote. And then he
did the same at Sears, where he was also on the board. And at the First National Bank, where he was also on the board. And at Northwest Industries,
where he was also on the board. And at the *Chicago Tribune*, ditto. All came
through. One *Tribune* executive noted later that Commonwealth Edison was
always among the first and most generous contributors to the pet causes of
other corporations. So when Tom Ayers asked for help, he had a lot of chips
to call in.

The board members who were sold by Ayers's presentations talked it up
among their other boards. Donald Graham of Continental Bank, one of
Ayers's original South Loop collaborators, sat on the boards of Marcor—

holding company for Montgomery Ward & Company—and of United States Gypsum Company and did an effective selling job there. Jim Downs was a director of Chicago Title & Trust Company, and helped sell that board. And so the word spread. "There were probably 20 guys who were on each other's boards," recalled Miles L. Berger, a real estate consultant and for years the chairman of the Chicago Plan Commission. "Three or four were uniform to four or five boards. That made raising capital a lot easier. You're sitting at a board meeting and you say, 'We're doing this great project, you've got to put some money in it.'"

There were also drinks at the Chicago Club at the end of the day and luncheons in the private dining club in the First National Bank Building, which conveniently looked down on the rail yards. Ayers was frequently joined by John Perkins and Charles Willson from Continental Bank and by Phil Klutznick, who was regarded with awe among the Chicago business corps for his legendary feats in developing Park Forest and pioneer shopping centers and for his reputation as a philosopher-diplomat. The other executives, powerful as they were in their fields, did not get phone calls seeking advice from the prime minister of Israel or the U.S. secretary of state.

Despite all of these built-in advantages, raising capital was not easy. In 1972 the goal had been $15 million to $17.5 million. But that was assuming the city would buy several hundred acres of South Loop land and lease it to the new corporation. Daley's apparent reluctance to do that made $15 million seem unrealistic; the group set a new goal of $30 million.

On September 12, 1973, John Perkins gave a breakfast in Continental Bank's elegant dining room for prospective investors and influential community leaders. The cardinal was there and labor leader Bill Lee and the president of Marshall Field Company and Louis Martin from the *Chicago Defender*. Architects Bill Hartmann and Bruce Graham showed their models, and Phil Klutznick gave a lengthy speech on the history of the modern city, the sources of its ailments, and the reasons why Chicago needed a South Loop New Town.

The guests were given a stock prospectus, stockholders' and subscription agreements, and financial projections prepared by the law firm of Mayer Brown & Platt and the Arthur Andersen & Company consulting firm. The subscription agreement specified that the stock was not transferable, that the fund-raising procedures exempted the new corporation from registration under federal and state securities acts, and that the purchaser had been duly warned of the risks. "The undersigned subscriber . . . has had personal discussions concerning the Corporation," the agreement said, ". . . and it understands that the principal purpose of investing in the Corporation is to support and contribute to its civic improvement purposes rather than to obtain any return on investment, and that the securities involve a very substantial element of risk while offering the possibility of only a limited return if the Corporation is financially successful."

Klutznick wanted his dissertation on cities and the South Loop New Town to be part of the package, but it was 22 pages long. Charles Willson edited it into a punchy six pages and combined it with Skidmore's architectural renderings and maps and Arthur Andersen's financial data in a bright, smart-looking booklet. The plan described in the booklet was essentially the unrealistic South Loop scenario produced a year earlier: city ownership of the land, even though this now was a remote prospect; densely packed superblocks; a typical unit of 1,000 square feet with two "comfortable" or three "snug" bedrooms at a sales price of $26,000; and a wildly optimistic sales and rental rate of 1,500 to 2,000 units a year. The booklet proposed a pilot development of 3,000 to 5,000 units. In another two decades, it predicted, the South Loop New Town would have 40,000 to 45,000 units on its 600 acres.

Within a few months of that September luncheon, Ayers had $1-million commitments from eight of the corporations he had targeted as major investors: Edison, Continental Bank, First National Bank (Chicago's second biggest), First Federal Savings and Loan Association of Chicago, Illinois Bell Telephone Company, Sears, Standard Oil Company of Indiana, and Peoples Gas Light & Coke Company. All of the big eight, except for Illinois Bell, were represented on the board of the Chicago Central Area Committee, producer of the Chicago 21 Plan. Illinois Bell was slower to respond than the other seven; its officers worried about a risky $1-million investment by a utility company that had to go to great pains to justify rate increases to consumer advocates and state regulators. Illinois Bell was a generous supporter of efforts to improve public schools and of causes aimed at helping the city's poor. It was having a hard time fitting this South Loop New Town into that category. Eventually, however, the fact that all the other good-guy corporate CEOs were participating persuaded Illinois Bell to join the million-dollar group.

Two other investors contributed $500,000 or more: Marshall Field Company, whose State Street store was particularly vulnerable to any Loop deterioration ($600,000), and Montgomery Ward's holding company, Marcor ($500,000).

Some old rivalries came into play. A. Robert Abboud, vice-chairman of First National Bank and soon to become its chairman, came up with the requested $1 million but did not become an active participant in South Loop planning; he thought Continental Bank and its president, John Perkins, were too influential. Robert M. Drevs, chairman of Peoples Gas, made sure his corporation invested as much as Commonwealth Edison; he didn't want another highly publicized all-electric development, like Marina City. (It worked; all of the townhouses in the first half of Dearborn Park had gas heat and appliances.) John W. Baird, chairman of the distinguished real estate company Baird & Warner and good friend and tennis partner of Ferd Kramer, chairman of the equally distinguished real estate company Draper & Kramer, bought no shares. "I figured it was locked up for Draper & Kramer," he said years later. "I thought they would get all the gravy."

Five months after they started their fund-raising drive, Ayers and his colleagues had secured an impressive $10 million. Then came a dramatic slowdown. The tight clique of downtown corporate leaders who knew each other well and were deeply involved in civic affairs had come through. Most, though, were chipping in with $250,000 or less, not the hoped-for $1 million to $500,000. Others, including some that Ayers and his colleagues hoped would be big investors, were turning them down. Some were headquartered in the suburbs and were only occasional participants in the Loop lunch scene and civic do-good projects. Some had corporate financial problems and thought it unseemly to throw their stockholders' money at a risky venture with no direct payoff to their firms, especially when the money at risk was not a tax-deductible charitable donation. And some felt that housing development, worthy as this particular enterprise might be, should be undertaken by experienced development firms, not by corporate committee. The list of prominent turndowns included United States Steel, Zenith Radio Corporation, Borg-Warner Corporation, Prudential and Kemper insurance companies, the giant printing company R. R. Donnelley & Sons, and two venerable Chicago-area food concerns, Jewel Companies and Kraftco Corporation.

Toward the end of 1973, attorney Robert M. Berger of Mayer Brown & Platt drew up articles of incorporation and bylaws for a corporation with a maximum return of 6.5 percent on investment. The name: Chicago 21 Corporation, after the big plan that had introduced the concept of a South Loop New Town to the city six months earlier. The articles of incorporation were filed with the Illinois secretary of state on January 7, 1974.

Throughout the previous autumn, the South Loop group had been assembling names for a new board. Some were obvious: representatives from the major investors and others who had been working on the project since its earliest days. They gave the board the influence and stature Chicago 21 would need in City Hall and among the financial institutions that would have to provide construction loans and mortgage money. But the social upheavals of recent years had made it clear that a gaggle of influential CEOs was not enough; there would have to be broader representation of the community at large—broad by the standards of the early 1970s, at any rate. "We sat down and we very carefully planned that board," John Perkins recalled. It had to have some women and some blacks, but these had to be thoroughly acceptable to the corporate community and carry some weight in City Hall, too; no troublemakers need apply.

By year's end, a board of 22 had been assembled. Most represented major investors. Three were black. Two were female. One of the women was Mary Ward, the socially prominent widow of J. Harris Ward, Ayers's predecessor at Commonwealth Edison; she had qualifications of her own: She ran Bright New City, an annual forum of lectures and seminars on improving Chicago's physical amenities. The other was Carey M. Preston, vice president of the Chicago Board of Education, president of the Chicago Urban League, executive secretary of a national sorority of black professional women, and, on top of all that, a crack real estate salesperson. Later she joked: "I filled in quite a few blanks for them."

The other two blacks were Louis Martin of the *Chicago Defender* and George E. Johnson, president of Johnson Products Company. Johnson had invested $200,000 in Chicago 21 and was enthused about the possibility of an interracial neighborhood that would knit the largely black South Side neighborhoods with the Loop. Martin and Johnson were part of the informal discussion group Ayers had pulled together to talk about stable integration in a new South Loop community. Ayers had recently recruited Johnson for Commonwealth Edison's corporate board.

Ayers was particularly pleased that John Cardinal Cody and the labor leader William A. Lee had agreed to join the board. He had been courting them since the summer of 1973. The cardinal even invested $200,000 in behalf of the Archdiocese of Chicago; "I am enthusiastic about this whole project," he wrote to Ayers. It certainly must have occurred to him that a big, new, middle-class community in the South Loop could revive a few withering near-downtown parishes. Lee was a fixture on a host of civic boards and mayoral commissions. It was assumed that he could secure labor's support—or at least its non-hostility. And from his standpoint, participation in civic ventures could head off any flirtation with nonunion contractors.

The board of the brand-new Chicago 21 Corporation met for the first time on January 17, 1974, in Continental Bank's dining room and elected, as arranged, Tom Ayers as chairman; John Perkins as president; Warren Skoning, vice president of real estate for Sears, as vice president; Harvey Kapnick, chairman of Arthur Andersen & Company, as treasurer; and Charles Willson, director of area development for Continental Bank, as secretary. Phil Klutznick was chosen to head an executive committee that would have hands-on control of planning and development; other members were Ayers, Perkins, Skoning, Kapnick, Willson, Louis Martin, Ferd Kramer, Mary Ward, and E. Stanley Enlund, chairman of First Federal Savings and Loan Association. It was a leadership roster ideally suited to financing, building, and selling a residential community. Klutznick had already developed new towns. Ferd Kramer knew how to market and manage them. Perkins and Willson had access to high-ranking city officials. Louis Martin had superb credentials in the black community, Mary Ward in the city's cultural and artistic circles.

Phil Klutznick didn't waste a minute in giving the group a timetable: By the end of 1974, the new Chicago 21 Corporation should have $30 million in capital and enough land for the prototype development of 3,000 units. He still believed that he could persuade the mayor to buy the property and lease it back to the corporation. Construction should begin within two years—by January 1976. The corporation would build just the prototype and then promote competitive development of the rest of the rail yards.

A week later, Chicago 21 awarded its first contract: $250,000 over 18 months to South Loop Associates, a creation of architects and planners from Skidmore, Owings & Merrill and Klutznick's firm, Urban Investment and Development Company. It was the same team that already had been working on the plans for more than a year. Klutznick was uneasy about the appearance of impropriety; as head of the executive committee, he was recommending a contract with his firm and with Skidmore, whose senior partner, Bill Hartmann, also was on the Chicago 21 board. But both, he felt, were the logical choices. Skidmore's Hartmann and its lead planner, Roger Seitz, were the principal creators of the big Chicago 21 Plan; now they were eager to amplify and refine their ideas for a South Loop dream town. But Klutznick insisted, every chance he got, that Skidmore was to be the "coordinating" architect only; other firms with more experience in residential work would design the various housing types specified in Skidmore's vision. As for his own involvement, Klutznick stressed that he had resigned as chairman of Urban in 1972. That was true, but he headed Urban's executive committee, and everyone who worked there considered him the guiding spirit behind it. Still, Urban was the only development company in the Chicago area that had its own little think tank, a pet project of Klutznick's; it had been working without pay on the South Loop project for more than a year, so giving it a share in a $250,000 contract did not seem improper to the Chicago 21 board. Besides, Klutznick's reputation for integrity was impeccable.

Mayor Daley, satisfied that the business group finally had some capital and was getting organized—two qualities he prized—directed his top planning officials to work with the new South Loop Associates. Phil Klutznick attended the initial session on January 25 and emphasized the need for momentum. He repeated the timetable he had given to the Chicago 21 board, including land acquisition in one year and ground breaking in two years. If the city was reluctant to buy the land for a first phase, he said, perhaps Henry Crown and George Halas could be persuaded to donate the 51 acres they were eyeing.

That last point was not the only one that struck Lew Hill, the city's canny commissioner of development and planning, as unrealistic, if not downright naive.

His response to Klutznick and the South Loop Associates indicated how much groundwork Chicago 21 still had before it. The 51 Halas acres were separated from the rest of the Loop by two decaying blocks along Dearborn Street, the old printing district; assuming Chicago 21 did get that land, he said, what did the group propose to do about that stretch of blight?

If Chicago 21 expected local government to pick up the costs of constructing new streets, sidewalks, parks, schools, sewers, and the like, city officials were going to have to justify those expenses. Hill needed a conceptual plan from Chicago 21, an analysis of the public costs and benefits, proposed development standards, projections of the income levels of the people who would live there. For example, could city schoolteachers and police officers afford it? The mayor hoped they could.

Quality schools would be essential to attracting middle-class residents. The Chicago Board of Education might be willing to set up a model system within the new neighborhood, Hill said, but it would be up to Chicago 21 to take the initiative in developing the plans and lobbying school officials.

Hill's chief deputy, Martin Murphy, added—correctly—that Chicago 21's brochure already was obsolete in its financial estimates, prepared 18 months earlier. Moreover, the density—100 units per acre—was unrealistically high, and it was extremely unlikely that Chicago 21 could sell or rent its projected 1,500 units a year. Murphy and Hill had spent hours hashing over the South Loop New Town with the city's real estate consultant, Miles Berger, when all three attended a land-use seminar at Harvard University the previous year. They felt strongly that the market, not some architectural vision, should dictate what the new town looked like, and the market said: townhouses, townhouses, townhouses.

Despite the various messages of caution, it was the dense superblock plan and the rosy financial projections of 1972 that were trumpeted at a gala April 4 luncheon announcing the formation of the new corporation. The cohosts were Mayor Daley and Tom Ayers, and the site was the historic Bismarck Hotel, Daley's favorite dining spot and headquarters of his Cook County Democratic Party.

The mayor predicted that the South Loop New Town would be the "most exciting, the most attractive and the most liveable urban family residential area in the United States." Tom Ayers talked about blacks and whites and Hispanics living harmoniously in this model community, walking to jobs, raising their children in a healthy, secure environment. Phil Klutznick said the development would infuse the Loop with vitality, which was important to the entire region because "if the heart of the city is ill, the suburbs must follow." John Perkins spoke, and Louis Martin. Cardinal Cody offered a prayer. Labor leader Bill Lee was there, and Carey Preston, and most of the other members of the new corporation's prestigious board.

It was such a festive gathering, with so much goodwill and optimism expressed all around, that no one was prepared for the stinging rebukes that came rapid-fire.

5

"An Awful Lot of Aggravation"

WHILE THE CHICAGO 21 LEADERS WERE MAPPING STRATEGIES IN THE BOARDROOMS AND dining clubs of the Loop's financial centers, another set of leaders was doing likewise a few blocks away in the far less imposing offices of the Citizens Information Service of Illinois, the educational arm of the League of Women Voters.

The group was largely Hispanic, with a smattering of whites and blacks. Most came from Pilsen, an old neighborhood that began across the river from the southwest corner of the rail yards. At the turn of the century, Pilsen had been a thriving industrial-residential area packed with newcomers from Bohemia and Poland who walked to their jobs from small apartment buildings and flats above stores.

Pilsen was still a port of entry in 1974, but mainly for Mexicans. Most of the industrial plants were deserted. The housing was worn out; money for repairs was virtually nonexistent. Development specialists from Chicago's Jewish Council on Urban Affairs were trying to revive Pilsen and other aging, decaying neighborhoods to the south and west; their goal was to restore the combination of industry and affordable housing that had made those areas self-sufficient in the first half of the century. The job trends of the 1970s, with industry spreading out in parklike suburban sites, made their hopes seem overly romantic. But, following the axiom that you need a villain to arouse people, they thought they had an ideal enemy in the Chicago 21 Plan and the newborn Chicago 21 Corporation.

Pilsen activists recruited allies from other impoverished inner-city areas,

48

including the dismal Cabrini-Green public housing development just north-west of the Loop and the largely Hispanic communities west of Cabrini-Green. Shortly before the Chicago 21 Corporation's April 4 announcement luncheon, they formed the Coalition of Central Area Communities. In angry press conferences and protest rallies, they charged that the South Loop New Town would drive up rents and property values in Pilsen and nearby areas, forcing out low-income minority families. A viable Spanish-speaking community would be destroyed. Fidel Lopez, an architect from Pilsen, complained about the refusal of financial institutions to make housing loans in coalition communities and the failure of city government to repair streets and sewers and parks. Garbage removal and police and fire protection were woeful.

"The new community will get services the coalition communities sorely need," Lopez told architecture critic Nory Miller. "Our taxes will be paying for those services. Why is there a drought of money to Pilsen and the others, but lots for this nonexistent community?"

The coalition vowed to block any attempt by the city to use its new federal community-development grants to help Chicago 21. A delegation camped outside Tom Ayers's office and threatened to stay until he gave a satisfactory response to their complaints.

The accusation that the new South Loop community would hog scarce tax and investment dollars came from sources with more influence than Pilsen. The *Chicago Tribune* published a supportive editorial after Chicago 21 Corporation's April announcement luncheon, but the *Chicago Sun-Times*—voice of the city's liberal community—was skeptical. The new corporation should also focus on "its responsibility to the congested neighborhoods that will be adjacent to the supercity," the newspaper said in an editorial. The Daley administration "must insist that the corporation, which could reap enormous profits from the new community, co-operate in development of necessary social services in the total area to be affected. . . . In point of fact, unless the total area is considered the supercity plan simply won't work."

A new nonprofit organization called TRUST (To Reshape Urban Systems Together), funded by prominent foundations and dedicated to promoting neighborhood development, raised some of the same questions put forth by the Pilsen group. Given the scarcity of resources for rebuilding old neighborhoods, a TRUST report said, was it wise to spend so much money creating a new one? Wouldn't it be better to improve the houses and streets and parks in existing communities? A South Loop New Town might even hasten their decay by siphoning off their middle-class residents.

TRUST's concerns were understandable. The withdrawal of investment by government and by financial institutions from racially changing neighborhoods and minority communities—"redlining"—was a major scandal in Chi-cago and many other cities in the early 1970s. By 1977 it would lead to new federal laws forbidding racial and ethnic discrimination in lending practices and requiring banks to invest in their communities. But the Chicago 21 lead-ers thought a South Loop New Town was part of the solution, not the prob-lem. Whatever money the city spent there would quickly be returned in real estate taxes from an area that was producing virtually nothing in tax revenue. That new money could provide the means, on a continuing basis, to help re-build decaying areas. Also, the new community would revitalize the Loop, Chicago's leading generator of jobs and tax money. These arguments, though, were too long-range and speculative to appease people whose needs were current, especially if they were aroused by skilled organizers.

Phil Klutznick's immediate reaction to the criticism was hurt outrage. He dashed off an angry letter to the president of the Jewish Council on Urban Affairs—an old friend and a board member of Klutznick's company—that asked, in essence, if he knew what his community consultants were up to out in the field.

Klutznick complained to James Hoge, editor of the *Chicago Sun-Times*, and to Emmett Dedmon, its editorial director. The Chicago 21 Corporation was trying to do one beneficial thing for the city, he said—not cure every conceivable urban problem. And where did the *Sun-Times* get the notion that the corporation could "reap enormous profits" from the new town? Had the editors and editorial writers bothered to read its stock agreements?

To his old friend and Chicago 21 colleague Ferd Kramer, Klutznick wrote about his frustrations with the TRUST report: "One is compelled to ask a simple question. Recognizing that what we do in the South Loop New Town will not be perfect, what are the alternatives? . . . Certainly, the acreage that is railroad tracks can lie there for many years as an eyesore or it can be uti-lized for development . . . . Merely leaving this acreage in its present state is not an appropriate answer. It will damage not only itself but everything that it surrounds by growing deterioration. Frankly, I am shocked by the whole exercise."

He didn't know who was behind the TRUST report, he wrote, but "I hope it was not the Metropolitan Housing and Planning Council." That was a dig at Kramer he couldn't resist. The two, in fact, rarely passed up chances to jab each other. The Metropolitan Housing and Planning Council was a vener-able, influential private agency that Kramer chaired. It was supportive of the South Loop plans and had nothing to do with the TRUST report, as Klutznick probably knew.

Klutznick's protests did not silence the *Sun-Times*. Jim Hoge responded by publishing a lengthy opinion piece by Richard F. Babcock, a Chicago lawyer and past president of the American Society of Planning Officials. Babcock labeled the proposed community "Fortress Loop." Chicago's business leadership suffered from "civic myopia," he wrote. It "simply can't see very far beyond the Loop. It still perceives the city as downtown. Grandeur in or near the Loop remains the path to urban salvation."

Phil Klutznick shot back with a four-page, single-spaced letter to Babcock, with copies to *Sun-Times* executives all the way up to the publisher, Marshall Field V. Granted, he said, Chicago had grave problems with schools and parks and slums; but a lot of business leaders already were trying to improve them. This was true; nearly every Chicago 21 board member, for example, was active on one or more committees working on urban problems. "I ask you a simple question," Klutznick wrote to Babcock. "Would you abandon the railroad yard to non-use or to decay or to disruptive uses or would you try to provide wholesome and decent neighborhoods in over 600 acres that are available?"

While Klutznick tried to handle his critics with his sharply worded letters, Tom Ayers and several other Chicago 21 board members took to the negotiating tables.

Ayers met a number of times during the spring and summer of 1974 with representatives of the Coalition of Central Area Communities. At first the sessions consisted mainly of scoldings from the coalition. Its chairman, Cezar Olivo, gave Ayers an ultimatum: The coalition must have veto power over any Chicago 21-sponsored development involving more than $100,000 or it would do whatever was necessary to block the project.

Ayers remained calm. He had been scolded and threatened before when he mediated open-housing disputes and during protests against Commonwealth Edison's nuclear-power program.

"We put up with an awful lot of aggravation," he said of those meetings. "It really griped the hell out of me. But I'd been down that road before. I'd had the experience of being yelled at. I know you don't have to be frightened but can sit and listen and talk about it."

The coalition did not get its veto power. As it turned out, there was something it found more valuable: money. Harold Jensen, who as vice president for real estate of Illinois Central Industries was presiding over the creation of a residential and commercial high-rise forest near the mouth of the Chicago River northeast of the Loop, was an influential member of the Chicago Central Area Committee. He was also sensitive to neighborhood concerns. Jensen arranged for the Central Area Committee to give planning grants of $12,500 each to any neighborhood that raised matching funds. Only two did that: Pilsen and Community 21, a consortium of groups northwest of the downtown area. Both hired professional planners to help chart and implement development strategies, with productive results.

The outcome was particularly productive for the young Pilsen architect Fidel Lopez, who eventually became manager of neighborhood development for Continental Bank and helped steer investment dollars to once-redlined communities.

The most informed criticism leveled at Chicago 21 Corporation in its early months centered on the plans themselves, not the philosophy behind them. An article in the October 1974 issue of *Inland Architect*, a magazine subsidized by the talented and mischievous architect Harry Weese, who enjoyed taunting big firms such as Skidmore, focused on the Chicago 21 model. "It is supposed to be the 21st Century," wrote Nory Miller. "But isn't it the 1920s version of the future: the homogeneous, characterless, immensely scaled, coarse-grained vision of a dog-eared science fiction novel?"

Miller quoted a number of architects who made similar comments. "Why are they trying to stuff so many people down there?" asked one. Laurence Booth, a rising young star who was producing wonderful residential designs, advised slashing the density from 100 units an acre to 25. "Most of the acreage should be developed as townhouses, with open space balanced among private, community and urban green," he said. Various configurations could be coordinated: stacked townhouses and free-standing homes, rowhouses with basement apartments and coach houses off mews, even a few towers in parkland.

Dorothy Rubel, newly retired as executive director of the Metropolitan Housing and Planning Council, was enthusiastic about residential development on the South Loop rail yards and recommended that it have high priority for public funding of basic infrastructure, parks, and schools. But, like the architects interviewed by Nory Miller, she did not like the proposed density. It would be 10 times the city's average, she wrote in an analysis of the plans, and twice that of Chicago's most densely populated one-quarter square mile.

Two of her recommendations were especially noteworthy and prophetic. For maximum impact, she said, the new community must include the land along the Chicago River. The waterfront should be developed for recreational purposes, a beautiful connector to the Loop. Bill Hartmann, Bruce Graham, and the other Skidmore architects working on South Loop plans agreed wholeheartedly. But Rubel did not think the Chicago 21 Corporation alone could amass sufficient land. She urged the creation of a quasi-public development corporation empowered by the state to sell revenue bonds for assembling, clearing, and packaging land tracts. New York's Urban Development Corporation should be a model.

Another Rubel suggestion was more radical. Because the new develop-ment would not attract and hold families like those who had been leaving for the suburbs unless it offered something better than the typical Chicago pub-lic school, she proposed "immediate exploration of a city contract with an out-standing suburban school system, such as Winnetka or Evanston, to establish a branch in the new town." Or, as an alternative, "a city contract with an in-stitution such as Northwestern University, the University of Chicago or the University of Illinois at Chicago to plan and operate school facilities serving the South Loop New Town and appropriate neighborhoods nearby."

In mid-1974, however, the new Chicago 21 Corporation had too many pressing, immediate concerns to lobby for a state-empowered development corporation or a new school system.

The April 4 announcement luncheon propelled George Halas and Ber-trand Goldberg into a whirl of meetings and telephone calls to push their own plans for the South Loop rail yards. Neither one tried to buck Chicago 21; the group was too well connected for that. Instead, they tried to sell their projects as pieces that could fit neatly into a renovated South Loop.

George Halas, now 79, embarked on a furious round of activities. Usually accompanied by his son-in-law, Ed McCaskey, he met with the publishers, editors, and editorial writers of the *Chicago Tribune*, the *Sun-Times*, and the *Chicago Daily News*; with Mayor Daley; with the city planning chief, Lew Hill; with John Perkins and Charles Willson of Continental Bank; with Tom Ayers; with Warren Skoning of Sears; with Ferd Kramer; and several times with Phil Klutznick.

Halas told them all that he was arranging an option to buy the 51 acres behind shuttered Dearborn Station for a stadium for his Bears. He was confi-dent of the financial backing of Ray Kroc of McDonald's and Col. Henry Crown of General Dynamics. In a letter to Daley shortly after the Chicago 21 luncheon, he wrote: "I believe the stadium will be a catalyst to stimulate the Chicago 21 Plan. . . . With your approval, Chicago will have a great stadium and will become the sports capital of the nation."

Halas told Klutznick that his option price of $3.25 an acre was less than half of what the railroads initially demanded. Klutznick admired his bargain-ing skills. Then Halas mentioned that he would need a developer for the sta-dium. Would Klutznick undertake that job? Now Klutznick admired the old coach even more; it was the sort of nervy thing he himself would do.

"I told him that in light of my voluntary commitment to Chicago 21, there could be a conflict of interest," Klutznick wrote in a memo to the Chicago 21 group. "Mr. Halas made it quite clear that his meeting with the Mayor was a friendly one and that the Mayor was deeply interested but did not give him a green light. All that he did was to suggest that he wanted him to see Lew Hill. . . . George has had his meeting with Lew, which he again said was friendly, but he had no firm commitment. . . .

"I pointed out that the piece of land they were talking about was in a sense a key piece from the point of view of developing the whole railroad track area. . . . He hastily said that as far as he is concerned as long as it is reachable by public transportation anywhere in the area would suit his purposes."

Klutznick asked his chief planner at Urban, Norman Elkin, to meet with Halas and McCaskey and their attorneys to explore alternate sites. Elkin came up with two near-Loop locations that Halas liked: the Near West Side and the Near Northwest Side. Both had big stretches of vacant or underused land; both were close to suburban rail depots and to expressways. The next day Elkin and Skidmore architects Bill Hartmann and Bruce Graham met with Lew Hill, who agreed that a South Loop rail yard location would not be compatible with a family-oriented residential development. He liked the Near West site; the University of Illinois could use it, as could nearby high school teams. But the mayor did not want to use city-backed bonds to help pay for a stadium, Hill said, whatever the site. Without help from those low-interest bonds, he thought the Halas group didn't have a chance to make it financially.

Bertrand Goldberg was a more worrisome problem. He was taking his River City models and films on the same rounds Halas had made—to city officials, newspapers, civic groups, the Chicago 21 leadership. He urged Tom Ayers and his board to adopt River City as their first phase. The president of Chessie System, which owned the stretch of riverfront land that Goldberg had in mind, contacted Ayers and John Perkins with the same plea. But River City scared them: Those enormous apartment towers would undermine their family-oriented plans and flood the rental market. Goldberg was planning on a federally subsidized mortgage; if River City flopped—and they feared it would—the U.S. Department of Housing and Urban Development might convert it into another Robert Taylor Homes or Cabrini-Green, practically at the doorstep of their new town.

Goldberg told everyone who suggested this scenario, including city officials, that he didn't mind if River City ended up with great numbers of subsidized families. People were people. But if his plans were carried out as he envisioned them, he said, no one had to worry about failure. The key to River City's success would be its very density and its "democracy of architecture."

Goldberg wrote to Tom Ayers on May 13, after they had met, reiterating that his plan would represent 15 to 20 years of construction and $2 billion in investment. He and his backers already had an option at $10 an acre on 100 acres, all of it along the river. "River City wants Chicago 21 to take steps to release this land from its planning negotiations with Lew Hill," Goldberg wrote. "It seems this can be done by recognition of River City as the first project of Chicago 21. Or, alternatively, Chicago 21 may wish to joint venture with River City."

The Chicago 21 group resented what they felt was his undue pressure and the pressure they were getting from his backers at Chessie. On May 22, John Perkins sounded out Lew Hill at breakfast and came back with a reassuring report: Hill said Goldberg is pushing very hard, but he believes River City is too huge and too dense and would be disastrous if it fails, an embarrassment to the city.

Still, Ayers worried about that letter from Goldberg. He asked Newton N. Minow, Klutznick's personal attorney, the former chairman of the Federal Communications Commission, and one of Chicago's most respected legal and civic leaders, to draft a reply. Ayers wanted to be certain that he said nothing that implied Chicago 21 was trying to undermine River City. Using Minow's suggested wording, Ayers wrote:

> We are working with City officials who believe, as we do, that an overall, coordinated plan for the area is a prerequisite to successful development. Once an overall plan has been agreed upon, development can begin and Chicago 21 is committed to encourage private companies and ventures to participate in such development in accordance with the plan.
>
> It would be self-defeating to divide the planning efforts into fragments which might or might not interface with one another. You have asked that we "release" certain land from our planning; this we cannot do because we neither own nor control the land. While we hope that you and your associates can await a more definitive plan, Chicago 21 has no authority to stop you from dealing with the public authorities directly. You are perfectly free to proceed on your own in discussions with the City.

A few days later, Goldberg's principal financial backer, Jerrold Wexler, called Klutznick. Wexler wanted to assure him that he wouldn't do anything contrary to Chicago 21's plans. "I told him there were some people who were getting put out about the kind of pressure that was involved," Klutznick wrote in a memo to his colleagues. "Jerry made it clear that he was going to do what he could to put an end to the pressure."

With both Halas and Goldberg put on hold, at least for a while, Klutznick turned his energies to his other big annoyance in the spring of 1974. Nearly two years had passed since he had first asked Mayor Daley for a written commitment that the City Council, the Park District, and the Board of Education would provide infrastructure and public amenities for a South Loop community. Without government picking up those costs, the whole venture was hopeless. The Skidmore architects and the Urban planners who formed South Loop Associates reported that Lew Hill and his staff were increasingly encouraging and helpful in their meetings, but there was no indication that a written commitment was forthcoming.

Charles Willson, who was coordinating Chicago 21's fund-raising, was also nervous about the absence of city action. Nearly $12 million had been pledged by mid-1974, but lately the response was "less than scintillating," Willson reported to the executive committee. The goal of $30 million by December 31 seemed wildly unrealistic. Potential investors needed assurance that the city would do its part in developing the South Loop New Town.

The chance of getting that anytime soon evaporated suddenly. For more than a year, Daley had been plagued by criminal charges against close political associates. A more hurtful spate of news reports had appeared in recent weeks, accusing him of steering city business to his four sons and questioning their professional qualifications. The mayor was furious, red faced, and sputtering at City Council meetings and sessions with reporters. On May 13 he suffered a stroke, his first serious illness during nearly 20 years as mayor. Three weeks later he underwent vascular surgery. He was away from his office until September, recuperating at his Michigan lakeshore retreat. Virtually all progress ceased on South Loop plans and on most other initiatives in which City Hall had a role. The city's guidelines for the new neighborhood, specifying maximum density and other requirements, had been promised for August 1. They did not appear.

Even the choice of a name for the new community was proving to be a hassle. South Loop Associates hired a name consultant—a ridiculous extravagance, in the view of Ferd Kramer, who was starting to chafe at the overhead the Skidmore-Urban group was piling up. The consultant's list included such oddities as Friend Town, Oasis, Fellowship, Mecca, and Rail Town. Marquette Place, after the 17th-century French explorer of the Chicago River, was better; so was Burnham Place, after the urban planner who promoted Chicago's lakefront parks. A Chicago 21 subcommittee finally settled on one of its own suggestions: Greenville. Then Carey Preston reminded the board of the disgraceful Treaty of Greenville of 1795 that snatched part of Ohio and Indiana from Native Americans. The search for a name continued.

Planning sessions between Lew Hill and his city team and Chicago 21's South Loop Associates got down to business again in the fall, after Daley's return to his office. It was likely, Hill made clear, that the city's guidelines for development—when they finally appeared—would specify a maximum density of only 50 units an acre, not the 100 envisioned in Skidmore's site plan.

Hill passed along another important message in a breakfast with John Perkins, Chicago 21's conduit to City Hall. The mayor had a reelection campaign coming up; the primary was in February 1975, the general election in April. Liberal, independent Democrats led by Alderman William Singer were mounting a strong primary challenge; the administration's handling of minority concerns would be a major issue. Chicago 21 needed to bring Hispanics and more blacks into its planning process, Hill said, and to make certain that its professional staff, when one was hired, was interracial. Otherwise, the city would have a difficult time investing in the development. Hill suggested that Chicago 21 get advice from two blacks who were close to Daley: State Senator Cecil Partee and Earl Neal, a real estate attorney who frequently served as a special city corporation counsel. Both men, Perkins wrote in a memo to Klutznick, "were solid people who had a sensitive and balanced approach to community problems and were well accepted in the total black community."

Klutznick agreed that the two could be helpful—not only in giving counsel, but also in keeping strident voices at bay. "I do think we need their advice before we move into discussions with additional representatives of the black and Latino community," he wrote. "I would hate to have a community convention get into the discussion on [the city's] policy statement."

The corporation's first birthday came and went in January 1975 with still no city guidelines or assurances on providing infrastructure. Nor did the business group have a site. On March 25, 1975, a fed-up Phil Klutznick halted all planning until the city provided a policy statement on land acquisition and infrastructure.

George Halas was also fed up. For a year, he had patiently tried to solicit city and Chicago 21 backing for a stadium on his 51 acres. He couldn't get the mayor to say yes, but neither did he say no. On April 11—10 days after Daley coasted to reelection and a sixth term—Halas announced publicly that he wanted the Bears to relocate to northwest suburban Arlington Heights, near Arlington Park Race Track.

Daley was livid. Let them go, he said, but they could no longer call themselves the "Chicago" Bears. "If they try," he said at a press conference, "they'll get the biggest contest they ever had."

John H. Perkins, the South Loop group's liaison to City Hall.

Halas's threat turned out to be Chicago 21's salvation. On May 1, Phil Klutznick and John Perkins had a watershed meeting with Daley and Lew Hill, "the best working meeting we have had," Klutznick wrote in a memo to other Chicago 21 leaders. When he mentioned the need for local government to pay for parks, a school, and other infrastructure, "at no point did the mayor disagree." Daley instructed Hill to cooperate with Chicago 21 in every way possible.

A few weeks later the mayor let George Halas know that he would not co-operate on a South Loop sports stadium. In a wistful letter to his attorney, Donald Lubin, Halas said he would be willing to transfer his option to Chicago 21. "There is just a slight touch of reluctance in giving up this property," he wrote. "With the adjacent subway and nearby expressways, you know it is the finest stadium location, which could be the center of attraction for the whole northern area of Illinois and adjacent states." He asked only to be reimbursed for his expenses and deposit—a total of $100,000.

"He might well have negotiated a higher price for the option," Lubin's partner Bernard Nath said later. "If he had wanted a million more, something like that, it was there. But he never asked for it."

Dearborn Park site prior to construction, with abandoned railroad buildings at left. Courtesy Dearborn Park Corporation.

Perhaps Halas had decided to be a hero, Nath speculated. In stepping aside, he would win Daley's gratitude and support in acquiring a new stadium site and building there. If that was his hope, it never materialized. Halas continued his search for another site, off and on, until he died in 1983. His grandson Michael McCaskey, who succeeded him as Bears president, also looked around from time to time and tried to pressure another Chicago mayor for help: Richard M. Daley. Twenty years after the 1975 exchanges between Daley and Halas, their heirs enacted an almost identical exchange that threatened to drag on into the next millennium. Meanwhile, the Bears remained at Soldier Field, paying rent to the Chicago Park District. Maybe that was what the first Daley had in mind all along.

Six weeks after their May Day meeting with the mayor, John Perkins and Phil Klutznick were back in Daley's office, joined by Tom Ayers. It was agreed that a prototype development would be built on the Halas site. Chicago 21 would acquire his option, with his bargain price tag of $7.3 million. The business group came away with the impression that Daley was agreeable to paying for streets, sewers, water connections, and other such necessities and still open to using revenue bonds to pay for the land. Typically, he did not offer to put this in writing, and the executives had learned by then it was pointless to urge him to do so.

The site was only 51 acres, nowhere near the 200 or 350 or 600 envisioned in various reports and plans since Tom Ayers and his two visitors had first talked about developing the rail yards five years earlier. It wasn't on the river, which the Skidmore architects, Dorothy Rubel of the Metropolitan Housing and Planning Council, and other land-use experts considered the choice site. But it came with that low price tag maneuvered by Coach Halas, and it lay on the portion of the rail yards closest to the Loop's financial and retail centers.

The Chicago 21 team could now concentrate on the bricks-and-mortar issues of what to build on its newly acquired wasteland.

Ferd and Phil, Together Again

reminded Tom Ayers of "two neighborhood cur dogs, snarling and spitting. I tell you, it was wonderful to watch."

To anyone else, the ferocious pair were the very essence of the successful chief executive of their era: impeccably turned out in gray pinstripes with snow-white shirts and muted silk ties, short thinning hair combed neatly back, straight and trim, confident and elegant. Kramer was tall and spare. His addiction to tennis seemed to have knocked a few decades off his 73 years. Klutznick was shorter and five years younger, with a striking resemblance to Jack Benny—when Benny was wearing his ultra-dignified mien.

By the time Chicago 21 Corporation was formed in 1974, Ferd Kramer and Phil Klutznick had been working together off and on for nearly 35 years. Their association was rooted in mutual respect and affection, and admiration for each other's integrity. They were also fiercely competitive, warily circling each other looking for slipups. Their arguments were legendary. Carl B. Bufalini, a Continental Bank development specialist on loan to Chicago 21, thought each was the only one who could handle the other. "When Phil would start ranting and raving, Ferd would jump in," he recalled. "When Ferd would get on one of his rampages, only Phil could bring him down. The others were always so polite, so indirect in dealing with each other."

At ages when most people with their financial resources had retired or were preparing to, they still sizzled with energy and ambition. They didn't eas-

60

ily suffer fools. Usually, though, Klutznick was more tactful in expressing his displeasure than Kramer.

Ferd Kramer and Phil Klutznick were the only members of Chicago 21's inner circle who actually had done what the group was attempting. "Their presence calmed our stockholders," Ayers said. "The investors were confident that Klutznick and Kramer knew how to build housing. They knew I didn't know how. Neither did the rest of us on the executive committee."

So, as Chicago 21 faced momentous choices during the summer of 1975, Phil Klutznick and Ferd Kramer took center stage.

Ferd Kramer was raised in one of the grand Prairie Avenue mansions on Chicago's Near South Side that were home to the city's merchant princes and other business elite at the turn of the century. His father, Adolph Ferdinand Kramer, was born in Chicago one year before the 1871 fire. In 1893, young Adolph Kramer and British immigrant Arthur Draper formed the mortgage-

Ferd Kramer, *left*, and Philip M. Klutznick, old friends reunited in developing Dearborn Park.

banking and real estate sales and management firm of Draper & Kramer. They opened an office on Dearborn Street, where 88 years later Kramer's son, Ferd, built a soaring glass-and-steel headquarters building with three stacked atriums; it was designed by Skidmore, Owings & Merrill.

Ferd Kramer was educated at the University of Chicago from the age of 14, first in its laboratory high school and then as a business student in the university. When Prairie Avenue deteriorated and the great stone houses were chopped into tiny flats, the Kramers moved south to the Hyde Park community surrounding the university. Watching Prairie Avenue crumble ignited an abiding passion in young Ferd: He resolved that the South Side would rise again.

In the late 1940s, Kramer built Hyde Park's first renewal projects. In the '50s and '60s, he won national acclaim for his well-constructed, reasonably priced, racially integrated developments near the old Prairie Avenue district, on South Michigan Avenue, and along the South Side lakefront. He lived in one of them, Prairie Shores, though he also had developed fine apartment buildings on Chicago's affluent North Side lakefront. His employees and friends marveled at this wealthy man who chose to live in a modest flat on the Near South Side, an easy walk to bleak public housing projects.

Philip Klutznick was reared in a kosher, Yiddish-speaking home in Kansas City, son of a cobbler from Poland. He remembered dropping his first coin into a collection box to reclaim a Jewish homeland when he was 13. The welfare and security of Israel became a lifelong concern. His energies seemed boundless. He was president of B'nai B'rith International, the Jewish service organization, and then U.S. ambassador to the United Nations Economic and Social Council while he was dotting the Chicago area with pioneering shopping centers. He was president of the World Jewish Congress, and then U.S. secretary of commerce under President Jimmy Carter while he was immersed in developing the South Loop. To some Jewish organizations he was a pariah for arguing that the Palestine Liberation Organization should be brought into the Mideast peace process. The verbal abuse hurt, but it didn't quiet him or deter him.

When Chicago 21 was organized, Phil Klutznick's son Thomas was running the family firm, Urban Investment and Development Company, and directing the creation of the 74-story Water Tower Place, a vertical shopping mall, office building, apartment building, and hotel that established Chicago's North Michigan Avenue as the nation's premier mixed-use development district. But Water Tower Place was Phil's baby; he picked the site, negotiated its purchase, and had the vision that shaped it.

As young men, Ferd Kramer and Phil Klutznick were enthusiastic supporters of President Franklin D. Roosevelt's new programs for construction of low-rent housing—Kramer in Chicago, Klutznick in Omaha. They admired each other's work. When Kramer was summoned to wartime Washington by Roosevelt to become deputy coordinator for the Division of Defense Housing Coordination, responsible for building what amounted to entire new towns near strategic installations, he hired Klutznick for his old job, program supervisor of defense housing in the Midwest. Two years later Kramer returned to Chicago to help run the family business, and Klutznick replaced him in Washington. In 1944 Roosevelt named Klutznick commissioner of the U.S. Public Housing Authority.

The Kramer-Klutznick collaboration continued after the war. Klutznick moved to Chicago to head American Community Builders; Draper & Kramer was one of two firms that arranged financing for Park Forest, the new town American was building south of Chicago, and for its shopping center. Later, Draper & Kramer handled the financing and managed most of Klutznick's shopping malls, including Water Tower Place.

Klutznick and Kramer shared a zeal for high-quality, integrated communities, but they often differed on how to achieve them. During the endless rounds of Chicago 21 meetings, recalled Tom Ayers, "Phil would get to talking lyrical. Ferd was a more pragmatic fellow. Phil was for the big plan, involving Washington and all. Ferd wanted to walk one step at a time."

In one of Klutznick's many long memos to his colleagues, he wrote that the new community must "meet a social need for rental facilities at the right price." It should be affordable to Loop sales clerks, schoolteachers, police officers, bus drivers, nurses—people priced out of other new near-downtown housing. To manage that, he said, Chicago 21 had to cut frills and seek every available subsidy. It should keep pressing Daley to buy the land with city bonds, provide streets, sidewalks, parks, and other basics and award some of his new federal community development grants to the South Loop New Town.

Ferd Kramer wanted only two forms of subsidies. First, the basic infrastructure, as Klutznick said; after all, the city would quickly get that money back in real estate taxes. Second, federal rent subsidies available through a state agency, the Illinois Housing Development Authority. Kramer had a practical reason for seeking these "Section 8" rent certificates: A subsidized building would assure a reliable income stream virtually from the day it opened; in fact, it should be the first Chicago 21 building on the market. But the only Section 8 program that interested Kramer was the one for people 62 and older. He did not want subsidized housing for families.

Kramer had no trouble convincing the executive committee that he was right. Tom Ayers and the others knew they had to have some subsidized housing; in their brochures and in speeches to civic groups, they had promised an economically diverse population. Low-income older people would supply that diversity without scaring away a single soul. The Chicago 21 leaders were already nervous about whether middle-class families, especially white middle-class families, would want to live on the fringe of the sleazy South Loop. Mixing in poor families, and the social problems that might come with them, could kill hopes of racial integration and possibly kill the project altogether. Besides, their original goal—endorsed by the city in its new South Loop development guidelines—was to create a downtown neighborhood of middle-class families.

The feedback they were getting was hardly reassuring. When Phil Klutznick asked for marketing tips from an analyst at First Chicago Realty Services, like First National Bank a subsidiary of First Chicago Corporation, she wrote: "Refer to the development as Chicago 21 only, never as the South Loop New Town. . . . *South* has a bad connotation in Chicago, and using the word with *Loop* is suicide."

A marketing survey commissioned by South Loop Associates reported that the overwhelming majority of every group questioned—city dwellers and suburbanites, blacks and whites and Hispanics—"pointed to some negative quality about the area."

Morris Janowitz, the University of Chicago sociologist who was advising Chicago 21, spoke eloquently about the importance of an economic mix of families, but the example he cited was not encouraging. South Commons, on Chicago's Near South Side near Lake Meadows and Prairie Shores, was designed to be a model of racial and economic integration. Its 1,500 high-rise, mid-rise, and townhouse units included subsidized apartments that were indistinguishable from the others. When it opened in the late 1960s, South Commons was about 30 percent black and 20 percent subsidized. Eight years later, despite good management and an attractive setting, it was rapidly losing unsubsidized tenants, especially the white ones. South Commons was projected to be nearly all black within a few years, with about two-thirds of its units subsidized by the federal government.

Ferd Kramer argued that the federal mortgage guarantees, development grants, and other subsidies Phil Klutznick wanted probably would require a sizable amount of low-cost housing for families. Chicago 21 also would need an environmental impact statement, subjecting it to a long series of reviews and hearings. It would lose control over what it could build and who would live in its new neighborhood. Kramer handed out copies of the April 1976 issue of *Practicing Planner* magazine, which described the woes of the big, multisubsidized Cedar-Riverside development near Minneapolis's central business district. A federal judge had just halted all work because of complaints about its environmental impact statement. Is this what the Chicago 21 investors wanted?

They did not, of course. The fewer government rules and regulations, the better. Dealing with Daley and his City Hall was fine; they knew and understood each other. Washington was something else. Still, the latest figures from South Loop Associates were unsettling. The 1973 brochures had trumpeted an average sales price of $26,000 a unit. Early in 1976, South Loop Associates recalculated and came up with a figure that was almost 70 percent higher. Also, Chicago 21's investment drive was sputtering out at $13.9 million, less than half of its goal. A total of 32 corporations had invested. Charles Willson, supervising the fund-raising, reported that recruiting new investors was difficult because it appeared to the public that absolutely nothing had happened since the festive Chicago 21 announcement luncheon two years earlier. Without big government subsidies and more capital to provide its own subsidies, Chicago 21 would have to attract a more affluent group of residents than originally planned. Phil Klutznick didn't like it, but his dream of a Loop workers' village was fading.

While Chicago 21's leaders were debating the merits of subsidies and an income mix, the urban planners and architects of South Loop Associates were waging a small war of their own. Norman Elkin and the rest of the planning contingent from Urban wanted housing that looked familiar, cozy, comfortable. The architects from Skidmore wanted fresh, exciting designs. Like Bertrand Goldberg with his River City plans, they relished the opportunity to create new ways for people to live and relate to the central city—thus their glassy skywalks, multilevel retail plazas, minitrains gliding through 700-foot-long buildings. As far as Elkin was concerned, the architects were stuck back in the 1950s and 1960s, under the spell of Le Corbusier and his conviction that architecture should drive city planning. Elkin thought the Skidmore designs were cold and oversized. They reflected the way the architects thought people should live instead of the way people themselves wanted to live. As for that six-story, 600-unit, 700-foot-long building, Elkin said, "We sat down with Ferd, and we figured out we would be in receivership by the time we got to the third floor."

Elkin and his ally Glenn Steinberg were disciples of Jane Jacobs and Oscar Newman, who advocated in their writings that urban planners and architects should aim for a sense of community, for "eyes on the street" and "defensible space." Sidewalks and people looking out of windows in rowhouses promoted security and neighborliness; skywalks, underground passages, and apartment towers surrounded by open meadows did not. Skidmore, Elkin said, was "the three blind Mies of architecture," a near-sacrilegious reference to Ludwig Mies van der Rohe and the clean, powerful structures he and his followers had created in Chicago.

In this dispute, Kramer and Klutznick were in solid agreement on the side of Elkin and the others from Urban. So was Tom Ayers, never a fan of the futuristic designs in the Chicago 21 Plan. "We were building a Model T," he said. "If somebody wanted to build a Year 2000 car, why that was fine, but we just wanted something that was reliable, that people would want. You know, architects like to build monuments. Well, that's kind of unfair for me to say. But they do want to do things in their own way."

Ayers liked the way Kramer and Klutznick challenged the architects. "They could talk to them in a way that I had no ability to, because I didn't know enough about the business," he said. "Boy, they could knock the socks off them on a few things."

Twenty years later, Skidmore's Bruce Graham still was unhappy about the lost opportunity. Mainly, he blamed Ferd Kramer and Tom Ayers for draining the excitement from the early concept. He thought they were too squeamish, not just in insisting on familiar-looking housing but also in set-

Architects' final master plan of Dearborn Park, looking south from a renovated Dearborn Station, summer of 1976. Courtesy Skidmore, Owings & Merrill.

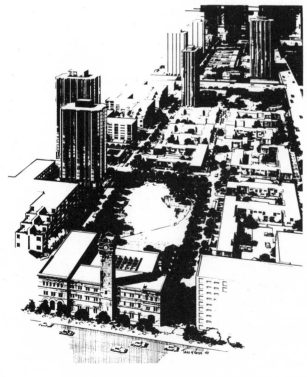

tling for 51 acres instead of campaigning aggressively for city and state help in getting a much bigger site that included the riverfront. "I've known a lot of good developers," he said. "They're all suicidal. They love risk taking. The Chicago 21 leadership was not suicidal."

With just 51 acres, the minitrains had to go. So did the landscaped riverfront and the commuter boats. The city's South Loop guidelines specified a maximum average density of 60 units an acre, compared with 100 in the early plans; the massive tiers of stepped-back townhouses and the multitude of high-rises were out, too.

The architects went back to the drawing boards and did master plan after master plan. Elkin and his Urban staff kept turning them down, asking for something simpler, more traditional. Finally, by the summer of 1976, a plan took shape that was acceptable to Urban and the Chicago 21 executive committee. It had just a few high-rise buildings, a row of mid-rises with six or seven stories, and clusters of townhouses and two-flats; the last was an old Chicago favorite. All would be clad in warm red brick, grouped around courtyards, connected by walkways, and softened by abundant greenery. There were no overpasses or underpasses, nothing overpowering. Nothing that hadn't been built in Chicago before.

The new community would be constructed in two segments. The first was the 24 acres north of Roosevelt Road. It would have 1,456 units, two-thirds of them rentals in high-rises and mid-rises; the rest would be for-sale high-rise and mid-rise condominiums and townhouses. The plan grouped taller buildings along State Street (the site's eastern border) and Polk Street (the northern border). Culs-de-sac would shield the community from Roosevelt Road, which was a viaduct over railroad tracks, and from Clark Street, a heavily traveled, partially elevated north-south route to the downtown that formed the western border. Clusters of 125 townhouses, 100 two-flats, and several parks nestled in the interior. A mid-rise building with 190 rent-subsidized apartments was reserved for people 62 and older. The plan had families in mind. One-fourth of the units had three or four bedrooms, twice the average in Chicago residential construction in recent years; one-third had two bedrooms. Construction was to start on April 1, 1977—15 months later than Klutznick's original date.

Site plan of northern half of Dearborn Park, summer of 1976, including high-rise and mid-rise buildings near Roosevelt Road that were eventually dropped. Courtesy Skidmore, Owings & Merrill.

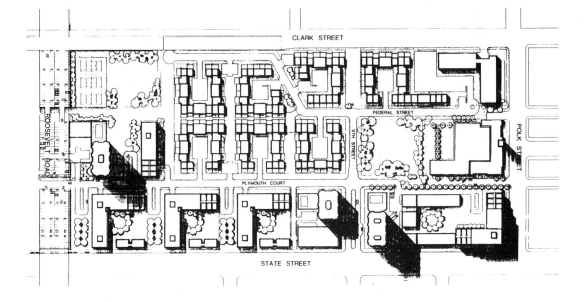

The second segment, with 1,544 units on 27 acres, would be virtually a mirror image of the first, except that it would have 50,000 square feet of retail space and 205 townhouses instead of 125.

Architects with residential experience would be invited to design the various types. Klutznick, eager to head off any charges that Chicago 21 was shutting out noninvestor firms, insisted on this. The rest of the executive committee agreed; Skidmore was justifiably famous for its strong skyscrapers, but not for housing. The goal was to hit the market with a variety of residential styles simultaneously.

As details of the site plan seeped out to the news media and to architects and neighborhood organizations throughout the city, a new round of criticism erupted. The Chicago 21 leadership was accused of dullness and lack of vision; of turning its back on the city by walling off State Street; of trying to prevent South Side blacks from driving through the new community by cutting off north-south through streets and allowing only two access streets, both of them east-west; of grouping rental buildings together to isolate their residents, who were more likely than the townhouse owners to be black.

The Coalition of Central Area Communities reconstituted itself as the Coalition to Stop Chicago 21. It labeled the plan racist and elitist.

It was not racism, however, that drove the plan, but an overriding conviction that the project would fail unless prospective residents felt safe living there. Traffic and security consultants hired by South Loop Associates had strongly recommended abolishing Chicago's traditional grid street pattern and using only 9th Street in the northern half of the 51 acres and 14th Street in the southern half for auto access. The consultants also wanted taller buildings along State Street, interspersed with fences and shrubs. The planners from Urban and the architects from Skidmore agreed wholeheartedly with these proposals. Heavy auto traffic and easy access by the drunks, panhandlers, and porn-shop devotees who wandered through much of the South Loop, especially South State Street, were not, they felt, compatible with a cozy family atmosphere.

Race was a major concern in a different respect. Lew Hill, the city's planning chief, was prodding his Chicago 21 contacts—John Perkins and Charles Willson of Continental Bank—to add a Hispanic board member and minority-owned consulting firms. Willson and Phil Klutznick were impressed with Fidel Lopez, the Pilsen architect who had helped form the Coalition of Central Area Communities. Other Chicago 21 leaders thought Lopez was too much of a firebrand to join their board. They wondered whether he had sufficiently "arrived."

Willson was annoyed. "Whether or not he has 'arrived' I suppose is a matter of individual judgment," he wrote in a memo to his boss, Perkins. "Many people feel that President Ford hasn't arrived as President and many wish Richard Nixon had not." Fidel Lopez, he said, had "a sensitive social conscience and sees clearly the Latino picture. . . . He communicates well with the Anglo sector, reflecting a high degree of culture and composure."

Willson also liked Sebastian Rivera. A "well-respected, bright attorney," he wrote, "self-made, articulate and of a conservative mold. He has been appointed to several commissions by the Mayor and obviously is well received at City Hall."

That did it. On March 1, 1976, Sebastian Rivera joined the Chicago 21 board. Fidel Lopez did not.

Louis Martin, one of three black board members and president of Sengstacke Newspapers, suggested hiring the black-owned Chicago Economic Development Corporation for additional market surveys. It was done. Martin also offered to scout minority construction firms, with the help of the Chicago Urban League.

Adding minority consultants was easy compared with another race-related matter. The executive committee spent many hours discussing the delicate subject of how to prevent the new community from becoming largely black. Most members danced around the topic, according to Carl Bufalini, Chicago 21's chief of staff, except for one. "Ferd Kramer, bless his heart, ran right into it," Bufalini said. "He told us, 'Look, if you want to keep a balanced community, you've got to set quotas.' Of course, everybody else said, 'We can't *set quotas*!'"

For years Kramer had been giving preference to whites on the waiting list to maintain an overall ratio in the Lake Meadows–Prairie Shores development of about half black, half white. He thought Chicago 21 should be prepared to do likewise. No such system existed at South Commons, and it was losing its whites. But Lew Hill in City Hall and Louis Martin warned of political and legal consequences if Chicago 21 instituted racial preferences in so public a project. Martin even warned against putting the topic on the agenda at meetings. He advised that, "if at all possible, this be a subject discussed privately only," Willson wrote in a memo to Phil Klutznick.

When the Chicago Economic Development Corporation's report was circulated among executive committee members in October, it seemed to justify Chicago 21's worries. Among its conclusions: There is "an American tipping point" at which whites leave a neighborhood as blacks move in; experience indicates this tipping point is about 20 percent. So, "if racial stability is a goal, arrange to maintain Black occupancy levels at 18 percent or less." Mixing market-priced housing with identical units of subsidized housing does not work. "Whenever possible select Black and White occupants of matched socio-economic status. . . . Rent to young, high-income Blacks."

The report did not explicitly recommend a quota system for approving residents, but it did advise that "Without control there has been a total failure to achieve interracial communities."

It had good news, though, about the possibility of attracting that magical 18 percent of suitable black buyers and renters. Because of Chicago's dire shortage of decent housing available to middle-class blacks, most of them were either trapped in segregated ghettos or paying a stiff premium to escape. Chicago 21 would do well to tap into this vast pool of potential occupants.

State Senator Cecil Partee, one of Daley's trusted black advisers, had been saying the same thing. At his suggestion, Chicago 21 hired Charles A. Davis Associates, a black-owned firm, to promote the South Loop New Town among affluent blacks. John Perkins hosted luncheons at Continental Bank for black professional women and the Chicago chapter of a black social sorority; Chicago 21 board member Carey Preston had been a national officer. Talk up this project among your friends, Perkins told them.

Ferd Kramer, meanwhile, was beginning to wonder if the new town would be affordable to enough people, black or white, to fill its 3,000 units. He was boiling at the way bills were piling up. Chicago 21 already had commissioned more than $1 million in professional services, which he thought was outrageous. Why spend so much time and money on studies and surveys and meetings and consultants to smooth relations with black and Hispanic neighborhoods, when Chicago 21 was not going to uproot anyone?

Kramer wrote, but never sent, a letter to Carl Bufalini: "We have now been involved in the development on the site of the railroads south of the Loop for two years. With the exception of acquiring the option on the first 51 acres, we still appear to be quite a long way off from breaking ground. I should like to point out that in the planning and development of the 130 acres occupied by Lake Meadows and Prairie Shores, no such lead time was taken. . . . It seems to me that entirely too much is being spent on research and paperwork that is of little value."

Guidelines could be "firmed up within a week," he wrote, "and then presented to architects who [would] present a preliminary plan within 60 days, showing not only the site plan but also the number of units, the number in each type of building, the size of the apartments, parks, recreational facilities, and convenience shopping."

Kramer didn't send the letter, but he did complain to Phil Klutznick, who persuaded him to give it a bit more time.

The planners of South Loop Associates felt that Kramer didn't appreciate the difference between this project and the high-rise, all-rental apartments of Lake Meadows and Prairie Shores. Those projects pre-dated the protest movements born during the civil rights crusades. Chicago 21 was being scrutinized in a way that Kramer never was when he built Prairie Shores. Tom Ayers and Phil Klutznick agreed that a cautious, cover-every-base approach was wise. Besides, the education and security studies were partially paid for by grants from Chicago Community Trust, a private foundation, and the Illinois Law Enforcement Commission, a public agency.

The education proposals were especially promising, and for all Chicago, not just the South Loop. The new Chicago school superintendent, Joseph P. Hannon, wanted to create a model system in the area that could be replicated throughout the city. He dazzled Chicago 21 shareholders at a meeting in March 1976 with plans for career-oriented programs at the high school level that would draw on the resources of Continental Bank, Illinois Bell Telephone Company, the Federal Aviation Administration, the Chicago Apparel Center, the city's acclaimed medical schools and hospitals, and the lakefront museums not far from the Chicago 21 site. A new Center for Urban Education would relate the schools to life in the city and would work to improve both. A new South Loop elementary school would double as an educational, recreational, and cultural center for parents.

Evans Clinchy, Chicago 21's Boston-based education consultant, contributed an intriguing idea: Offer a choice to parents, but within the public school system. A new South Loop school would join three or four existing schools in surrounding neighborhoods to form a single attendance area. Each school would have a distinct educational philosophy: a Montessori system in one, an open-classroom system in another, a rigorous traditional approach in a third, and so forth. Parents within this district could apply to any of the schools, partly on a first-come, first-served basis but maneuvered to assure racial and economic diversity. Busing would be needed for most students.

Glenn Steinberg, overseeing school plans for South Loop Associates, was enthusiastic. He thought the concept could transform public education in Chicago and improve the social climate as well.

An evaluation by Skidmore concluded that the 90-year-old Dearborn Station, which came with the rest of the railroad property, was suitable for restoration. It would be ideal for a school and community center and a charming showcase for the development. The Chicago 21 leaders agreed and asked Skidmore for a design package.

As these plans took shape, Phil Klutznick grew increasingly concerned about the absence of a written commitment from the city that it would pay for infrastructure, parks, and a school. Early in 1976, Lew Hill had hinted to South Loop Associates that Chicago 21 should be prepared to pay for streets, sidewalks, streetlights, sewers, and water connections, as well as the land. This would add an average of $4,440 to the cost of each unit when borrowing charges were factored in, according to Elkin's staff. John Perkins picked up another message from City Hall: Lew Hill "felt somehow there was a killing to be made on the development."

This was probably just a tough negotiating stance on Hill's part, directed by the mayor. Daley, as was his style, did not want to state unequivocally that Chicago 21 should forget about city revenue bonds to pay for land acquisition. He wanted the group to realize this on their own. Charles Willson had argued all along that it would be more efficient and cheaper in the long run if Chicago 21 bought the $7.3-million site and then sold to the city, at Chicago 21's cost, the acreage for parks and a school. He offered Hill a trade-off: Chicago 21 would buy the 51 acres and forget about any additional land purchases with revenue bonds; the city would pay for peripheral and internal infrastructure, converting old Dearborn Station into a school, and buying and landscaping the parks. That arrangement suited the mayor. He sent word that it would be done.

The mayor helped with another matter. Architect Harry Weese, whose creative ideas for the city had once made the cover of *Esquire* magazine, was rounding up support for saving the historic office buildings directly north of the Chicago 21 site and converting them into loft residences. He loved the long-span, timber-and-wrought-iron train shed behind Dearborn Station, oldest of its type in the United States. He drew plans for recycling it as a racquet club, flower market, and boutique strip and thought the Chicago 21 leaders were a bunch of fuddy-duddies for not agreeing that this would enhance their property. Weese and other preservationists applied to put the shed on the National Register of Historic Places, which would make demolition difficult.

But Daley did his stuff. While the application was pending, the city granted a demolition permit to Chicago and Western Indiana Railroad, still the official owner. The Weese group won a temporary order in a U.S. district court to block it. Four days later, at the formal request of the railroad and Chicago 21 Corporation, the restraining order was lifted. The sheds were demolished in May 1976.

December 1976 began with a burst of activity. Phil Klutznick, agreeing now with Ferd Kramer's assessment, wrote a long memo complaining about "too much input from experts and others without a tight control within our own organization." He warned about mounting costs and ordered a number of trims, including—to the regret of future residents—only 850 off-street parking spaces for the northern 1,456 units instead of the already-too-meager 975. "After all," he wrote, "this is supposed to be a public transportation site." He eliminated the below-ground garages planned for the townhouses and cut their storage areas. The two-flats disappeared, replaced by a few more townhouses and mid-rise apartments.

At Klutznick's urging, the executive committee adopted the agenda Kramer had suggested six months earlier: By mid-January, Skidmore would select architects for each of the building styles, ask them to have preliminary designs and proposals ready by mid-February, and aim for bids from contractors by March 31. It was a tight schedule, but the committee and the board of directors felt good about getting under way at last.

On December 16, South Loop Associates gave its site plans and a pro forma (a cost and marketing projection) to Chicago 21 shareholders at their annual meeting. When some expressed concerns that the project might run at a loss in its early years, Ayers said the corporation would do its utmost to provide the 6.5 percent return. But he reminded them that there was "a large degree of pro bono publico" in this venture. One shareholder rose to say that anyone who couldn't afford to lose his investment shouldn't participate.

The meeting ended on an upbeat note. At the suggestion of Norman Ross, a First National Bank officer and popular Chicago radio and television commentator, the shareholders approved a name for the development: Dearborn Park, paying homage to Chicago's premier architectural street and also to its history. Fort Dearborn, named for Revolutionary War hero Henry Dearborn, who later became President Thomas Jefferson's secretary of war, had protected the little settlement at the mouth of the river the native population called Checagou from 1803 until it was burned down by the Potawatomi nation during the bloody Fort Dearborn Massacre of 1812. American soldiers rebuilt it four years later, and the community that grew around it was incorporated as the village of Chicago in 1833.

The shareholders also voted to change their name from Chicago 21 to Dearborn Park Corporation. One reason, Carl Bufalini later joked, was to confound the Coalition to Stop Chicago 21.

Two cautionary notes did not seem worth worrying about at the moment. Herbert Johnson, a Continental Bank executive on the Chicago Board of Education, told John Perkins that no one on the school board except Carey Preston knew about School Superintendent Hannon's big plans for the South Loop; Hannon had never brought the matter before the board. And Harold Jensen, vice president of real estate for Illinois Central Industries, said the new development could not operate with financial stability unless Daley's promise to provide infrastructure was in the form of a contractual ordinance; Daley might seem immortal, but it was likely that the project would span several administrations.

Four days after the shareholders meeting, Mayor Richard J. Daley stopped in to see his doctor on North Michigan Avenue. He had been bothered by chest pains that morning as he presided over the dedication of a new Chicago Park District gymnasium. Daley phoned his son Michael from the doctor's office, and while talking to him he slumped over and died.

The leaders of the Dearborn Park Corporation, like most of Chicago, could not imagine the city working without him.

7

"I Am at My Wit's End"

MAYBE IT WAS THE SUDDEN DEATH OF THE MAN THEY HAD COUNTED ON TO SHEPHERD them through the thickets ahead that left Dearborn Park's leaders in such a frazzled state as 1977 began. Or the anxiety over finally getting down to the business of building, after five years of talking and planning and raising money. Whatever the reason, the year was starting out miserably.

At an executive committee meeting on January 6, Chairman Tom Ayers introduced his choice for Dearborn Park's first full-time, paid chief executive: Raymond C. Wieboldt Jr., a grandson of the founder of Chicago's Wieboldt Stores and chairman of the Wieboldt Foundation. A pleasant man who was well known in Chicago's civic and philanthropic community, Wieboldt had run a major construction firm for 20 years until it fell on hard times. He had been highly recommended to Ayers by executives at Inland Steel Company, a Dearborn Park investor; he had headed Inland's development subsidiary after folding his construction business.

Phil Klutznick, presiding over Dearborn Park's executive committee, asked for a vote on Ayers's motion to elect Wieboldt president of the corporation. John Perkins, the Continental Bank chief executive who had been serving as unpaid president, would shift to vice-chairman. Everyone voted yes except Ferd Kramer, who abstained. He was furious that committee members were expected to decide the matter in Wieboldt's presence and without a mention of his salary. (He learned later it was to be $70,000 a year, which he thought was too high.) Besides, Kramer wasn't sure Wieboldt had the right experience to oversee a big, complicated residential development.

75

A few days later, Kramer had another reason to be irked. He had been trying to get Klutznick to pay attention to an analysis prepared by his Draper & Kramer staff of the financial assumptions submitted in December by Dearborn Park's consultants from Urban Development and Investment Company. In effect, Kramer had asked his firm to second-guess the work of Klutznick's firm.

Klutznick did not put the Draper & Kramer analysis on the executive committee agenda. To make matters worse, on January 11 Kramer got a rather brusque letter from George Darrell, Urban's executive vice president, addressed to "Dear Fred." It wasn't signed.

Kramer promptly responded, "I have your unsigned letter addressed to Fred Kramer, whom I presume is I. . . . The work that my office did, and which I had ready to present to the executive committee if Phil had wanted it to be presented . . . needed to be done . . . because we felt some of the assumptions that you made were unrealistic." A meeting Kramer had scheduled with Urban had been canceled by Darrell's office, he wrote, and he had been unable to get a new appointment.

Kramer was convinced that Urban had priced the high-rise rental buildings substantially above what Chicago's market would accept. He thought overhead was running too high; nearly one-third of the projected costs for the first phase were nonconstruction expenses. In another respect, he felt the planners from Urban had been too conservative; to compete with suburban developments, he wanted more parking and an indoor recreational facility with tennis and racquetball courts and a gymnasium—even if it meant running at a loss the first few years. Phil Klutznick had flatly rejected Kramer's proposals. They were luxuries Dearborn Park couldn't afford and wouldn't need, he said; the nearby resources of the Loop and the lakefront would be adequate substitutes. The two had been arguing these points for well over a year; Klutznick, who could easily dominate a meeting, got his way. "He was so dynamic," said Carey Preston, remembering those spirited Dearborn Park sessions. "Sometimes I felt he was in love with the sound of his own voice. But he did know how to get things done."

A few weeks after Wieboldt's appointment, Kramer quit. He sent a letter to Tom Ayers, criticizing the presentation of Wieboldt as an accomplished fact. "If this decision is not important enough for a full blown discussion and final decision in executive session, I can see no need for an executive committee," he wrote. "I therefore tender my resignation from the board and the executive committee."

In a separate letter to Klutznick, he complained about "the numerous occasions on which you have made it very clear that you were not interested in my opinion . . . climaxed by interrupting my comments in the recent meeting with [architect Bill] Hartmann.

"You and I have had a wonderful relationship both in the government and public affairs and in business. . . . I have only the highest regard for your ability and your opinions and I think you have the same regard for me . . . but for some reason or other, this has not held true on matters pertaining to Chicago 21."

It was inevitable that high-powered chief executives, accustomed to running their own businesses, would clash on a collaborative effort such as Dearborn Park. Ayers and Klutznick knew they had to heal this rupture with Kramer, the only one of their group with experience in financing, marketing, and managing residential developments as well as building them. Klutznick took on the task with his customary diplomatic skill. In a "My dear Ferd" letter, he said he understood why Kramer felt aggrieved, and he acknowledged that mistakes had been made. "It has been clear to me for some time that you are terribly unhappy . . . . I think there has been too much time that we have both permitted to pass without sitting down and talking to one another. . . . We have been friends too long and worked together too long to permit things of this sort to emerge. If you are prepared to do so, I am prepared to pay for a lunch, since I owe you many, at which we can sit down and really go over some of these problems. Let us not let an old friendship fall apart without doing something to put it back together again."

It worked. Kramer withdrew his resignation. Reviving his beloved South Side was more important to him than a bruised ego.

Klutznick had another problem. City Hall was in shock after Daley's death. Acting Mayor Michael Bilandic, a mild-mannered lawyer who lived near Daley in Bridgeport and had become the mayor's City Council floor leader after Alderman Thomas Keane went to jail, was trying to get a grasp on the job. His cabinet members and their underlings, unsure what would happen to them or what they were expected to do, did nothing. Meanwhile, Dearborn Park needed to get its plan approved in the City Council, and various city departments had to get started on infrastructure planning and installation.

Klutznick was worried, too, about the possible repercussions of Daley's way of doing business. Dearborn Park had nothing in writing confirming Daley's handshake agreements to pay for streets, sewers, parks, a school. In the months after Daley's death, a nonstop stream of supplicants visited Bilandic's office to say, "But Mayor Daley promised . . ." Klutznick did not want to be lumped into that mass.

In the corporation's early days, he had asked his friend and lawyer Newton Minow, partner in the influential law firm of Sidley & Austin, to recommend legal counsel. Minow had a special interest in South Loop development and wanted to help it along. As a Northwestern University law student in the 1940s, he had written a paper on reclaiming unused railroad land for productive purposes. He picked two young lawyers in his firm, James L. Marovitz and Jack Guthman. Marovitz, who had done legal work for Klutznick's suburban developments, became Dearborn Park's counsel in real estate and contractual matters. Guthman, a fund-raiser and organizer in Daley's mayoral campaigns and a friend of both Bilandic and city Planning Commissioner Lew Hill, took charge of legislative and regulatory matters. Marovitz remained the corporation's lawyer for the rest of its existence. For Guthman, the Dearborn Park assignment eventually led to national prominence as an authority on zoning and other legal issues associated with big developments.

Both were regulars at Dearborn Park meetings. Guthman spent a half dozen years unraveling snarls with the city Departments of Public Works, Development and Planning, and Streets and Sewers; with the Chicago Park District; with the Cook County Assessor's Office; with all the City Council committees that had to approve Dearborn Park plans; with the Illinois Housing Development Authority and the U.S. Department of Housing and Urban Development, which took 20 months to decide whether Dearborn Park needed an environmental impact statement (the final answer: no); and with the Chicago Plan Commission, which had to approve a detailed Planned Unit Development application before work could begin. Marovitz created condominium associations and their bylaws, drafted and scrutinized contracts, helped assess all manner of residents' complaints, and steered the corporation through threatened (and a few actual) lawsuits.

Guthman arranged a February 28 introductory meeting with Bilandic and Dearborn Park leaders. The new acting mayor said he wanted to help in every way possible: Final plans would be unveiled in a City Hall press conference in May; his cabinet would expedite work on infrastructure plans; and—most welcome news of all—he would introduce an ordinance spelling out the city's responsibility for installing and paying for infrastructure.

The Dearborn Park group left the meeting elated. For months, their optimism seemed justified.

The Interstate Commerce Commission, after more than a year of dawdling, gave its approval for the discontinuation of the 51 acres for railroad purposes. Dearborn Park promptly bought the land for the Halas-arranged price of $7.3 million, more than half of its capital. "That was the thing that made us," Tom Ayers said later. If the price had been double that amount, as the railroads wanted, instead of the bargain the tough old coach engineered, Dearborn Park might never have emerged from the rail yards.

Top: Terrace Homes, developed by Daniel McLean in Dearborn Park's south neighborhood, with unusual combination of two-story townhouses built over single-story homes. Architect: Barton Associates. Photo by Michael J. Kardas.

Federal Square townhouses, popular with first-time buyers and singles, developed by George Thrush along Roosevelt Road in Dearborn Park's south neighborhood. Architect: Pappageorge Haymes. Photo by Michael J. Kardas.

Top: Dearborn Park's costliest residences, single-family Prairie Manor Homes developed by Daniel McLean, with features reminiscent of Frank Lloyd Wright's Prairie School. Architect: FitzGerald & Associates. Courtesy MCL Development.

Ornamental entrance of a Prairie Manor Home. Photo by Rick Stetter.

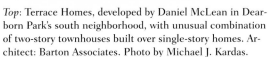

Lunchtime at Lindas Margaritas in the renovated Dearborn Station on Polk Street. Photo by Michael J. Kardas.

The Romanesque Donohue Building, built in 1883 as Dearborn Street's first printing house. Ninety-three years later, Printers Row's first residents moved in. Photo by Michael J. Kardas.

Colorful tile mosaic showing men at work on early printing presses adorns facade of New Franklin Building on Printers Row. It was converted to residential use in 1987. Photo by Michael J. Kardas.

Architect's conception of future use of Roosevelt Road viaduct, with shops and other commercial enterprises tucked under the roadway. Courtesy DLK Architecture.

◄ Aerial view of nearly completed Dearborn Park, looking northeast to the Loop and Lake Michigan. The elevated Roosevelt Road separates the northern neighborhood from the newer southern half. Photo by Lawrence Okrent, © 1995.

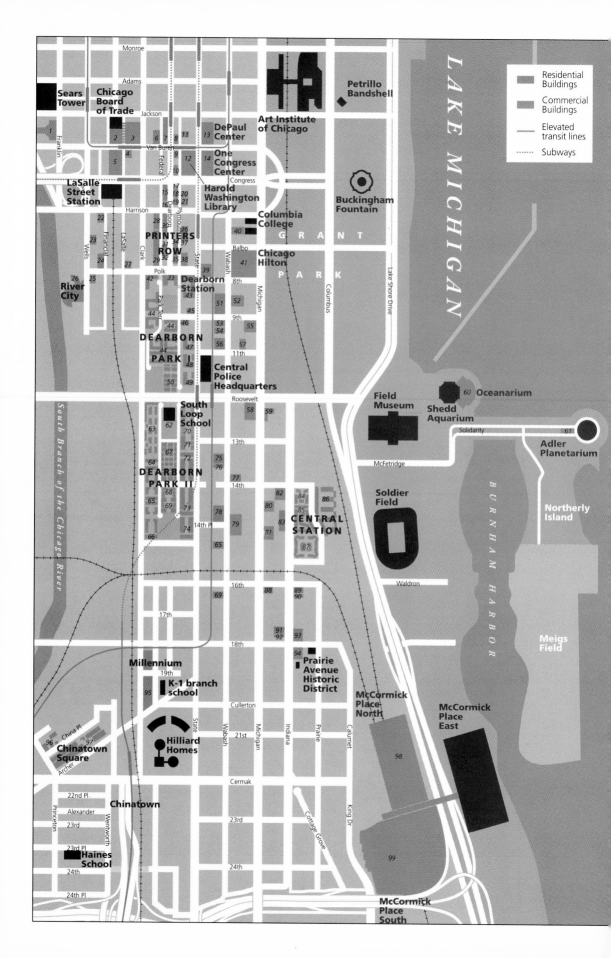

Near South Development, 1977–1997

1 311 South Wacker, office, 1990
2 & 3 Board of Trade additions, 1983, 1997
4 Atrium Bldg., office, 1985*
5 One Financial Place, office, 1984
6 South Loop Garage, 1989
7 Monadnock Block, office, 1992*
8 Fisher Bldg., office, 1982*
9 Old Colony, office, 1984*
10 Manhattan Bldg., 105 apts., 1982*
11 Chicago Bar Assn., office, 1990
12 Harold Washington Library, 1991
13 DePaul Center, office/university, 1993*
14 One Congress Center, office, 1986*
15 Hyatt Hotel Printers Row, 1987**
16 Pontiac Bldg., office, 1986*
17 41 West Congress, office, 1989
18 Old Franklin Bldg., 54 apts., 1984*
19 Terminals Bldg., 52 apts., 1986*
20 Peterson Lofts, 49 apts., 1995*
21 Mergenthaler Lofts, 50 apts., 1980*
22 Market Square, 82 apts., 1997*
23 The Regal, 84 apts., 1987*
24 Polk St. Station, 138 apts., 1996*
25 801 South Wells, 108 apts., 1990*
26 River City, office/446 apts., 1985
27 Folio Square, 63 apts., 1989*
28 Printers Square, office, 1983**
29 Printers Square, 356 apts., 1983*
30 Transportation Bldg., 294 apts., 1983*
31 Rowe Bldg., 9 apts., 1979*
32 New Franklin Bldg., 66 apts., 1989*
33 Dearborn Station, office/retail, 1987*
34 GracePlace, church, 1986*
35 Donohue Bldg., 95 apts., 1980*
36 Moser Bldg., 88 apts., 1988*
37 Pope Bldg., 91 apts., 1986*
38 Columbia College residences, 1985*
39 Two East Eighth, 330 apts., 1985
40 Columbia College campus, 1987*
41 Chicago Hilton & Towers, 1985*

DEARBORN PARK I
  42 The Oaks, 190 apts., 1979
  43 The Terraces, 220 units, 1983
  44 Townhouses, 144 units, 1979
  45 & 46 High-rises, 370 apts., 1979, 1980
  47–49 Mid-rises, 235 units, 1979–81
  50 McNeil townhouses, 51 units, 1985

51 Burnham Park Plaza, 281 apts., 1987**

52 The Loftrium, office, 1986*
53 Fairbanks Lofts, 36 apts., 1988*
54 916 South Wabash Lofts, 16 apts., 1990*
55 Michigan Avenue Lofts, 262 apts., 1997*
56 Eleventh Street Lofts, 52 apts., 1995*
57 Getz Theatre of Columbia College, 1986*
58 1212 South Michigan, 343 apts., 1982
59 Grant View Apartments, 110 apts., 1987*
60 Shedd Oceanarium, 1992
61 Adler Planetarium addition, 1991

DEARBORN PARK II
  62 South Loop School, 1988
  63 Federal Square, 117 townhouses, 1994
  64 Terrace Homes, 32 units, 1994
  65 Prairie Town Homes, 72 units, 1993
  66 & 67 Prairie Manor Homes, 42 houses, 1992–97
  68 Atrium Townhomes, 14 units, 1995
  69 Park Homes, 12 houses, 1994
  70 Chicago Homes, 36 houses, 1994
  71 Newgate Square, 41 townhouses, 1994
  72 & 73 Rowhouses, 72 units, 1990–93
  74 Metropolitan Mews, 48 townhouses, 1991

75 Filmworks Lofts, 86 apts., 1995*
76 Filmworks II, 10 townhouses, 1997
77 Wabash Corner Lofts, office, 1994*
78 Townhomes on Wabash, 16 units, 1997
79 Soka Gakkai Buddhist center, 1995
80 Letter Carriers Union Bldg., 1988
81 Trevi Square, 69 apts., 1996*
82 Senior Suites, 96 apts., 1996
83 Lake Vista seniors housing, 286 apts., 1983*
84–87 Central Station, 280 townhouses, 1993–
88 1603 South Michigan, office, 1992*
89 EastSide Lofts, 53 apts., 1996*
90 EastSide Townhomes, 10 units, 1997
91 Bicycle Station lofts, 53 apts., 1996*
92 Bicycle Station, 10 townhouses, 1997
93 Prairie District Lofts, office/130 apts., 1994*
94 Vietnam Veterans Art Museum, 1996*
95 Millennium townhouses, 32 units, 1996–
96 & 97 Chinatown Square, retail/residential, 450 units, 1991–
98 McCormick Place North, 1986
99 McCormick Place South, 1997

*   conversion or renovation
** renovation and new construction

Park Row, one of several townhouse styles in the Central Station neighborhood developed by Daniel McLean on railroad land east of Dearborn Park near Lake Michigan. Architect: FitzGerald & Associates. Courtesy MCL Development.

Vacant Dearborn Station and the abandoned rail yards that became Dearborn Park.
Courtesy Dearborn Park Corporation.

An amputated, deteriorating Dearborn Station, minus its sheds, as Dearborn Park sales opened in mid-1979. *At left*, the newly completed The Oaks, subsidized housing for older people. Architects: Dubin, Dubin, Black & Moutoussamy. Courtesy Dearborn Park Corporation.

First Dearborn Park townhouses in summer of 1981, 18 months after residents arrived. Architects: Hammond Beeby & Babka. Photo by Daniel Weinbach, Dearborn Park landscape architect.

The Terraces, massive 220-unit flagship complex on Dearborn Park's northeast corner. Architect: Skidmore, Owings & Merrill. Courtesy Dearborn Park Corporation.

The new community's informally named "Dog Park" with Sears Tower, *at left*, rising above The Oaks. Photo by Michael J. Kardas.

▼

▲ The Terraces and 27-story condominium building, forming the often-criticized "wall" along State Street. Photo by Michael J. Kardas.

◀ One of Dearborn Park's two high-rise condominium buildings, facing each other at the community's 9th Street entrance. The master plan specified six. Architect: Ezra Gordon/Jack Levin. Photo by Bob Shimer, Hedrich-Blessing.

The renovated Dearborn Station with galleria and roundhouse addition. In background are loft residences of Printers Row and Loop skyscrapers. Photo by Michael J. Kardas.

Terraced mid-rise building, with backyards in the sky, one of three identical buildings in Dearborn Park's north neighborhood. Architect: Booth Nagle & Hartray. Photo by Michael J. Kardas.

Three-story "garden homes" backing onto State Street in courtyards of mid-rise buildings. Architect: Booth Nagle & Hartray. Photo by Wayne Wille.

Conversation and companionship in courtyard of The Oaks. *From left*, Julia Vlachos, Ida Harding, Jean Valentino, Akhtari Begum, and Sativari Kamra take time out for a chat. Photo by Michael J. Kardas.

Patios of white townhouses flanking a shaded lane in Dearborn Park's north neighborhood. Photo by Ferd Kramer.

▼

▲ The "wild vernacular" of red brick, cream stucco, blue pipe rails, and hint of gabled roof of developer Jack McNeil's townhouses, final phase of north neighborhood. Architect: Michael Realmuto. Photo by Wayne Wille.

South Loop School, focus of an agonizing struggle between Dearborn Park and a low-income community to the south. Photo by Michael J. Kardas.

◄ An impromptu ring-around-a-rosy by mothers and toddlers in Dearborn Park's leafy north neighborhood. Photo by Wayne Wille.

▲ Familiar after-school scene in Dearborn Park: buses lining up to transport South Loop School students out of the neighborhood and back home. Photo by Michael J. Kardas.

Developer Daniel McLean's popular Chicago Homes in Dearborn Park's south neighborhood. The tall, narrow structures with high front stoops recall a century-old city style. Architect: Pappageorge Haymes. Photo by Michael J. Kardas.

◄ A red-white-and-blue Chicago Home opening onto State Street, decked out for the Fourth of July. Architect: Pappageorge Haymes. Photo by Michael J. Kardas.

Relaxing on the front stoop, an old city custom resurrected in Dearborn Park's Chicago Homes. Martin Kittaka and his son, Max, 5, enjoy the autumn sunshine. Photo by Wayne Wille.

Fourteenth Street entrance to Dearborn Park, one of only two vehicular entrances to the community. In background are Ogden Partners' copper-trimmed Rowhouses. Architect: Booth/Hansen. Photo by Wayne Wille.

Garages and off-street parking in courtyard of the Rowhouses, typical of Dearborn Park's south neighborhood. Architect: Booth/Hansen. Photo by Wayne Wille.

At home in the Loop: green lawns and tranquility in the
shadow of Sears Tower, with spacious single-family Park
Homes in the foreground. Architect: Booth/Hansen.
Photo by Wayne Wille.

Top: playtime in South Park, at the southern end of the community, with developer Daniel McLean's Prairie Town Homes, *at left*, and Ogden Partners' single-family Park Homes, *at right*. Architect: Roy Kruse for McLean and Booth/Hansen for Ogden. Photo by Wayne Wille.

Playground on Dearborn Park's southern border. Photo by Michael J. Kardas.

Top: Dearborn Park's southern neighborhood, viewed from the elegant South Park. Photo by Michael J. Kardas.

Courtyard of developer Daniel McLean's angular Prairie Town Homes, accented with horizontal stripes of brown brick and vertical teal panels, in Dearborn Park's south half. Architect: Roy Kruse. Photo by Wayne Wille.

Ogden Partners' Metropolitan Mews townhouses, some with fourth-floor "penthouses," built around a tree-lined center green at Dearborn Park's southeast corner. Architect: Booth/Hansen. Photo by Michael J. Kardas.

Printers Row residents Joshua Hamburg, 4, and
his mother, Gail, enjoying the sand and sun in
Dearborn Park's south neighborhood. Photo by
Michael J. Kardas.

Architect Bruce Graham of Skidmore asked four firms noted for residential work to submit designs for the four types of housing: Ezra Gordon/ Jack Levin for the high-rises, Booth Nagle & Hartray for the mid-rises, Hammond Beeby & Babka for the townhouses, and Dubin, Dubin, Black & Moutoussamy for the building for older people. Graham wanted red brick throughout, with trims of dark brown and angular bays and shapes. No units opening onto State Street, the architects were told; no first-floor windows on State, either.

The four firms were not enthusiastic about following the strict guidelines Graham gave them. Several talked him into variations. Ezra Gordon's bay windows, for example, became contemporary versions of the traditional, graceful Chicago bay rather than the severely boxed Skidmore interpretation. Thomas Beeby pulled the parking slots into the middle of the townhouse clusters, gave each home a little front yard, and organized them with a complex symmetry that relieved their boxy dullness. The townhouses were compact, carefully parceling out every square inch of space; yet even the smallest two-bedroom unit was 30 percent bigger than the three-bedroom, 1,000-square-foot houses in the unrealistic "South Loop Scenario" of 1972. Laurence Booth put stepped-down terraces on one side of each of his three L-shaped, six-story buildings. He added indoor parking, an aesthetic improvement he made affordable by keeping his building structures simple and economical. Some of the first-floor units in the mid-rises became duplexes opening onto tiny patios. Along the State Street side of each mid-rise cluster he placed a quartet of three-story "garden homes," terraced toward the interior court.

At first, Booth questioned what he called the "circle-the-wagons mentality" of the Dearborn Park leaders and their architectural guidelines. "They said they had spent a lot of time with security people, and they had to have only one street entrance, for security. And they had to have a fence along State Street," he recalled. "I think it was reasonable, for that time. . . . If you had an apartment window [at ground level] on State Street, it wasn't so cool. We put little buildings on State, so there was something against the street without being a slab. To Bruce's credit, he listened, and he said yes."

Booth lost his argument, though, to restore the traditional Chicago two-flats excised from earlier plans.

Ray Wieboldt arranged contracts with the architects for 3.48 percent of anticipated construction costs of $32.5 million for 939 units; Dearborn Park would need the cash from filling these before starting the rest of the 1,456 units planned for the northern portion of its site. Mayfair Construction Company was low bidder on all but the housing for the elderly; Corrigan Construction won that. One company skilled in residential work did not bid: Urban

Investment and Development's construction subsidiary. Klutznick, fearful of any perception that he would profit from Dearborn Park, didn't let his old firm participate. Wieboldt began negotiating final terms with Mayfair and Corrigan.

The question of how to maintain racial integration was even more of a concern now that the group was on the verge of producing housing. Phil Klutznick drew up a "managed integration" statement, intended as a guide to a future marketing staff. It declared that "Park Dearborn" (Klutznick frequently got the name backwards) wanted "a full mix of families with or without children, elderly and singles of all economic levels," recognizing that "the elderly and those at the lowest range of the economic scale" would need subsidies "if the mix is to be complete." Interesting, since no one but Klutznick at that point wanted so complete an economic mix.

The statement did not mention quotas, but it said: "It is the aim of the tenant selection guidelines and the sales program to achieve a well balanced community with an integration of races, creeds and economic levels to fully reflect the population of the city. In the pursuit of this objective, it must be clear that tenant selection and sale standards will be observed to assure that tenants and buyers are able to meet their financial responsibilities . . . and to achieve a community that avoids introduction of adverse elements which might tend to lower the moral or law abiding attributes of the community."

The statement never was brought before the executive committee, but Klutznick advised Ray Wieboldt to keep it on file. "It may serve us well some day in the future," he wrote in a covering letter, apparently anticipating lawsuits on tenant and buyer approval.

Tom Ayers had a more immediate concern. Dearborn Park would soon have to face public hearings before the City Council and the Chicago Plan Commission, a mayoral-appointed board of politically connected citizens with experience in real estate, development, or urban planning. Ayers wanted Dearborn Park to have a strong nondiscrimination policy in place by that time. In April, the executive committee approved his resolution pledging that "this corporation will take affirmative action to ensure that we as well as those we engage will provide access to housing . . . without restriction based on race, color, religion, sex or national origin; offer reasonable opportunity for minority businesses to provide goods and services to the corporation; recruit, hire, transfer, and promote persons in all job classifications without regard to race, color, religion, sex, or national origin; base decisions on employment so as to further the principle of equal employment opportunity. . . ."

No quotas were specified, but, at Ayers's urging, the committee agreed that some would be forthcoming. At the time, this was an unusual step for what was essentially a private endeavor. Ayers also directed the Dearborn Park staff to make certain that some of its funds were deposited in minority-owned financial institutions.

In another move to prepare for hearings, Dearborn Park hired a public-relations firm. Phil Klutznick, annoyed with what he felt were misrepresentations in the news media, had long wanted to do this. In particular, he was enraged by occasional references that identified him as head of Urban Investment and Development Company, which had a Dearborn Park contract. He was retired, he wrote repeatedly to newspaper executives; he did not run Urban—his son did.

On May 2, 1977, just over three years after Mayor Richard J. Daley, Tom Ayers, Phil Klutznick, and the others jointly announced the start of South Loop planning, the Dearborn Park leaders were in City Hall for a joint announcement with Acting Mayor Bilandic. The futuristic city heralded in the original Chicago 21 Plan, with its 40,000 dwellings linked by glass-enclosed walkways in the sky, had shrunk to a modest prototype of 3,000 units in pleasant brick buildings connected by concrete sidewalks on the ground.

Work would begin in a few months, Ayers said, on an initial phase of 939 units comprised of 144 townhouses; 370 apartments in two high-rise buildings, one rental, one for sale; 190 subsidized rental apartments for older people in a mid-rise building; and 235 units in three mid-rise complexes, two of them rental. There would be jogging tracks, three outdoor tennis courts, play lots, 3.5 acres of parks, and three outdoor swimming pools—two attached to high-rise buildings and one in the mid-rise clusters. Another 517 high-rise and mid-rise units would be built later, completing the north neighborhood.

Residents could begin moving in during the fall of 1978. Prices had not yet been established, but Ayers promised that they would be 4 to 10 percent lower than comparable new housing in Chicago. This time, the leadership said the development was planned for "mid-income families." There no longer was any mention of lower income levels.

Nor was there any sign of the ordinance specifying city payment of infrastructure, promised by Bilandic in February. Jack Guthman went to work in City Hall and reported that Bilandic and Lew Hill expected to give it to the City Council in June.

The Chicago Board of Education took care of one other critically important piece of unfinished business on June 8, with an action that would be cited again and again by future Dearborn Park residents. It approved School Superintendent Joseph Hannon's recommendation to put an elementary school into the vacant, run-down Dearborn Station.

A model of the new Dearborn Park community went on display at Continental Bank a few weeks after the Bilandic press conference and then moved around to other downtown lobbies.

On June 23, after a three-hour hearing, the Chicago Plan Commission gave its unanimous approval to the Planned Unit Development application drafted by Jack Guthman. This was no surprise. Guthman had made certain that the commission was thoroughly familiar with Dearborn Park; in any case, it usually liked what the mayor and Lew Hill liked, and vice versa.

The hearing, however, was hardly a calm affair. Protesters noisily jeered Dearborn Park's testimonials. Slim Coleman, coordinator of the Intercommunal Survival Committee, a group located miles away from Dearborn Park on the city's North Side, called the new development proof positive of the city's plan for wholesale displacement of poor people.

"I don't understand," said Plan Commission Chairman Julian H. Levi, a professor of urban studies at the University of Chicago, where his brother, Edward, had been president. In a voice heavy with sarcasm, Julian Levi said he was under the impression that Dearborn Park was being built on unused railroad land; he didn't realize, he said, that the tracks were populated with poor people.

When Tom Ayers mentioned in his presentation that Dearborn Park would be financed with private money, Robert L. Lucas, executive director of the Kenwood Oakland Community Organization, miles away on the South Side, called out, "Where did you get the money? The economy of the Western World was built on the backs of slaves. That's your private money." The city's poor "will follow you to the end of the earth," he told Ayers.

Chairman Levi retorted, "Anyone who listens to you for any length of time comes to one conclusion—they don't want to come within 80 miles of you."

James P. Chapman, an attorney representing the opposition, called Dearborn Park "the first step in the whitening of the Loop." No retort there; that was one goal of the investors, no doubt about it.

The careful groundwork Ayers had laid paid off. A lineup of blacks, Asian Americans, and Hispanics testified in behalf of the project; they represented organizations that were older, better financed, and more cooperative with Chicago's business and political structure than the protesting groups. Two came from Dearborn Park's nearest neighbors: Emil Peluso of the Near West Side Community Committee and John Y. Ing of the Chinese American Civic Council. The most newsworthy, as far as the press was concerned, was Leon Finney Jr., executive director of The Woodlawn Organization, Chicago's biggest and most aggressive black neighborhood group. Finney had been courted by Ayers and his colleagues for several years. He lamented the loss of

"350,000 white and black middle-income families to the suburban area" in the previous 16 years, draining the city of jobs and tax revenue. It was urgent, he said, to do something to keep these families—black and white—in the city.

One potential foe had been quieted months earlier. Alderman Fred B. Roti was not eager to have thousands of new voters inundate his First Ward, legendary for its huge turnout for the city's Democratic organization on election days and for its ties to the crime syndicate. For all he knew, these newcomers could be dreaded independent liberals. Roti expressed his unhappiness around City Hall, but in the months before his death Mayor Daley had instructed him to shut up. He did, and became a staunch proponent of Dearborn Park in its dealings with the city, the school system, and the Park District. (In 1993, as Dearborn Park was nearing completion, the helpful Roti was sentenced to four years in federal prison for racketeering and extortion.)

Another slap stung because of its source. The Citizens Information Service of Illinois, educational arm of the local League of Women Voters, released a 56-page report on Dearborn Park prepared by David Emmons, a sociology instructor at Roosevelt University. Most of it was a careful description of the corporation's organization, capitalization, and financing plans, with biographical data on its board members and their intertwined relationships. It noted that three had ties to firms doing business with Dearborn Park or likely to do business with it: Philip Klutznick, retired chairman of the planning consultant, Urban Investment and Development Company; William Hartmann, senior partner of Skidmore, Owings & Merrill, the coordinating architects; and Ferd Kramer, whose Draper & Kramer was in line for a management contract once Dearborn Park was built.

What angered the Dearborn Park leaders were such phrases as "[the plan] assures the presence of whites at a time when blacks are increasingly users of the Loop." The investors were attracted "not because they would make a lot of money, but because they would see in Dearborn Park protection for their own brick-and-mortar holdings." The site plans would "physically limit and psychologically discourage" outsiders from gaining access. And, "It remains to be seen whether the developers will employ the tactic others have been reputed to use: an aggressive marketing approach with potential white buyers coupled with a privately maintained quota on blacks."

Emmons's conclusions were accurate enough. Tom Ayers and John Perkins had made some of those same points in recruiting shareholders, and Ferd Kramer was manipulating tenant selection to maintain integration in Prairie Shores. But the Dearborn Park leaders resented the snide undertone in Emmons's report that made them seem racist and selfish, without a word about the benefits to the city and its tax base if the project succeeded. There was something more: They belonged to a generation that did not understand public scrutiny of private endeavors. They were investing their own capital and resources, using their best professional and civic judgments. What provoked these non-involved non-professionals to snipe at them?

The Planned Unit Development ordinance made its way effortlessly through City Council committees after the Plan Commission endorsement. On July 7 the full council gave its unanimous approval.

Five days later, new Mayor Michael Bilandic—he had won election on June 11 to complete Daley's term—planted a 28-foot sugar maple tree to symbolize the start of construction. In news coverage of the event, only the black-owned *Chicago Defender* noted that Dearborn Park "currently contains no plans for low-income family housing."

A month after city planning chief Lew Hill testified enthusiastically in behalf of Dearborn Park before the Plan Commission, he was back to turn thumbs down on another South Loop project, architect Bertrand Goldberg's River City. Goldberg and his backers—financier Jerrold Wexler and Chessie Resources, real estate arm of the railroad holding company Chessie System—wanted to build 6,000 apartments in six 72-story circular towers on 45 acres, plus 4.3 million square feet of commercial and industrial space. There would be athletic fields, fishing lagoons, a marina for 500 boats, a health center, a school, shops, jobs in the industrial area, and a horizontal people-mover system linked to nearby subway and bus terminals. Goldberg planned on federal mortgage guarantees and rent subsidies for lower-income families. Only 15 percent of the units would be for sale. This would be "the most modern and revolutionary community yet developed," he told the commissioners, "both in terms of architecture and style of living."

The contrast with Dearborn Park was stark, and it was clear which version city officials preferred. Lew Hill said city guidelines for South Loop development permitted a maximum of only 1,750 units for that site, and the 4.3 million square feet of commercial and industrial space was excessive for the area. The Metropolitan Housing and Planning Council, the influential private organization chaired for many years by Ferd Kramer, also testified against River City. The council didn't like the height and density and worried about the impact on the downtown area if the huge development failed.

So did the Plan Commission. River City's economics couldn't work, according to Miles Berger, a real estate consultant and the group's vice-chairman. If the Federal Housing Administration (FHA) had to take over, he said, "we saw River City as potentially another Cabrini" public housing project.

None of the Dearborn Park leaders testified; they wanted to avoid any appearance of a battle with Goldberg. But Phil Klutznick wrote to Ray Wieboldt shortly before the hearing, telling him that it might be timely for the "Park Dearborn" public-relations agency to compare its relatively modest density with that proposed by Goldberg.

The Plan Commission voted—unanimously, as usual—to reject River City. Depressed and bitter over what he felt was a defeat engineered by Dearborn Park and the corporate power structure it represented, Goldberg went back to his drawing board.

Lew Hill and Louis Martin of the *Chicago Defender* had been telling the Dearborn Park leaders for several years that they should have a black staff officer before construction got under way to head off protests and pickets. Finding someone suitable seemed to take forever. Finally, late in 1977, Tom Ayers introduced his choice to the executive committee: Robert T. Carter, a vice president of Inland Steel who had worked previously with Ray Wieboldt. He would be director of corporate communications.

Ferd Kramer was unhappy again. On November 17 he wrote to Tom Ayers, "With the employment of Mr. Carter at $35,000 a year, Dearborn Park is now spending $95,000 a year on community and public relations. . . . If the Dearborn Park project was displacing large numbers of minority families, I could see why a major effort should be put on public relations, but this is not the case and we have built successful projects that were much more controversial than Dearborn Park without spending anything like this amount of money."

Problems far more severe than adding another $35,000 to overhead were accumulating as construction finally got under way that fall of 1977, almost two years after Phil Klutznick's original target date. Demolition costs had come in at $22,000 above the estimated $205,000 because the city wouldn't allow rocks to be crushed on the site; they had to be hauled off. The corporation had to build 17 bulkheads in an abandoned tunnel system under its site, adding another $132,500. It had to pay for Mayfair Construction's performance bonds, a $160,000 bill it hadn't expected. Annual real estate taxes during construction were projected at $195,000.

More bad news. Ray Wieboldt had not yet been able to negotiate a final agreement with Mayfair, which now estimated that its costs for the high-rise and mid-rise buildings and an initial batch of townhouses would run $1.5 million over its March bid of $28 million.

And the infrastructure ordinance promised by Mayor Bilandic in February and then for certain in June still had not appeared.

Late in November, the real estate departments at Chicago's two biggest banks, Continental and First National, had devastating responses to Dearborn Park's requests for construction loans. Both wanted evidence that the corporation would mount first-class advertising and marketing campaigns. Both said Dearborn Park would need more capital—at least $6 million, perhaps as much as $10 million—before this first phase was concluded. And both wanted written assurances from the city that it would pay for infrastructure.

Meanwhile, Chicago newspaper reporters—and a number of Dearborn Park shareholders—were pressing to find out the sales and rental ranges. None had been given. Roy Wiley, Dearborn Park's media consultant, was assured by its staff that he would have them by mid-December. He scheduled a December 19 press conference for the announcement. But with the Mayfair contract not yet signed, no one could give Wiley the numbers. He had to cancel the press conference.

The next day, frustrated that he still had not been able to negotiate an agreement with Mayfair, Ray Wieboldt halted all construction work.

Word spread quickly around Chicago's corporate boardrooms and in City Hall that the Dearborn Park group didn't know what it was doing. Mayor Bilandic called John Perkins to ask if it was true that the project was in deep trouble. Lew Hill and his staff put aside work on the infrastructure schedule and got busy with other things.

On January 7, 1978, Phil Klutznick, about to leave for Europe to preside over a meeting of the World Jewish Congress, wrote a memo to Tom Ayers, John Perkins, and Ferd Kramer. He was chagrined; there was no way Dearborn Park could meet the timetable it had trumpeted. "The mayor is not the only one who is asking questions," he said. "There is word all about the development fraternity that we have trouble in our construction programs."

In his absence, he said, he didn't want any contract finalized with Mayfair until Ferd Kramer had an opportunity to review it.

"I am at my wit's end," he wrote. "Unless we get this thing changed there will be more red faces and less accomplishment than in anything I have ever been associated with. I know that goes for you people as well."

Six weeks later, Ray Wieboldt resigned. Tom Ayers and Phil Klutznick, desperate to restore credibility to Dearborn Park as quickly and surely as possible, turned to their most experienced colleague and persistent nag. The firm of Draper & Kramer was hired as development manager for $12,000 a month, in effect replacing Wieboldt and the planning team from Klutznick's old firm, Urban Investment and Development Company. Urban's contract with Dearborn Park had ended with the approval from the Chicago Plan Commission.

Ferd Kramer immediately hired a talented young real estate project manager who had worked for him and Phil Klutznick on several Urban projects, Sheldon L. Kantoff; his salary would come from Draper & Kramer's $12,000-

a-month fee. Next, Kramer contacted the three-year-old firm of Schal Associates, specialists in the new field of construction management. Its cofounder, Richard Halpern, had been construction officer in charge of Sears Tower. Kramer offered Schal $350,000 over two years, plus expenses, to be his eyes and ears on the job. These fees would be paid by Dearborn Park Corporation.

"I was brokering steel when Ferd called, out of the blue," Kantoff recalled. "I met him for breakfast the next morning. He asked, would I be interested? I said, of course. I didn't even talk about money, it sounded so challenging, so exciting."

For Richard Halpern and Schal Associates, as with Jack Guthman, Dearborn Park turned out to be a career builder. In future years Schal played a key role in some of Chicago's biggest, most prominent construction projects and branched out around the world.

After the squabbles and frustrations of management by part-time committee, a group of canny professionals was now in charge.

A Fresh Start, and Fresh Snow

8

AFTER A FEW WEEKS AS DEARBORN PARK'S PROJECT MANAGER, SHELDON KANTOFF WAS ready to tell Tom Ayers and the rest of the board to call the whole thing off. He had no contract with Mayfair, the primary construction company. No ordinance from the city spelling out responsibilities for installing and paying for streets and other infrastructure; in suburban developments where he had worked, this was usually in place before construction started.

Even more alarming, he had studied the year-old projections from the departed consultants at Urban Investment and Development Company, and agreed with Ferd Kramer that they were too simplistic and optimistic. Kantoff was convinced that Dearborn Park would not be able to lease its rental buildings fast enough to meet its loan payments. And two-thirds of the first-phase units were rental.

Kantoff told Ferd Kramer he thought Dearborn Park could not survive without switching the entire development to the quick cash returns of condominium sales. The executive committee was fearful of such a profound change. People might be willing to try out life in the South Loop on a rental basis, but would enough of them risk buying there? And Dearborn Park already had ruled out subsidized family housing; if it eliminated rentals as well, it might look as if no lower-income families were welcome. In the interests of solvency, though, the committee decided to build the high-rise and mid-rise condominiums before starting on the rental versions.

Richard Halpern of Schal Associates, Dearborn Park's new construction consultant, also was appalled at the mess he confronted. After reviewing architects' specifications, contractors' bids, and what was going on in the building industry, he told the executive committee that, with no changes, this first phase of Dearborn Park would cost $6 million more than the 1977 estimate of $32.5 million.

The 144 townhouses were the chief offender. Latest estimates were "dramatically over market value," Halpern said, running about $2 million above the 1977 construction estimate of $7.6 million.

The townhouses already had been subjected to a round of cost cutting late in 1976 by Phil Klutznick. Committee members wanted them to be decent and attractive, but they worried that they might overestimate the market for their housing. If they failed, their investors—the most influential business people in Chicago—would be humiliated. They were obsessed with staying financially viable. A few dozen empty townhouses could kill them.

They told Halpern to sign a $24.9-million contract with Mayfair for the two high-rises and the first two mid-rise buildings, as he had recommended, and to proceed with "major design changes in structure and mechanical systems" of the townhouses.

Sheldon Kantoff and Michael Oppenheim, Halpern's deputy, went to work with townhouse architect Thomas Beeby. They revised the drawings, switched to less costly construction methods, and substituted grayish concrete bricks for the dark red clay bricks that coordinating architect Bruce Graham of Skidmore had wanted throughout Dearborn Park. By March 1978, Halpern was able to give the executive committee a new cost estimate of $36.9 million for its initial 939 units. Sales would begin early in 1979 instead of late in 1978, reflecting the time lost in changing managers and contracts.

No one had bothered to tell Bruce Graham about the townhouse revisions. When he found out, he exploded. "The brick color was the single most important element tying the various housing units together," he wrote to Ferd Kramer. "In my opinion, our original goal for an integrated design has been destroyed. We are told that the change was necessary to save costs . . . . If we had been consulted, we probably could have found other places to cut."

His firm had devoted years to the planning and design of this project, Graham wrote. But ever since Sheldon Kantoff had arrived, it had not been consulted on design decisions. "I will not stand idly back and relinquish our established position of Coordinating Architect to others who have not had the benefit of our experience."

The drab color, it would turn out later, was the least of the problems with the townhouses. Kramer and Phil Klutznick let the decision stand but told Kantoff to talk to Graham the next time he contemplated changes.

It took a while for the Dearborn Park regulars to adjust to Shelly Kantoff and Mike Oppenheim. For one thing, the two newcomers did not look like the rest of the group, who all tended to blur together in their dark, well-tailored suits, white shirts, and subdued ties. Mike Oppenheim wore turquoise-and-silver jewelry and Western boots. Shelly Kantoff had wild black curly hair and a mustache. "But I changed my wardrobe," he said later. "I got a gray suit."

Kantoff and Oppenheim were brash and smart and for the most part got what they wanted from the executive committee, which seemed relieved to turn its worries over to them. Still, working with these powerful corporate chiefs, accustomed to controlling their own companies, was "tough, really tough," as Kantoff recalled it.

"I had to be absolutely prepared for everything," he said. "I did a lot of homework before I met with these guys. I made sure I was right, that my numbers were right. These were hard businessmen, and you had to be a hard businessman to deal with them. You had to know what you were talking about. I could never allow myself to be embarrassed, because they would eat me up."

Ferd Kramer and Phil Klutznick continued their bickering, mainly about things of little import. "They would fight and fight and fight," Kantoff said. "But they were still great friends. It was almost like a marriage."

Kantoff learned to do what was politically correct in Chicago. The alderman for the area, Fred Roti, had a cousin who wanted to put a hot dog stand on the site during construction. Kantoff agreed. Dearborn Park's insurance, like that of nearly every big publicly assisted project in Chicago, was provided by Near North Insurance Agency; the firm was founded by George Dunne, president of the Cook County Board and successor to Richard J. Daley as chairman of the Cook County Democratic Party. Fortunately, Near North's prices and services were competitive and reliable. Ferd Kramer's firm handled insurance, too, but Kramer never asked to be considered, according to Kantoff. "Ferd didn't want any part of that stuff. His ethics were way up there. All the people involved with this were absolutely first class. Their promise was perfect. They didn't play games."

The corporation paid for the early construction work with its capital, but it was imperative to get construction loans at affordable rates, and soon. E. Stanley Enlund, chairman of First Federal Savings and Loan Association of Chicago and head of Dearborn Park's finance committee, had been working with Kantoff and Kramer to satisfy the conditions set by the big banks. One response came quickly. The executive committee gave Kantoff the $2.9 million over two years he requested for newspaper and magazine advertising, radio commercials, billboards, brochures, models in Loop buildings and other public places, and a public-relations program. Two high-quality agencies were hired, Bernard E. Ury Associates for publicity and public relations and Haddon Advertising. City living in a suburban setting would be the theme, with emphasis on security, greenery, convenience, cultural and educational amenities—and a school in place when the first residents arrived.

The banks also wanted a written commitment from the city that it would supply the infrastructure. Yet no one in City Hall had acknowledged that Dearborn Park was moving again. Jack Guthman, Dearborn Park's attorney and lobbyist on government-related matters, had an idea. He wanted Dearborn Park leaders to meet informally with Mayor Bilandic and Planning Commissioner Lew Hill, away from City Hall, so Bilandic could get a thorough briefing on the progress of recent weeks. Guthman's chance came early in February when Ayers, Perkins, Bilandic, Hill, and Guthman himself were in Detroit to look at the Pontiac Silverdome as part of a stadium study committee appointed by Bilandic. Guthman brought the five of them together in a revolving bar in Detroit's Renaissance Center. It must have been a quite an evening. By the time they left, Bilandic and Hill were resold on Dearborn Park.

A few weeks later, on March 2, Hill sent Guthman what the Dearborn Park group had sought for years. "The following statements concern public investment and improvement efforts . . . in and around the Dearborn Park project," Hill's letter began. He then spelled out what the city would do: improve peripheral streets; landscape the parkways; install traffic signals; build interior streets and sewer and water lines; plant trees along the streets; build sidewalks; and buy land within the 51-acre site for parks to be developed by the Chicago Park District. Also, the city would "remain committed to the concept of developing a public school facility within Dearborn Station." The vagueness of that last promise should have set off alarms.

These commitments, Hill wrote, applied to the entire site. But, for the time being, the city would work only on the northern area. "Other public responsibilities south of Roosevelt Road will be held in abeyance until such time as [Dearborn Park Corporation] indicates that it is prepared to initiate private site improvements."

The commitment to work on the southern portion as well as the northern was not incorporated into a city ordinance. Again, the Dearborn Park group was more trusting than it should have been.

Hill attached an infrastructure schedule with sewer work beginning in May 1978 and streets, streetlights, and parkways in October. City work on this northern portion was expected to cost $6.5 million, with federal highway funds covering about half.

With that, Stan Enlund and his committee could nail down their financing. Enlund's First Federal Savings and Loan and John Perkins's Continental

Bank joined 50–50 in a $45-million construction loan at the prime rate plus 1.5 percentage points, with the provision that "the rate shall at no time exceed 10 percent per annum." Servicing fees were waived. This was a tremendous break, better than anyone could have foreseen. Prime plus 1.5 was at least 0.5 percentage point below the usual rate for construction loans. The 10 percent cap was phenomenal. During 1978 alone, the prime rate advanced 14 times to 11.75 percent. By mid-1981, when the loan matured, the prime was a killing 18.9 percent.

For permanent financing, which would provide mortgage money for residents and pay off the construction loans, Ferd Kramer made plans for a $30-million pool at, he hoped, 9 percent. He knew all of the people who ran the 20 or so institutions he would solicit—banks, savings and loans, union pension funds, insurance companies. Several on his list were minority owned, including Seaway National Bank of Chicago. Its chairman, Ernest Collins, had recently joined the Dearborn Park board, replacing Louis Martin from the *Chicago Defender*, who resigned when he moved to Washington.

Enlund and Kramer worked to lure First National Bank into the fold. The city's second biggest bank, after Continental, was a major Dearborn Park shareholder but had not actively participated in its plans. Its chairman, A. Robert Abboud, felt John Perkins and Continental were too prominent, and he had concerns about the project's viability. Despite appeals from Ferd Kramer, whose firm was a client of First National, and from John Perkins, who wrote to Abboud that "in no way are we [at Continental] . . . trying to do more than get the leadership group together," Abboud did not relent. First National did not participate in the loan pools.

A financing plan with bargain interest rates was a major factor in Dearborn Park's strategy to give the best housing value in the Chicago region. A second factor was the low return to investors—no higher than 6.5 percent, when 15 or 20 percent was expected from a successful residential development. To assure that residents and not speculators would get the benefit from Dearborn Park's lower prices, Ferd Kramer insisted on an unusual clause in sales contracts: Buyers could not rent out or resell their units for two years. Exceptions had to be approved by the Dearborn Park management, with Dearborn Park Corporation getting repurchase rights at the original price plus the increase in the Consumer Price Index.

By mid-March, construction was well along on the building for older people and beginning on the high-rise condominiums. Robert Carter, Dearborn Park's vice president for community relations—in reality, minority relations—warned the executive committee that pressure to hire minorities would heat up as the buildings grew more visible. It had been nine months since the committee approved Tom Ayers's affirmative action resolution, and the promised goals still had not been set. A committee resolution told Carter to create a minority-hiring program, adding that "It was recognized that some additional costs might be incurred as a result."

Carter quickly put together a Dearborn Park Affirmative Action Committee, with representatives from the Chicago Area Minority Purchasing Council, the Chicago Urban League, the Martin Luther King Jr. Movement, the Latin American Task Force, and Charles A. Davis Associates, a black-owned management consulting firm.

It couldn't act fast enough. On April 20, the *Chicago Defender* printed the first in a series of articles critical of Dearborn Park's failure to hire minority contractors. "Blacks 'Shut Out' in Dearborn Project," said a front-page headline. The story noted that "the proposed development was the center of a bitter controversy last summer when several community groups claimed it was intended to be a white-only fortress to protect the financial district from blacks."

The project was especially important, the *Defender* said, because it was financed with private funds and "therefore raises the question of the responsibility of the private sector to minority contractors and suppliers and to the extremely high minority unemployment rate."

A *Defender* editorial asked:

What is the obligation of the private sector toward solving racial inequality? Is financial profit the sole criterion for determining action or inaction? Should banks and independent retailers and manufacturers be required to solve the social problems they helped create?

. . . This highly touted and highly visible project is funded entirely by private funds from the biggest banks, retailers, manufacturers and churches in the city. Although the first phase has been underway for months, Dearborn Park planners are still "talking about" affirmative action for minority contractors and craftsmen.

If this was a federally funded project, HUD, the Labor Department or some other agency would have descended on the planners with an ultimatum long ago. They cannot here.

So who is going to put pressure on the planners? We believe that pressure must be generated from within by the banks, retailers, manufacturers, etc., whose money is in Dearborn Park. They must do it out of a sense of social responsibility.

If that doesn't work, then the minority community has no alternative but to take economic sanctions against those banks and retailers into whom they pour millions of their own dollars each year.

Carter's sources told him to expect picketing and disruptive action at the construction site momentarily.

Two weeks after the first *Defender* article, the executive committee accepted Carter's recommendation that 10 percent of all construction dollars go to minority-owned businesses and that one-third of the workforce be black, Hispanic, or Asian.

Carter, assisted by Richard Halpern of Schal Associates and James W. Compton, president of the Chicago Urban League, proceeded to create a minority-owned construction industry. Compton assigned several of his staff members to work full time recruiting skilled laborers and possible contractors. The Urban League convened several sessions for minority business enterprises. "Halpern and the others would make presentations," Compton recalled, "They got them involved in bidding and did the necessary orientation and nurturing."

The results were astonishing. On June 7, barely seven weeks after the *Defender* articles appeared, Carter reported to the executive committee that "the negative image of Dearborn Park in the minority community has been turned around." Two black general contractors would build townhouse clusters for $1 million each. Five minority subcontractors had been awarded a total of $300,000 in business. Another $225,000 was pending. The goal of 10 percent of construction expenses to minority-owned firms would be attained in a few months. Minority employment already was at the 33 percent goal.

By the end of 1978, contracts for $4.2 million had been awarded to minority-owned companies. Minority employment was 40 percent.

There were problems—and some subterfuge. A minority-owned carpet company, for example, received a contract, hired a white-owned company for the work, and then turned over most of the money to its white shadow. Mistakes were made in townhouse construction that eventually cost the Dearborn Park Corporation dearly.

By the time Dearborn Park was completed, in the mid-1990s, Chicago had a skilled and active minority construction industry. "Today, you can award in the minority community and many of the contractors are at least on the same level, and some a lot better, than the mainline contracting fraternity," said Halpern. "In fact, I don't look at minority contractors as minority contractors. They're contractors, period. But in 1978 it was very early, and perhaps awards went to people that didn't have as much experience as they should have and as much business backing. It was a difficult time. There was a lot of mentoring and joint venturing. We had to do a tremendous amount of hand-holding and monitoring."

The Dearborn Park staff was working out of offices in a building owned by Continental Bank in Chicago's LaSalle Street financial district in the spring of 1978. With less than a year to go before sales opened, or so the group thought, the pace of activity was ferocious. In April, contracts were awarded for a hefty $341,000 for landscape design and installation around the new buildings. Bruce Graham and his planning team from Skidmore wanted mature, abundant greenery with little hillocks and hollows for visual appeal on the flat site. These would also help blot out the railroad tracks and elevated streets to the west and south, the empty, decaying buildings to the north, and the weirdness of State Street to the east.

In July, Ferd Kramer's many months of heavy lobbying and untangling of bureaucratic snarls paid off. The Illinois Housing Development Authority awarded 190 of its federal Section 8 rent-subsidy certificates to the building for low-income people aged 62 and older, one for each unit. Section 8 certificates were scarce, demand was great, and the housing agency fretted because Dearborn Park had moved ahead with construction before getting its approval. In any case, the state agency agreed with Kramer that the need for good, affordable homes for elderly people was urgent. Housing of this type was nonexistent, in fact, in the downtown area. The building was scheduled for occupancy early in 1979, and Kramer already had given it a name: The Oaks, in honor of the young trees that would be planted around it.

But the infrastructure work was not proceeding as the city had promised. Sewer work began in August instead of May. Two months later it stopped, for reasons the Dearborn Park group never did ascertain, except that the crews were busy elsewhere. Sewer and water connections were supposed to be ready by the end of October. Now that was impossible. Street work had not begun.

Shelly Kantoff, who had the new title of general manager of Dearborn Park, got a bleeding ulcer to go with it. He realized he wouldn't have streets and sidewalks ready when people began moving in, but he surely needed sewers and water. "I became a pest in City Hall," he said of those days. "That was my job, the company pest."

Construction on the buildings slowed in July, but not for long, thanks to the influence of the Dearborn Park board. A letter from Material Service Corporation to Kantoff advised him to expect reduced shipments of ready-mix concrete and bulk cement because of an acute shortage that was likely to continue for a year or more. Kantoff called Phil Klutznick, who called Tom Ayers, who called Lester Crown, head of Material Service and a Dearborn Park shareholder. A few days later, Ayers reported that "Les indicated we would be a number one priority, and should not be affected by the shortages."

It was time to put together a sales and management team. Several years earlier, the planning consultants from Urban Investment and Development

Company had asked Ferd Kramer and John Baird to form a joint enterprise to lease rental apartments and commercial space in Dearborn Park, sell its condominiums, and manage the completed buildings. Baird was a longtime friend and tennis partner of Kramer's and, like him, a senior statesman in Chicago's real estate industry. Tall, sophisticated, invariably in a bright bow tie, the Harvard-educated Baird was president of Baird & Warner, which his great-grandfather Lyman Baird had helped form in 1860. John Baird was a veteran crusader for open-housing laws and practices. He had built and marketed a successful, integrated townhouse and high-rise development on Chicago's Near West Side and was involved in other revitalization projects around the city and in the suburbs.

Kramer and Baird proposed a five-year contract calling for a 50–50 split of sales commissions of 3 percent, a leasing fee of $100 for each rental unit, and a management fee of 4 percent of gross income of the rental property or $12 per unit, whichever was greater, and $15 a month per unit for condominiums, plus cost-of-living increases.

In a covering letter, they urged that Dearborn Park's plans be revised immediately to include an indoor facility for racquet sports, a health club, an ice rink, and a gymnasium, even though this would mean losing money in the short term. "We feel it is crucial that this amenity package be provided up front," they wrote. "We realize that economically the first 1,000 units could not justify this expenditure, but it would firmly establish our commitment to tenants and owners that this development is moving forward."

Phil Klutznick was irate. He thought they wanted too much money and ordered Urban's staff to give him comparisons with similar contracts. "Frankly, the more I read this proposal, the more I am convinced that they either do not want the job or else they want everybody to take a risk except themselves," he wrote in a memo to Urban. "My attitude is conditioned in part by the utter boorishness and stupidity of some of the criticism, but more importantly, the holier-than-thou attitude of people who should know better.

"P.S. I do not believe John Baird conceived this proposition."

Well, the indoor sports facility *was* a pet project of Ferd Kramer's. But John Baird concurred. The Urban staff reported that the Kramer-Baird proposal was in line with others in the Chicago area. Nevertheless, the two made downward adjustments. The management fee fell to 3.5 percent of gross income for rental buildings and $8.55 a month for condominiums, with no cost-of-living increases. Now, Klutznick was told, the contract was lower than those checked by Urban. In a three-page, single-spaced memo, he said he had questioned the terms only to avert criticism of the two firms and of Dearborn Park for engaging them without soliciting other bids.

Toward the end of 1978, the management team set tentative prices. Rents ranged from $310 a month for a studio apartment to $750 for a three-bedroom unit. Sale prices ranged from $49,900 for a one-bedroom, 780-square-foot high-rise condominium to $110,900 for a four-bedroom, 1,706-square-foot townhouse and $145,900 for a terraced, four-bedroom, 1,900-foot unit in a mid-rise building. All were within the goal of 4 to 10 percent lower than comparable new housing in the region.

Only a few advertisements had appeared, but these—and the news reports of the previous few years—generated more than 1,500 inquiries to the Dearborn Park offices during 1978.

In November, Richard Halpern reported that construction costs were only 2 percent over his March estimate, despite an annual inflation rate running at 7.6 percent—and heading into double digits.

A move-in schedule was prepared: January 1979 for The Oaks, March for the first townhouses, April for the first mid-rise condominiums, and June for the high-rise condominiums.

The Chicago City Council added to the year's good news on December 20. It authorized the Public Building Commission, a joint city-county agency with power to sell bonds, to pay $536,000 to Dearborn Park Corporation for two park sites in its northern neighborhood and for the part of Dearborn Station that would become a school. But talk of a new educational system that would be a model for all of Chicago had vanished with the departure 18 months earlier of the planning team from Urban Investment and Development Company. Now there was just the fervent hope that a decent school would be ready by the start of the 1979 school year.

Phil Klutznick was so happy about the progress that he told Kantoff to start work on the second high-rise, an all-rental, 27-story building with 250 units. With its 75 studio and 125 one-bedroom apartments, it would be geared to singles and young couples who couldn't afford to buy the generally larger condominiums in the high-rise across the street. Klutznick also was looking forward to completing the northern portion of Dearborn Park with a third high-rise building and a "flagship" complex at the northeast corner, a showcase site. Bruce Graham wanted his Skidmore firm to design this one rather than farm it out as it had done with the other buildings.

The year was about to end on a high note, a happy contrast to the close of 1977. And then the blizzards hit. A snowfall that began on New Year's Eve went on, and on, for about two weeks. Chicago got 89.7 inches that winter, a city record. Temperatures didn't rise much above zero. Nothing melted. Autos were buried, garbage collection virtually ceased, traffic barely moved. The city's snow-removal forces couldn't cope. People grew grumpier by the hour.

Then the hapless Mayor Bilandic, who already had infuriated the city by appearing on television and saying things really were all right, ordered the elevated trains to bypass stations in largely black neighborhoods in an attempt to speed service to outlying areas, which were white. Black residents erupted in their first broadly based political revolt.

Unfortunately for Bilandic, he faced a mayoral primary in February. By springtime, Dearborn Park Corporation was dealing with its third mayor: Jane M. Byrne, a Daley protégée, head of the city's Consumer Affairs Department, and the first woman to preside in City Hall. Planning Commissioner Lew Hill, who had worked on Dearborn Park ever since Tom Ayers's first meeting with Richard J. Daley, had left city government in mid-1978 to head the Chicago area's Regional Transportation Authority. He was succeeded by his chief deputy, Martin Murphy. Like nearly everyone else in City Hall, Murphy was nervous and uncertain about dealing with Jane Byrne, who had a reputation for being extremely bright but also extremely volatile.

Murphy and his staff asked for a meeting with the new mayor to explain Dearborn Park's history and the city's commitment to it. They arrived with maps, sketches, and photographs and proceeded to set them up. As one of the planners recalled the session, Byrne asked: "What's all this stuff?" He launched into a speech about the benefits of the project, but she cut him off. "She turned to her chief of staff and said, 'Make a list of these guys. Write their names down. I want to know who it is that wants $6 million from me.' I was the guy on the bottom rung. I thought I would get booted out."

He wasn't, and she could be forgiven. Chicago's all-male business and political establishment was so stunned by her election that for months most of its members avoided contact with her, not knowing how to act. She was convinced they were plotting to strip her of authority and conduct their city dealings without her. She wasn't so far off base. But Jane Byrne had a flair for encouraging projects with promotional possibilities. She was soon won over to the Dearborn Park vision. Infrastructure work, which had slowed to a trickle the previous fall, resumed when the snow melted.

Construction work also had to wait for a big thaw. The opening of sales was pushed from March to July 21, with occupancy beginning in the fall. The Oaks, though, would be ready in the spring.

An advertising campaign hit high gear in May 1979 with a full-color, eight-page insert in the *Chicago Tribune* and in other displays in the *Chicago Sun-Times*; newspapers aimed at Chicagoans of Hispanic, Asian, and African descent; a special section in *Chicago* magazine; and inserts in Chicago-area editions of *Newsweek, Time, Sports Illustrated*, and *Fortune*. Billboards announcing "Dearborn Park: Chicago's Next Great Neighborhood" went up along expressways to the suburbs. Commercials aired on 15 radio stations popular with the 25-to-45 age bracket. Dearborn Park was extolled as "A neighborhood filled with trees, parks, and playgrounds, right in the heart of the city." And, "the Loop and the lakeshore, just blocks away. . . . you can walk to work . . . . Enjoy opera, ballet, concerts, sporting and cultural events." And, "A new neighborhood, where people of all ages can live and share in its growth."

One phrase from earlier ads and brochures was cut. The low bid for renovation of Dearborn Station came in at $6.2 million. The Public Building Commission's renovation budget was only $3.2 million. The promise of a school "on site before the first residents arrive" disappeared. Everyone at Dearborn Park, however, thought the matter would be resolved before the 1980 school year began.

By summertime, landscape architect Daniel Weinbach was ready to decorate the site with pink and white flowering crabapple trees, slender birches, groupings of vivid maples and oaks, lacy honey locusts and lindens. He picked them for their toughness as well as their looks. These were sturdy city fellows, immune to pollution. There still were no streets and sidewalks, but—to the joy of everyone connected with Dearborn Park—the city's sewer work would be finished in time for a November occupancy of the first buildings.

Interest was percolating. Kathryn Moery lived in a western suburb with her husband, John, and their two small children. One day she took them to the Museum of Science and Industry and saw a model of Dearborn Park; what a delightful idea, she thought—raising children in a downtown setting that looked like a suburb. Timothy A. Donovan was riding on a commuter train from a southern suburb when he noticed townhouses going up close to the Loop; what a time-saver, he thought—no more train schedules. Maureen Murphy knew about Dearborn Park because she worked on the city's planning staff; she lived in north suburban Evanston, and Mayor Byrne had just told city employees that they had to live in Chicago if they wanted to keep their jobs. Jeanne and Edward Barry wanted to sell their house in Chicago's South Shore neighborhood now that the last of their four children was out of high school; DePaul University, where Jeanne worked, had a session for faculty and employees to interest them in Dearborn Park. Ruth Pomaranc was newly divorced; she and her husband had raised their children in a high-rise apartment on Chicago's North Side lakefront and then moved to a spectacular condominium on the 83rd floor of the John Hancock Center. Now she wanted a house, on the ground, and someone told her that affordable ones were going up just south of the Loop.

Inquiries were pouring in to the marketing staff at the rate of 300 a week.

The Dearborn Park leadership, however, was as anxious as ever. Were these possible buyers, or just curious? Were enough of them white? Would they be able to get a racial balance? How?

On the eve of the sales opening, a member of the marketing staff noticed something peculiar about everyone in the office. All were white. John Baird telephoned a crack salesperson at another Baird & Warner office: Carey Preston, vice president of the Chicago Board of Education, officer of the Chicago Urban League, former national officer of a black sorority, member of Dearborn Park's board and its executive committee, and "always everybody's favorite token," as she described herself. Would she please come to Dearborn Park to sell?

Yes, she would. Another crisis averted.

Sheldon Kantoff bought long red carpets and stretched them over the mud, up ramps, and into the nine furnished models ready for display in the still-unfinished buildings. He thought they added an aura of adventure, romance. Maybe no one would notice the absence of streets and sidewalks.

9

Neighbors Across
a Mud Sea

NINE A.M. SATURDAY, JULY 21, 1979: FRANK LIVINGSTON, HEAD OF THE DEARBORN
Park marketing team, waited nervously in the sales office set up in one of the townhouses. "We didn't know whether anybody would show," he said, recalling that moment. "We were that insecure."

Two hours later, Livingston was helping the sales staff assign numbers to the crowds streaming through the townhouse door. No one from the joint Draper & Kramer and Baird & Warner marketing force had seen anything like it. They couldn't possibly keep up with the flow. Visitors were asked to please come back in an hour or two, when their numbers would be called.

Maureen Murphy arrived from north suburban Evanston on Sunday morning and was astonished. "I had no idea it was going to be so mobbed," she said later. "I had to get my number, like at a deli. And I'm waiting and waiting. I remember Carey Preston came up to me when I was next in line. I said I would like to look at a one-bedroom, and she said, 'They're all sold' and walked away.

"I was just heartbroken. I finally got one salesperson to give me a couple of brochures, and I walked over to look at the models in the high-rise. The first floor wasn't in yet. We had to go up these ramps. But I was just blown away. It was so wonderful. The layout was terrific. And the price—you just couldn't beat it."

All 29 one-bedroom units in that first batch of Dearborn Park housing had been reserved with $1,000 deposits in just one day. Faced with the new City Hall edict that she must move into Chicago to continue working for the **101** city, and the "really quite shabby stuff" she had seen elsewhere in her price range, Maureen Murphy did something she had never done before. She talked to a city official, who talked to John Baird. A few weeks later she had a telephone call: Two of the one-bedroom contracts had fallen through; which one did she want? "Only once in my life have I ever used clout," she said.

Another prospective buyer who was disappointed that first weekend was Frank Livingston. He and his wife were enchanted with a four-bedroom apartment with a big terrace on the fifth floor of the mid-rise building. They tried to put down a deposit but found someone had already done that: Ferd Kramer and his wife, Julia.

When the sales staff finally closed shop on Sunday evening, they had compiled a remarkable record. Of the 341 units offered for sale that weekend—144 townhouses, 120 high-rise condominiums, and 77 condominiums in the first of three mid-rise buildings—two-thirds had been reserved by prospective buyers. Almost 1,200 visitors had trooped through the models. About 60 percent of the people who had made deposits were single; that was a surprise to the Dearborn Park leaders, who had deliberately put their bigger units on the market first to appeal to families with children. To their great relief, though, the depositors were a racially integrated group—and in proportions they considered ideal to assure continued integration; about 70 percent were white, 20 percent black, and 10 percent Asian or Hispanic. No need to try to manipulate waiting lists with that crowd.

The weekend was so spectacularly successful that on Monday morning Frank Livingston canceled ads scheduled for the following Saturday and Sunday in the *Tribune*, the *Sun-Times*, and neighborhood newspapers.

Two weeks later, 2,800 visitors had seen the models and 90 percent of the 341 units had been reserved, at a total value of $27 million, assuming everyone who made deposits eventually bought. Many did not, but the waiting list was long enough to fill those vacancies. More scheduled ads were canceled. The advertising agency was unhappy; it was not recovering its up-front costs.

The sales force, meanwhile, continued to supply intriguing numbers. Dearborn Park was attracting few of the young middle-class families its founders originally had in mind. Most buyers were single professional people who worked in the Loop and lived in Chicago, usually in a rental apartment. Only 40 percent were married couples. Only 8 percent of the buyers had children living with them, and most of those children were not yet of school age. But this was to be expected, with no school in the area. When prospective buyers asked about that, salespeople told them the city and the Chicago Board of Education had promised to put an elementary school on the premises; it probably would be ready in a year. In the meantime, the school system would bus children two and one-half miles north to Ogden School, a model of integration and academic excellence. Most Chicago high schools operated on an open-enrollment system; the only good ones based admission on academic standards, which was fine with Dearborn Park buyers. But there were few teenagers among the early residents, and those few attended private schools.

The most frequently asked question involved security, not schools. The culs-de-sac that eliminated through traffic and limited auto access to only one street had been ridiculed and denounced as elitist. But to the people who would actually invest their money and live in that forlorn setting, they were needed reassurance.

Even so, a common complaint from visitors to the models was the isolation, even eeriness, of the surroundings. The elevated streets to the south and west made the muddy little community-to-be look depressed, as if it sat in a basin. Dearborn Station at the northern edge was dark and empty. Beyond it were several blocks of broken sidewalks and even drearier buildings, their windows gaping black holes in sooty walls, their doors standing open to vandalized lobbies. Only to the east was there some life, and that was in several cheap residential hotels catering to down-on-their-luck single men. The one comfort in the vicinity was the big Chicago Police Department headquarters across State Street, but that was a mixed blessing. Police officers came and went at all hours, but so did some strange characters booked for appearances in the building's courtrooms or newly released from police lockups. The Dearborn Park site was "not exactly esthetically dynamic," as the *Tribune* wryly observed.

Yet the sales certainly were dynamic. On August 13, three weeks after the opening, Dearborn Park Corporation had to air a new radio commercial: We're sorry; we're sold out, but more housing will go on the market in a few months. Watch for our ads.

The unexpected demand prompted a quick decision. The second mid-rise building, intended to be rental, would be sold as condominiums instead. Sheldon Kantoff, who had wanted this change all along, ordered better-quality cabinets and carpeting to match those in the first mid-rise. By October, he and Ferd Kramer had persuaded the rest of the Dearborn Park group to switch the final two buildings in this first phase to sales—a 250-unit high-rise and another 79-unit mid-rise. Upgrading the three would cost $1.6 million, but the cash from the sales would improve the corporation's financial position when payments came due on its construction loan. Kantoff had never liked the economics of a 250-unit rental building; if it filled slowly, overhead costs would be devastating.

That left only one rental building in the 939-unit first phase—The Oaks, for low-income people 62 and over. It was also the only one ready for occupancy that summer of 1979. As Ferd Kramer had predicted, it was filling rapidly. Its 180 one-bedroom and 10 two-bedroom apartments were light and airy, with compact kitchens and big windows overlooking landscaped courtyards, sitting areas, and gardens. Federal rules required tenants to pay monthly rents of 30 percent of their income, minus medical expenses; the U.S. Department of Housing and Urban Development supplemented that amount to bring the total rents to an average of $460 a month. But the population of The Oaks was not quite in line with what federal housing officials wanted. By August it had 110 white occupants, 48 blacks, and a total of 5 Asian Americans and Hispanic Americans. An urgent message was passed from Washington to Illinois housing officials to Robert Wolak of the Dearborn Park marketing staff: Find 5 more Asians and 12 more Hispanics. Wolak placed ads in newspapers that circulated in Chinatown, in the Spanish-language *La Raza*, in the *Philippine Times*, and in the *Chicago Defender*, just in case the black percentage dipped. He papered Chinatown and Hispanic neighborhoods with leaflets about The Oaks and asked its new minority residents to tell their families to promote it in churches and stores and on the job.

A month later, only a few of the 190 units in The Oaks were still available. Wolak found his Asian-American tenants but was still searching for more Hispanics. The Dearborn Park leaders congratulated themselves on their decision not to seek rent subsidies and go through a similar rigmarole with the rest of their buildings.

Elsewhere in the city, soaring construction costs and interest rates were destroying the new-housing market. Little was being built. What was built was not selling. During 1979 and the first quarter of 1980, new-home sales in Chicago plunged 60 percent.

Gasoline prices were escalating faster than any other major component of the Consumer Price Index, up 40 percent in 1979 and 39 percent in 1980. Being able to walk to work in the Loop became a powerful inducement to buy in Dearborn Park.

Another was the pool of mortgage money assembled by Ferd Kramer. In the spring of 1979, mortgage interest rates hit 11 percent and kept climbing. In visits, telephone calls, and a persistent stream of follow-up letters to several dozen potential lenders, Kramer argued passionately that this first phase of Dearborn Park had to be a rousing success, and in a short period of time. For that to happen, it would need below-market mortgage rates. The momentum from a smash-hit early phase was essential to development of the rest of the 51-acre site and to the creation of a catalyst that would transform the entire Near South Side, downtown Chicago's only weak flank. All of the companies he was contacting would benefit enormously, as he kept telling them, and telling them, and telling them.

By the end of June, he had $12 million in mortgage money at a fixed rate of 10 percent from five institutions—First Federal Savings and Loan, Northern Trust Company, Harris Bankcorp, Aetna Life and Casualty Company, and State Farm Life Insurance Company. By the end of August, the pool had swelled to $23 million for 30-year, fixed-rate mortgages at 10 percent, plus a 1.5 percent service charge to borrowers, with a down payment of 20 percent of the purchase price. A few mortgages were available with 10 percent down at 10.5 percent interest. By that time, rates elsewhere were 12 to 12.5 percent. In 1980, conventional mortgages for new homes climbed to 14 percent. In 1981, when Kramer's 10-percent pool finally ran out, they were 16.5 percent.

As the November 1 move-in date for the first buildings approached, the Dearborn Park executive committee was eager to get going on its second phase, the 517 units that would complete the north neighborhood. Next up would be the "flagship," as the committee called it, a 220-unit complex at State and Polk streets. This was the community's most prominent site, at the northeast corner, next to Dearborn Station. Skidmore, Dearborn Park's coordinating architectural firm, would do that one itself.

No one knew when work could begin in the 27 acres to the south. Dearborn Park was having problems with city officials pleading poverty. Years of fat payrolls and adroitly hidden deficits under Mayor Daley had screeched to a halt with cuts in federal programs and, in the wake of the near collapse of New York City, tighter scrutiny by the New York firms that rated municipal credit. Mayor Byrne said the city could not afford the estimated $7.5 million in infrastructure and peripheral improvements needed in the south area.

Then the Chicago Park District announced that it had no money to landscape the 3.5 acres of mud designated to become parks in the north neighborhood. An indignant Ferd Kramer began a series of visits to park and city officials, pressing to have something ready by the spring of 1980. It did not look hopeful.

And, after a depressing meeting with Mayor Byrne and city Planning Commissioner Martin Murphy, Tom Ayers reported that the plan for a school in a renovated Dearborn Station was dead. Rehabilitation costs were prohibitive. The city, in fact, didn't know what to do with the part of the station it had bought for the school. Byrne had already demolished the station's waiting rooms.

Not all the news was so bleak. Dearborn Park's affirmative action program was winning praise as a model for developers. Richard Halpern of Schal Associates, Tom Ayers, and Robert Carter, the Dearborn Park officer who organized the effort, accepted awards from the Chicago Urban League, Black Contractors United, and the Chicago Economic Development Corporation, a black-owned consulting firm.

In October, Halpern reported that construction costs for the 939 units in the first phase would total $40.8 million. That was nearly 10 percent over his March 1978 budget, but not bad, considering the scorching inflation rate and the $1.6 million spent to upgrade the rental buildings to condominiums. Halpern had been paid $479,000 in fees and expenses to oversee the first phase. For the remaining north-area buildings, he was given a new contract as construction manager at 2.95 percent of construction costs, plus expenses.

So there was Dearborn Park on the day its first residents arrived: no school, no charming community center in a charmingly restored Dearborn Station, no parks, no shops, no recreation center, no medical clinic—none of the alluring amenities its leaders had wanted in place to welcome the newcomers. The streets weren't finished, and there were no sidewalks. But some housing was ready; the sales had been terrific; and Dearborn Park was about to become a Chicago neighborhood, nine years and seven months after Tom Ayers, Donald Graham, and Gordon Metcalf looked out of Ayers's window and resolved that something had to be done with those awful tracks.

Marsha Klevickis will never forget the first week she and her husband, Michael, spent in their new three-bedroom Dearborn Park townhouse. "There were rats, open fields, the old station with broken windows," she told reporter Connie Lauerman of the *Chicago Tribune*. "No sidewalks. A lot of unfinished units. One night we were looking out into the dark, and our neighbors' dog was whimpering. He was nervous, too. It sounded like a wolf howling in the wilderness."

Bette Cerf Hill, from her sixth-floor corner condominium, remembered looking down at "a mud sea. We couldn't buy milk or bread anywhere nearby, but we could buy construction workers' gloves from a van parked below."

Thomas Burns, a city employee who moved in with his wife and 13-year-old daughter, told Sandra Pesmen of *Crain's Chicago Business* about his qualms that first week in November, looking at the mostly unfinished townhouses around him. "I thought, this is a risk. We don't know what kind of neighborhood this will become."

Yet the setting awed him. "When you stand in my backyard and look out, you see Sears Tower, the Board of Trade, and the First National Bank in the background. It's quite a contrast," he said. On Sundays, when there was almost no downtown traffic, the birds came out. "One morning I opened my drapes and saw two pheasants in the vacant area between us and the river. I've seen quail and ducks and geese and a wild turkey."

Marsha Klevickis remembered another sighting. "There was a real genuine hobo camping west of us, in the fields near the railroad tracks. There was some feeling that we should have the area declared a protective wildlife sanctuary to protect all the strange birds out there—including our hobo."

They were pioneers, and they bonded to each other and their muddy village with the same spirit of adventure and accomplishment that inspired settlers of the midwestern prairies 150 years earlier. Within weeks of the first move-ins, they had established a babysitting cooperative, a food-buying cooperative, a plant-buying cooperative, exercise classes every Tuesday and Thursday, a schedule of potluck suppers, a jogging club, a biking club, a roller-skating club, a child-care network (in cooperation with the older people, men and women, of The Oaks), and a school-for-Dearborn-Park committee. Blackie's, a tavern that once served passengers from Dearborn Station and was hoping for a rebirth, sponsored a women's softball team.

"This was just like a big resort, honestly," said Kathryn Moery, who came from the western suburb of Willow Springs with her husband, John, and two preschool children. "There was such a nice spirit, everybody loving where they lived, with the city at their feet." She had always yearned to move downtown, she said, but never before had there been a way to do that at a price they could afford and in a setting suitable for children. "It was the fulfillment of a dream that had been germinating for years. The satisfaction of being downtown meant I could just work through anything."

Marsha Klevickis told the *Tribune* that the camaraderie reminded her of her childhood in a small town in Wisconsin. "What happened is like what happens in the army or in your freshman year in college. We all were uprooted. It was a raw area, and we all got involved." Marsha, a lawyer, and her husband, a federal government supervisor, walked to work. One reason they left their North Side city apartment was the expected arrival of the first baby born in Dearborn Park.

The newcomers were a resilient lot. Jeanne Barry, director of public relations at DePaul University, and her husband, Edward, arts critic for the *Tribune*, bought a high-rise apartment with a magnificent view of the city skyline. Shortly before they moved in, Jeanne went to measure the windows for drapes. A big rat blocked her path past Dearborn Station. "He was a beautiful animal," she recalled. "A gleaming black coat. He wasn't going to move.

He was King Rat. And I wasn't going to challenge him." She stepped aside, nodded to King Rat, and walked through the mud to her new home.

Maureen Murphy brought her boyfriend to see her new apartment before she moved in. "When I first told him I had bought it, he said, 'You did *what*? You bought *where*? Oh, I hope you get out of your contract.'"

She wanted to buy a bottle of wine to celebrate, so they stopped at a liquor store in the Roosevelt Hotel, one of several near Dearborn Park that ungraciously were called flophouses. "It was horrid," Maureen recalled. "But I loved getting him upset. I said, 'Oh, look, I can buy toilet paper here, too.' He was so disgusted."

The surroundings didn't bother her. "I felt it was a safe investment because I knew who the backers were," she said. "But it also turned out to be one of the nicest social experiences. You don't usually get that in housing. That was totally unexpected. I moved into a building pretty much at the same time everybody else did, so there was a kind of freshman effect. That was very binding."

Ruth Pomaranc, who had spent all of her marriage and child-rearing years tucked away in high-rise city apartments, paid $95,000 for a three-bedroom townhouse and relished looking up at the Sears Tower from her patio. Her grown children were concerned about their newly divorced mom alone in a house on the fringe of a seedy area, without the customary doormen and security of expensive apartment buildings. "My children were afraid I was going to be raped and mutilated and God knows what the first night," she said. "And of course I never had any problems, ever. My daughter was particularly worried. But she lived in New York City."

Genell Harris was renting a studio apartment on the Near North Side when the building converted to condominium; the asking price for her one-room flat was $80,000. She bought a bigger, one-bedroom condo in Dearborn Park for $53,900. It was closer to her job in the federal-building complex in the Loop, so she saved money on bus fares. And she liked the environment. "It's not that we're fenced in," she said, "but when you walked home you felt you were entering your own little community. It always felt so safe. I traveled a lot on my job, and I always felt good just walking into Dearborn Park."

Tim Donovan, who had noticed Dearborn Park going up as he commuted into Chicago from a suburb, bought a four-bedroom townhouse with his wife, Noreen, and two children. "I was so sick of commuting," he said. "A lot of my life became free."

Two of the new residents were to play prominent roles in the South Loop's future: Judith Hoch and Bette Cerf Hill.

Judy and her then-husband, Guy Hoch, moved into a three-bedroom condominium in the high-rise building early in 1980 with their 18-month-old son and 4-month-old daughter. They came from Austin, an old neighborhood on Chicago's West Side that was undergoing a familiar Chicago transformation. It was white, then integrated, then black. Much of the housing had deteriorated, and the crime rate was rising. They wanted to raise their children in a racially integrated setting, and Dearborn Park seemed like one of the very few spots in Chicago where they might be able to do that. Temporarily out of the workforce to raise her small children, Judy Hoch had no trouble finding outlets for her energies.

"I remember Judy sitting on a bench with her two little kids, nabbing people who went by," said Kathryn Moery, a teacher also temporarily at home with small children. "She always had something for us to sign, some new project to get us involved." First there were the broken sidewalks on Dearborn Street north of the new development. "You could fall through them," Judy recalled. She circulated petitions to get them fixed. She was part of the babysitting cooperative and the food cooperative and lined up day-care services with the retired people at The Oaks. In a few months, she had found the cause that would consume her for a decade. She organized the South Loop School Committee and began a campaign to force city and school officials to fulfill their promise of a school in Dearborn Park.

Bette Cerf Hill moved into the same Dearborn Park high-rise in the spring of 1980. She came from the North Shore suburb of Wilmette, where, a single parent, she had raised three daughters. She had promised herself that as soon as the youngest had entered college, she would be off to the city, which she loved.

She was familiar with Dearborn Park because she worked just a few blocks north of the site, for the Landmarks Preservation Council of Illinois in the landmark Old Colony Building. The area was mainly "a scuzzy skid row," as she called it, but she saw its potential—the vacant old buildings that could be rehabilitated, the blighted tracts of land that could be developed. She decided that what the South Loop needed, now that it was getting Dearborn Park, was an organization that would promote it throughout the Chicago area and also promote sound planning for its future. Working out of her kitchen, she and a colleague from the Landmarks Preservation Council, Barbara Lynne, made the rounds of property owners and businesses, from the corporate chiefs of Dearborn Park Corporation to the vice president in charge at the huge Hilton Hotel a few blocks east on Michigan Avenue to the real estate syndicates that controlled the unused railroad property. They talked and wheedled and sold—and extracted enough money to create the nonprofit South Loop Planning Board, destined to play a major role in the development of the area.

A year after the first residents arrived, Dearborn Park's public-relations agency, Bernard E. Ury Associates, surveyed buyers and reported that a person moving in was likely to be 25 to 44 years old, was a professional working in the Loop who previously rented in Chicago, had at least four years of college (an amazing 80 percent), and was buying a first home. This Dearborn Park was more affluent and had fewer children than the one envisioned by Phil Klutznick when he talked about a village of sales clerks, bus drivers, nurses, and schoolteachers. About half were married. Only 12 percent came from the suburbs. Whether Dearborn Park could take credit for keeping them in the city was not known, but it looked as if that would happen in coming years: About 85 percent said they would look first in Dearborn Park if they wanted a bigger dwelling.

The racial breakdown had shifted only slightly from the first weeks of sales. By the end of 1980, Dearborn Park was 67 percent white, 28 percent black, and 5 percent Asian or Hispanic. The "tipping" that its founders had worried about was not occurring. They apparently had achieved stable integration without resorting to manipulation. The Chicago Commission on Human Relations received several complaints alleging discrimination from people whose mortgage applications had been rejected, but its investigations concluded the rejections were based on objective financial considerations.

Among the new black residents were Jacqueline Vaughn, president of the powerful Chicago Teachers Union; U.S. Representative Cardiss Collins; and the novelist Cyrus Colter. George Muñoz, president of the Chicago Board of Education, moved in. So did a flock of city officials, including Walter Knorr, the comptroller. Urban planners, some working for the city and some for consulting firms, were attracted to Dearborn Park. A number of architects and journalists arrived, and a contingent of lawyers from downtown firms. The big federal buildings one-half mile to the north sent a throng of buyers, as did the financial centers of nearby LaSalle Street.

The most-in-demand building was The Oaks, which had a waiting list of 300 within a year of its opening. Ferd Kramer, who had been elected president of Dearborn Park Corporation in May 1980, in addition to his role as development manager, was threatened with a lawsuit by a black applicant who had been turned down at The Oaks. Kramer said she didn't meet tenant standards, but federal housing officials disagreed and insisted on strict enforcement of open-housing laws and regulations. Kramer would not be able to maintain integration at The Oaks by giving preference to whites, as he had done for two decades at Lake Meadows and Prairie Shores. Judging by its waiting list, he told the Dearborn Park executive committee, The Oaks would be predominantly black in a few years. And so would Lake Meadows and Prairie Shores.

Dearborn Park Corporation began 1980 without the man who had been its forceful conceptualizer for nearly nine years. Phil Klutznick left for Washington to join President Jimmy Carter's cabinet as secretary of commerce.

The new year brought another significant change. Years of financial finagling masterminded in City Hall caught up with the Chicago school system. City residents—the entire state, in fact—were stunned to learn that misleading financial statements had masked a deficit of almost $500 million. Joseph Hannon resigned as school superintendent. The plan for a Dearborn Park school had lost its only influential advocate within the school system.

Hopes for a supermarket in Dearborn Station faded, too. John Baird tried valiantly, but rehabilitation costs, insufficient population, and a shortage of parking space killed prospective deals.

Financially, Dearborn Park was awash in good news. About 90 percent of the 420 units completed by mid-1980 had been sold. The 250-unit high-rise building was about to go on the market. Sheldon Kantoff announced that the conversion to sales would transform a projected $5-million cash deficit for 1980 into an $8-million surplus.

In a development critical to Dearborn Park's future, First Chicago Corporation, parent of First National Bank, got new leadership. A. Robert Abboud left and was succeeded as chairman by Barry F. Sullivan, fresh from New York. Sullivan was impressed by Dearborn Park and the involvement of the Chicago business community. He wanted First Chicago to be a major player. Richard L. Thomas, president of First National Bank, joined Dearborn Park's financial planning team and, as a first contribution, provided a $4-million loan to complete construction of the north area.

The city finished the streets and sidewalks in June 1980, about a year behind its planned date. Tom Ayers ordered full speed ahead on the flagship complex. Bruce Graham showed the model, an L-shaped, 11-story, red-brick building with a terraced roofline and 198 apartments. A row of 22 townhouses with individual patios formed a third wing. An interior courtyard sat above a two-level, 420-car garage whose parking spaces would be sold on a condominium basis. Construction was expected to cost $18.3 million. This would be the most expensive Dearborn Park building to date, priced from $68,000 for a one-bedroom unit to $170,000 for the largest townhouses.

The final two buildings in the north neighborhood, a 27-story high-rise and a six-story mid-rise, were scheduled for 1982 starts.

As 1980 ended, Dearborn Park Corporation prepared to turn over control of its building operations to condominium associations formed by the new owners. And, while it was no substitute for a supermarket, a grocery chain agreed to open a convenience store in one of the high-rise buildings.

To cap off a rousing start, Dearborn Park got a rave review from the prestigious Urban Land Institute, a Washington-based planning and development think tank. In its Project Reference File of October 1980, the institute concluded that the site plan by Bruce Graham and Roger Seitz achieved a difficult goal: a neighborhood setting compatible with a surrounding high-density environment.

"Since the project is located in a formerly nonresidential area with little visibility and no prior identity, it was essential to establish an immediate image and a sense of community," the report said. "The availability of all the building types in the first phase, together with mature landscaping, created an appealing neighborhood environment."

The institute singled out several features for special praise: the large terraces in the mid-rise buildings; the three outdoor swimming pools; "attractive, tree-lined walkways and bike paths, serving as unifying elements, creating an appealing pedestrian atmosphere"; and the ban on sales to buyers who would not live in their units.

The landscaping provided an effective buffer between the site and "unattractive adjacent uses," the institute said. It praised the street system for ensuring that the project was accessible "without being crisscrossed with through streets, which would destroy the internal community environment," and concluded that "The residents' perception of security within a comfortable neighborhood setting has been a significant factor in the success of the project."

Dearborn Park's lone fault, according to the institute: not enough off-street parking.

Some reviews dissented. Local critics lamented the lack of a dramatic focal point and denounced the culs-de-sac that the Urban Land Institute lauded. Nory Miller of *Inland Architect*, writing in the *Chicago Daily News*, complained that Dearborn Park was merely "a patchwork . . . designed for pleasant living, playing it too safe—tossing together proven ingredients."

But anyone who wanted more adventure had only to look a block or two north, where another renewal effort was under way. It was radically different from Dearborn Park. Together, linked by the little red railroad station, the two had a synergy that was all the more marvelous for its total absence of coordination.

10

"The Whole Street Was Just Empty"

THE BEGINNING, AS LAURENCE BOOTH RECALLED IT, WAS A TELEPHONE CALL ONE spring day in 1975 from his fellow architect Harry Weese, then president of the Chicago chapter of the American Institute of Architects. "Harry was on a rampage about something," Booth said. "What it was, I don't remember. But he wanted me to fly to Washington with him to do something about it."

That wouldn't have been unusual. Harry Weese was often on a rampage about a half dozen things at once—stopping demolition of a building he liked, fighting Chicago's obsolete building and zoning codes, promoting his ideas for a marina off Navy Pier or a racetrack jutting out into Lake Michigan, or whatever. From its timing, this trip probably was connected with Weese's campaign to put the Loop's 80-year-old elevated rapid transit system on the National Register of Historic Places and thus prevent its demolition. The city wanted to replace it with a new subway extension. Weese failed, but so did the city's subway plan. The venerable El was spared by default.

On the plane back to Chicago, Weese told Larry Booth to go to South Dearborn Street and look at the Transportation Building: a tall, thin slab, 22 stories high, as long as a football field, and only 60 feet deep. Built in 1911 to house many small companies involved with the railroad industry, it had been sitting empty for years. Weese's artist daughter Margo had given her father glowing reports of old commercial buildings converted into loftlike residences in New York City's SoHo district, and he wanted to do something like that with the Transportation Building.

Booth worked out of offices just north of the Loop. He lived in the Lin- **113** coln Park neighborhood near Chicago's North Side lakefront. This section of Dearborn Street in the South Loop was foreign territory to him, but Harry Weese could be persuasive. He went.

What he saw stunned him. "The whole street was just empty," he said. Empty, with vaulted sidewalks, litter and garbage blowing around, and forlorn souls who camped in the vacant hulks wandering about. But oh, those vacant hulks: They were run-down, dilapidated, and scarred with broken windows and crumbling facades, and they had trees growing out of caved-in rooftops, but they were gorgeous.

This was Printing House Row, where publishing and printing businesses began to flourish in the decade after the Chicago Fire of 1871, about the same time the railroads chugged into the city and built their switching yards and terminals just south of the printing district. As the businesses prospered, they commissioned new plants and offices from a number of the talented architects who had been drawn to the resurgent city. The result was a magnificent collection of tall, strong, architecturally significant buildings with intriguing facades lining three blocks of South Dearborn Street; the district spilled over into narrower lanes, one to the east and one to the west. After World War II, when the railroads began retreating, the printing businesses consolidated, modernized, and moved away to new quarters.

"What was great about it was that the street had a closure," Booth said. That was the rosy red Dearborn Station, 90 years old at the time and also vacant. A group of business and financial leaders, the Chicago 21 Corporation, was about to acquire an option on the station and 51 acres of tracks behind it to create a model residential community and, it hoped, spur development throughout the area.

Booth told Harry Weese they couldn't fix up just the Transportation Building. They went for advice and help to John Baird, president of Baird & Warner real estate company, and to developer Ivan Himmel, who had worked with Weese and Baird on re-creating Frank Lloyd Wright apartments in the western suburb of Oak Park. Their investigation of county records showed that Theodore Gaines, a lawyer, owned some of the most important properties in the South Dearborn district, and they invited him to join them. The five met for breakfast in Baird's office every Tuesday for a year—Gaines brought doughnuts—to plot something new for Chicago: adapting old commercial buildings into residences.

The group called on city Planning Commissioner Lew Hill, already deep into preparing guidelines for a new South Loop town in conjunction with the Chicago 21 group. Hill liked the idea immediately. He knew something would have to be done about the unsightly wrecks north of the Chicago 21 property, and he didn't relish the cost or the outrage the city would provoke if it tried to demolish this grand old chapter in architectural history. He already had estimates on tearing down the Transportation Building; it had attracted so many scavengers who stripped its mosaics, marble, and mahogany woodwork and anything else they could cart away that it now was considered a public health hazard. Razing it would cost $750,000, half of the city's annual demolition budget. If this group could figure out a way to spare the city that $750,000 bill, put the building back on the tax rolls, and at the same time knit the ravaged South Loop to the rest of the downtown, more power to them.

Hill took them to see Mayor Richard J. Daley, who, as Booth remembered, nodded and said, "Yeah, good idea."

That was all it took in Daley's City Hall. Cooperation was assured.

The big Transportation Building was the place to start. The quintet tried to find out who owned it; a trail led from West Virginia investors to a Dallas real estate company and then vanished in a savings and loan in Oklahoma. Nobody owned it, it seemed, but the Cook County Treasurer's office said the building's six years of unpaid taxes, penalties, and interest amounted to $2.7 million. Under existing law, Cook County required four more years of default before it placed the building on its auction block, assuring further deterioration.

John Baird had a plan: The city could condemn the building, assume the title, and wipe out the tax liability. If the Printing House Row Five could get a loan guarantee from the FHA, the city could then sell the building to them under an urban renewal program. After months of exploring dead-end alternatives, Hill finally agreed and set a giveaway price: $150,000.

That was the beginning. The five formed South Dearborn Renovation Associates, later renamed Community Resources Corporation. As they were planning their redevelopment strategy for the Transportation Building, Harry Weese bought the nearby Donohue Building, "a total mess," according to Larry Booth, for $150,000. "I bought 5 percent of it," Booth said. "Harry told me his wife, Kitty, would kill him if he bought it alone." The strict Chicago building code prohibited residential use of heavy-timber buildings such as the Donohue, which had been designed in 1883 to accommodate publishing and bookbinding firms and printing presses. But Daley had blessed this effort, so city Building Commissioner Joseph Fitzgerald engineered a revision in the code.

Next, the five chipped in to buy the 14-story Terminals Building a block north of the Donohue after Harry Weese insisted it was a bargain he couldn't refuse. "We told him to stop for a while, no more," John Baird said. "Then he told us the Rowe Building was available. I said, 'Harry, don't do it.' He said, 'I already have.'"

In 1976, at the start of their Printing House Row adventure, John Baird and Harry Weese visited Phil Klutznick of Chicago 21 and proposed joint planning for the two new South Loop communities. "Phil thought we were just crazy," Baird said. The five continued on their own, with the bigger, more influential Chicago 21 group watching them warily, hoping they would do nothing to spoil plans for a neat and tidy new town on the tracks south of Printing House Row.

While the five were working on financing for the big Transportation Building, they sought advice on what to do with the shorter but massive Donohue, built in the Romanesque revival style popular among turn-of-the-century railroad stations and courthouses. Duncan Henderson, a real estate developer with experience in New York conversions, suggested a cheap option: Lease or sell unimproved spaces. Artists and others who might like loft living could create their own residences.

A half dozen or so brave spirits thought that was a great idea. One was Vera Klement, who lived on the South Side near the University of Chicago, where she taught, and painted in a studio on the North Side. She moved into the Donohue in 1978, renting 3,200 square feet for $300 a month. She had long wanted to live where she worked; her vivid canvases were enormous, and this vast space, with its 14-foot-high ceilings, was perfect for them. She even had her own freight elevator at the rear to get them down to Plymouth Court, at the building's back entrance, for transportation to galleries.

A few enterprises were still operating in the building—a printing press, a typewriter-repair business, a machine shop. "When they closed for the day, the rest of us would be left rolling like marbles in this empty box," Vera Klement said. "There was no security. The door downstairs didn't lock. There were no parking problems, because there was no one here."

She began cleaning out her new home. "I filled seven enormous dumpsters with stuff. The floor had metal plates for holding heavy machinery. I pulled those off."

There was a toilet. She built her bathroom around it. A walled-off corner that had been a machine shop's office became her bedroom. She put in a kitchen where there had been an old sink.

With no lock on the door to Dearborn Street, people wandered in and out. "One old guy decided that the lobby, which had a little radiator, was his bedroom. Every night he banged around down there. My bedroom is right over that thing. He would wake me every night."

A few years later, she bought her space from Weese and Booth for $19,200, or $6 a square foot. She had made the dingy expanse extraordinarily charming. Light spilled in from big windows onto whitewashed ceilings crisscrossed by white pipes and onto four mighty whitewashed pillars and exposed-brick walls. An Oriental carpet defined her living room. She created a table by placing a slab of beautiful marble on an old sewing machine. She mixed well-designed old and new furniture, big plants, a piano, tropical fish, a cat.

The Donohue was Chicago's first residential loft, and Vera Klement's space became an attraction for local sightseers. "I would get these phone calls—could this group of 20 or 40 people, a bus load, come and look at my work? The temptation they dangled was that they were interested in my paintings, which no one ever was. I'd give them a little talk about the area, about being a woman and doing your own loft, being an artist, and the work. And then they'd say, and where do you sleep? They always asked that. Then they'd want to see the bed. It was hilarious."

The first new businesses in the reincarnated Printing House Row—or Printers Row, as newspapers began calling it—couldn't have been more appropriate. Wilbert Hasbrouck, executive director of the Chicago chapter of the American Institute of Architects, was leaving that post to open his own architectural firm. His wife, Marilyn, owned the Prairie Avenue Bookshop, which offered its fine selection of architectural books in a distinctive but remote setting, the once-grand Prairie Avenue on Chicago's Near South Side. She wanted more space and more accessibility to the Loop. One spring day in 1978, Will Hasbrouck mentioned their plans to Harry Weese. "He put his hand on my shoulder," Hasbrouck recalled, "and he said, 'Will, I'm going to solve your problem. I'm going to carve a piece out of the Donohue Building for you and Marilyn.'

"I brought Marilyn over to look at the space, and I thought she was going to cry. It was vacant, had been for years. There was a six-foot-diameter hole in the floor—you could look down into the basement. It was full of dirt, grime, and—stuff."

Marilyn Hasbrouck remembered the hole as 20 feet wide. "Bill said to me, 'That's cosmetics, cosmetics! You have no imagination!'"

Both were uncertain about locating in what was essentially an abandoned area. "We thought about it for a long time," Will said. "But Harry sold us. He was offering space for nothing. We bought mine and Marilyn's for what amounted to less than a year's rent." The renovation, much of which Will did himself, cost only about $70,000.

Marilyn Hasbrouck moved her bookstore into a street-level shop in October 1978, and her husband opened architectural offices in the floor above, in what had been a Linotype operation. The hardwood floor was scarred where pieces of hot lead had fallen. "The bay on the north end must have had 2,000 or 3,000 five-gallon tins partially filled with paint," he said. "It was a fire hazard like you never saw in your life. The south bay was a storeroom for out-of-print books, water damaged and stuck together. We had to get rid of all that stuff. The building was filled with that kind of debris."

He painted the pillars in his offices bright blue and added decorative capitals. The exposed-brick walls were trimmed in rose red. With her expanded space, Marilyn Hasbrouck built the largest architectural book collection of any store in the country. Students and tour groups trooped in and out. She drew customers from around the world, and not only by mail, though that was a big portion of her business. "I would get a call from Japan saying, 'What time you open tomorrow?' And then they would ask directions from O'Hare Airport to here." She bristled when local callers wanted to know whether it was safe to venture into the South Loop. Of course it was. Slightly weird, in those early days of Printers Row, but safe.

The summer after they moved their businesses into the Donohue, Will and Marilyn Hasbrouck bought a condominium in a mid-rise building designed by one of the Printers Row Five, Larry Booth, in the brand-new Dearborn Park. Their next-door neighbors were Ferd and Julia Kramer. Instead of a long commute from their southern suburb, they now could walk to work in 10 minutes. Their new home, Will said, was "as near to a perfect place for us as I've ever seen."

The most distinguished building on Printers Row was the Pontiac, named after an Ottawa Indian chief. It was finished in 1891, the oldest survivor of the pioneering and prolific Chicago firm of William Holabird and Martin Roche, designers of 72 commercial buildings in downtown Chicago in the four decades after the Fire of 1871. Its 14-story skeletal frame was sheathed in dark brick; imposing bays trimmed in red terra cotta ran continuously from its 3rd to 13th floors. It rose on the corner of Dearborn and Harrison streets, north of the Transportation Building, a prominent site. The Printers Row Five decided to make this a commercial building to qualify for a federal Urban Development Action Grant, which required a business component. Larry Booth and his new partner, Paul Hansen, did the conversion into modern office space.

The city applied for a $1-million grant, which the five wanted to use for decorative new sidewalks, trees and other plantings, and street and curb repairs. But there were a few hitches. Harry Weese had succeeded in entering Printers Row in the National Register of Historic Places, which protected its architectural treasures but also restricted what could happen there. The Illinois historic preservation officer telephoned Booth to inform him he could not install fancy sidewalks or plant trees on Dearborn Street; this was a historic industrial district, and industrial districts did not have trees or pretty walkways. "I'm usually pretty cool," Booth said. "But I went blithering." After he calmed down, he appealed to the director of the Illinois Landmarks Commission, who engineered a compromise. Trees were all right, but not decorative sidewalks. The city spent only $800,000 of the $1-million grant on Printers Row, enough to plant trees and repair broken curbs and sidewalks; the other $200,000 disappeared elsewhere in the city budget.

With its historic district designation, the intrigue over loft living, and Marilyn Hasbrouck's renowned bookstore, Printers Row generated newspaper stories—and more occupants. Larry Booth and Paul Hansen bought a small two-story corner building across Dearborn Street from the Pontiac,

The vacant, vandalized Transportation Building on Printers Row, 22 stories high and 290 feet long, before its renovation in 1981. Courtesy Dearborn Park Corporation.

painted it green, and transformed it into their architectural offices. A wrecker clearing out refuse on the upper floor found a skeleton, Booth recalled, still in its clothes. This became one in a long litany of Printers Row legends. Some examples: The sidewalk outside the Booth/Hansen & Associates offices was collapsing. One day a mason working in the basement heard a big crash. "All of a sudden," Booth related, "a guy came crashing through the dust. He said, 'Hey, I was waiting for a bus, not the subway.'"

Ulrich Sandmeyer opened a bookstore in the Rowe Building across from the Donohue. The space had been a bindery with a specialty fitting the South Loop's past. Piles upon piles of bound pornography were found in the cellar. "They had to shovel it out," Sandmeyer said.

In the cellar of the Mergenthaler Building, on Plymouth Court behind the Booth/Hansen offices, workers clearing out debris found what they concluded was a dungeon, neatly walled in.

Young restaurateur Michael Foley rented ground-floor space in the Pontiac Building in 1981. It had once housed a cafeteria. He later joked that he scraped six inches of grease off the walls. "I put every dollar I had in that restaurant," he said. "I spent a good many nights sleeping there the first year just to keep the bums out." A few years later, his stylish Printers Row Restaurant was a favorite at lunchtime with the financial district crowd and at dinner with people on their way to the nearby Orchestra Hall or Auditorium Theatre.

Work began on the Transportation Building early in 1981, financed by an $18-million FHA-insured loan. By that time Dearborn Park had been on the market for about 18 months and was home to nearly 1,000 people. Harry Weese's reuse plans took advantage of the Transportation Building's tall windows and high ceilings to create 294 light, airy apartments, all rental.

One-bedroom apartments were priced at $480 a month when it opened in 1983; not cheap, but a bargain for newly renovated, near-downtown dwellings. Comparable quarters on the city's Near North Side went for $700 a month. But John Baird was unsure whether enough tenants could be lured there to fill 294 apartments. When he had an opportunity to get federal housing subsidies for low-income families for 20 percent of the units, he grabbed it. By the time the subsidies expired 10 years later, the building and its Printers Row neighbors were solid hits. He didn't seek to renew them.

The renovation edged north of Printers Row, leaping over the broad Congress Parkway, which feeds into an expressway to the western suburbs. In 1982, architect Will Hasbrouck restored the magnificent, 16-story Manhattan Building, designed 90 years earlier by the father of the steel-skeleton skyscraper, William LeBaron Jenney. At the time, it was the tallest building in the world. With retail on the ground floor and 105 apartments above, it was the first residential conversion to jump north of Congress.

Dennis Coll bought two Dearborn Street landmarks north of the Manhattan, the Old Colony and the Fisher. The former was an 1894 masterpiece by Holabird and Roche with gracefully rounded corner bays. The Fisher, adorned with terra-cotta fish, salamanders, snakes, and crabs, was a fanciful 1896 gem by Daniel Burnham, who gave a century of Chicago planners and architects their commandment: "Make no little plans; they have no magic to stir men's minds."

Coll told reporter Deborah Silver of *Crain's Chicago Business*: "There I was, in the middle of massage parlors, porno bookstores, and drunks. A lot of my friends were ready to pay for a month's rent for me at the funny farm." Four years and $5.5 million in renovations later, his two office-retail buildings were 90 percent leased. "Lawyers and accountants had replaced the bookies," Silver reported.

One of Coll's first tenants in the Fisher Building was Dearborn Park resident Bette Cerf Hill and her new South Loop Planning Board, which took space formerly occupied by a porno bookstore. She had listened to so many warnings about the creepy connotations of "South Loop" that in 1984 she renamed her organization the Burnham Park Planning Board, after the Near South Side lakefront park and yacht harbor named for Daniel Burnham. It wasn't until 1994, when the area was firmly established and the planning group expanded its reach, that it took "South" back and became the Near South Planning Board.

Printers Row had a debut party in September 1981. In a newly renovated gallery in the New Franklin Building, Bette Cerf Hill and her associate Barbara Lynne helped a group of women stage a showing of *The Dinner Party*, by the feminist artist Judy Chicago. It consisted of a 50-foot-long, triangular-shaped table with 39 ceramic plates memorializing 39 notable women of history and mythology with variations on the vagina. An opening-night champagne reception was mobbed. *The Dinner Party* inspired derision and adoration and, above all, curiosity. It drew crowds to the new gallery—and the new South Loop. An exhibit held later, *Artists of the New South Loop*, featured works by the sculptors, photographers, painters, and potters who had settled into the apartment studios of Printers Row.

Still, Ulrich Sandmeyer remembered "more winos than yuppies on the street" when he and his wife, Ellen, bought ground-floor space next to the New Franklin in 1982. Both librarians, they had dreamed of owning their own bookstore. This site was ideal: accessible to an emerging residential community and to the thousands who worked just a few blocks away. The Sandmeyers refinished the hardwood floors, cleaned the brick walls, painted the pipes white and dark brown, and put in track lighting and high-tech metal shelving tilted to display books. Sandmeyer's Bookstore developed a reputation for travel books, children's books, poetry, drama, greeting cards, and an efficient mail-order business. One of its regular customers was Michael Foley, hunting recipes for his Printers Row Restaurant. "He would always be surprised if we didn't carry, say, *Veal Sausages of Northeast Transylvania* and had to order it," Ulrich Sandmeyer said.

Another regular was Harold Washington, who became Chicago's first black mayor in April 1983. He liked to spend quiet Sunday afternoons browsing in the store, ordering history—especially Greek history—and anything on politics.

In 1984, Bette Cerf Hill and Barbara Lynne organized an outdoor Printers Row Book Fair along a two-block stretch of Dearborn Street. It grew into an annual June festival that by 1996 covered five blocks and attracted 150 booksellers and 55,000 visitors with food and music, extensive displays, readings by authors, a tent for children's books, and stands of rare used books.

Other architects and developers added to the works of the Printers Row Five. Kenneth Schroeder put wedge-shaped bays with multipaned windows on the six-story Mergenthaler Building, once a factory, and created 21 stunning dwellings. Anthony Antoniou bought five buildings in a row and with architect Louis Arthur Weiss joined them into Printers Square on Federal Street, just west of Dearborn; it had 356 rental units, a 180-car garage, and 160,000 square feet of office and retail space. He persuaded the city to tear down some small buildings across the street for a parklike opening to Printers Row.

Larry Booth and Paul Hansen designed a loft church, GracePlace, in a small printing building across the street from the park that opened to Printers Square. Grace Episcopal Church and Christ the King Lutheran Church shared a ground-floor meeting room and a circular second-floor sanctuary. Behind the pulpit a piece of sheet metal also did double duty; it was a bracket holding a post and beam together, and a sanctuary cross. In 1995, the churches invited Synagogue Makom Shalom to join them. Loop Christian Ministries, a Christian Reformed Church, arrived in 1996. A group of Bahá'ís also worshiped there regularly. This ecumenical mix was enhanced with a toddlers' play group, a thrift shop, and services to the homeless. The ground-floor space doubled as a South Loop community meeting hall.

GracePlace was a convenient name. By avoiding the word "church," the edifice could also avoid violating a city ordinance that prohibited bars within 100 feet of churches. GracePlace's neighbor was a 100-year-old tavern called

Kasey's, lone survivor from Printers Row's former life. Owner Kasimir Weglarz sold it in 1986 to Bill White, who had owned a tavern in the yuppiefied Lincoln Park area. White refinished its two solid-mahogany bars, added a kitchen, and served homemade soups, prime rib, stuffed pork chops, and sandwiches. He preferred the Printers Row atmosphere to that of Lincoln Park. "It's not as transient," he said. "People stay; they know each other. There's more sense of a neighborhood, a little town inside a big city."

Developer Paul Stepan bought two buildings, the Duplicator and the Morton; in 1987 architects Larry Booth and Paul Hansen created a 161-room hotel by splicing their floors together and extending one building. It became the Hyatt on Printers Row, with an elegant restaurant, Prairie, that echoed Frank Lloyd Wright's designs.

Twelve years after Harry Weese sent Larry Booth to abandoned South Dearborn Street, Printers Row had 1,260 rental apartments and residential condominiums. Fifteen buildings had been renovated at a cost of $110 million. The development was boosted considerably by the federal Tax Reform Act of 1981, with its 25 percent income-tax credit for substantial restoration of a certified historic structure. This was cut to 20 percent in 1986. A 1983 Illinois law helped by freezing property-tax assessments at prerenovation levels for eight years for owner-occupants in renovated buildings within a historic district.

Larry Booth was not surprised that residents flocked to Printers Row. With 500,000 people working within walking distance, he didn't see how it could miss. To John Baird, who was selling the more sedate Dearborn Park at the same time he was developing its quirky neighbor to the north, the response was a surprise. He had worried, for example, about the Old Franklin Building, with huge steel beams cutting diagonally across some of its lofts. It turned out that people liked the look. "When all the units with beams were taken," Baird said, "someone asked us to install one in the apartment he wanted."

All of this was good news for Doreen Thomas and her son, Jeffrey, owners of Blackie's, a block west of the Dearborn Station. Her father, Alex De Milio, bought it in 1939, when it was known as a classy "cocktail lounge" serving passengers on stopovers from New York to Los Angeles. Doreen Thomas remembered Lana Turner visiting Blackie's between trains. One night, according to South Loop lore, Frank Sinatra punched a reporter in Blackie's. "We had some good nightlife during the 1940s and '50s," Doreen Thomas said. "Then it got bad. We were a simple shot-and-a-beer place for 20 years. Now we've got young professionals, advertising types."

On Saturday and Sunday mornings, Blackie's breakfasts brought Dearborn Park and Printers Row together for toasted cinnamon rolls, fried eggs, and crisp bacon. The main restaurant and bar held 82 people, but by the time Dearborn Park and Printers Row were fully occupied, Blackie's had outgrown its original space. It expanded twice, once for overflow and once with an art deco room for private parties.

Ivan Himmel, one of the Printers Row Five, opened Edwardo's, a pizza restaurant, in his Old Franklin Building. A collection of dry cleaners, real estate offices, and hair salons appeared. The Deli on Dearborn became the place to stop for a warm muffin on the way to work, the Moonraker for seafood in the evening. Sidewalk cafés and a Thai restaurant flourished, as did Trattoria Catarina, a gourmet Italian restaurant-and-carryout owned by Dearborn Park residents Catherine and Carmen Mugnolo. A pharmacy opened. The Gourmand, with fashionable coffees and scones and pasta salads, tolerated the Columbia College students who sat and read for hours and lived in Columbia's new dormitory—the restored Lakeside Press Building a block away. Starbucks Coffee Company opened a shop on the corner next to the Booth/Hansen office; now Printers Row residents felt they were a certifiably gentrified community.

Success had its drawbacks. When Ulrich and Ellen Sandmeyer opened their bookstore in the Rowe Building, its residents were artists and architects and photographers. A decade later, lawyers and traders from the financial district had replaced them. Wine and music disappeared from the condo meetings, and in came higher assessments as the affluent new owners voted for improvement after improvement. Ulrich Sandmeyer joked that, as the only owner who was not a millionaire, he became the only negative vote.

Marilyn Hasbrouck needed more space and in 1995 moved her Prairie Avenue Bookshop a few blocks northeast to Wabash Avenue. Her Donohue Building space joined a troubling list of vacant Printers Row storefronts. The higher rents, higher sales prices, and higher condominium assessments that accompanied Printers Row's success squeezed out a number of small businesses and frightened potential new ones. Marilyn Hasbrouck's 24-foot-wide, 72-foot-deep retail space, with basement storage, went on the market for $325,000. Across the street, a four-room, nicely appointed residential loft with a terrace was on sale for $369,000. Vera Klement, who had bought her unimproved space in 1980 for $19,200, estimated that in 1996 it was worth $384,000; Donohue condominiums were selling for $120 a square foot. She did not want to move, but her overhead was crushing—$10,800 a year in condominium assessments and $6,000 a year in real estate taxes. "My tragedy, as I see it, is that I found a place, made it livable at a reasonable price, and then I got clobbered," she said.

The last of the vacant Printers Row buildings, the Peterson, was converted into 49 residential lofts in 1995 and quickly sold out. The five men who met for doughnuts every Tuesday in John Baird's office 20 years earlier had managed to preserve some of the finest urban architecture in the world and in doing so created a lively and elegant entrance to Dearborn Park. The two neighborhoods, one rising fresh and new from rubble and railroad tracks, the other carved into the city's precious architectural heritage, were made for each other.

John Baird, active in both, was convinced that Printers Row was more important to Dearborn Park's success than vice versa, though his friend Ferd Kramer would argue with him about that. "We gave Dearborn Park the decent corridor to the Loop that it needed," Baird said. But he admitted that he might be biased, because working with those grand old buildings was simply so much fun.

In the early 1980s, the excitement generated by the South Loop communities prompted other residential development, just as Chicago 21 Corporation had intended back in 1974.

A Seattle-based syndicate put up a 30-story, $22-million building with 343 apartments known as 1212 South Michigan two blocks east of Dearborn Park in 1982. Two years later a group headed by Theodore Gaines, one of the Printers Row Five, built a 29-story, $26-million structure with 330 units called Two East Eighth, kitty-corner from Dearborn Park.

That same year, Bertrand Goldberg received approval from the Chicago Plan Commission to build a much-scaled-down version of his River City on the railroad tracks west of Dearborn Park. Still, even the first of his planned three phases was mammoth: a total of 446 apartments in a pair of S-shaped, poured-concrete buildings with a riverfront promenade, a 70-slip marina, a $60-million price tag, and an extraordinary 240,000 square feet of office and retail space.

Two years later, developer Jerome J. Karp converted an old YMCA hotel a block east of Dearborn Park into Burnham Park Plaza. Its 281 apartments were imaginatively designed by architect Kenneth Schroeder, who had done successful Printers Row recyclings. Costs totaled $34 million.

Mortgages on all four were insured by the FHA. Their combined 1,400 units, all rental, glutted the high-rise market in the South Loop. All had problems filling quickly enough, and at sufficient rates, to cover their high overhead and debt requirements. The three with commercial space had a terrible time renting it; for River City, this was disastrous. By 1989 all four had defaulted on their FHA-insured loans. The U.S. Department of Housing and Urban Development became the mortgagee, paying a total of $114 million to

their lenders. Federal officials worked out new repayment schedules, conducted periodic inspections and financial reviews, and managed to keep all
four afloat. River City and Burnham Park Plaza had no subsidized units; the
other two had 135 combined. Not surprisingly, River City's subsequent phases
were scrubbed.

Dearborn Park Corporation had made a smart move when it switched its
rental buildings to sales. Its lower-than-market-rate loans and mortgages, engineered by its well-connected leaders, had given it a competitive edge. But
not even the prudent, influential Dearborn Park team could escape the rav-
ages of inflation for long.

11

"Beating the Sidewalks" to Stay Alive

DEARBORN PARK HAD BEAT THE ODDS THROUGHOUT ITS FIRST YEAR AS A SETTLE-ment. It had no parks and no school and no grocery store, and the vacant Dearborn Station—the first thing strollers from the Loop saw—was an eyesore. Yet 90 percent of its 420 completed condominiums and townhouses had been sold. The Oaks, the building for people 62 and older, had a waiting list of 600 by the end of 1980.

The conservative men who ran Dearborn Park had worried for years that they were on the brink of financial collapse. They didn't get there until 1981. And then it looked as if they were stuck there.

Two new Dearborn Park buildings were ready for sales early that year, a mid-rise with 79 units and a high-rise with 250. The timing could hardly have been worse. Double-digit inflation had paralyzed the real estate industry. Mortgage rates were heading above 16 percent. Homeowners couldn't move because they couldn't find buyers. First-time buyers found great bargains in the older, formerly rental buildings that were flooding Chicago's condo market.

Construction had virtually ceased in Chicago. But Dearborn Park had three buildings on the drawing boards: the 220-unit flagship complex on Dearborn Park's northeast corner, next to the vacant station, and two buildings to the south, near Roosevelt Road—a high-rise and a mid-rise. Combined, they would add just over 500 units and cost about $35.5 million. Dearborn Park's chairman, Tom Ayers, presiding over its executive committee while Phil Klutznick was winding up a year in Washington as secretary of commerce, 127

128

"Beating
the
Sidewalks"
to Stay
Alive

thought it would be crazy to push ahead with a big building program when 329 new units were just coming on the market. For one thing, the interest on a new construction loan would be close to 20 percent, assuming they could get one. And Dearborn Park's 10 percent mortgage fund, a huge factor in its rousing start, was running out.

There was another worry. The newly completed high-rise had 75 studio apartments. This made sense for a rental building, which was what it was supposed to be when it was designed. But a need for cash and the collapse of Chicago's rental market had prompted a switch to condominiums. The studios had generous closet space and enclosed kitchen areas, but finding buyers who would pay $48,000 to $54,000 for basically one room could be a problem.

Ferd Kramer, Dearborn Park's president, project manager, and development manager, and generally regarded now as the fellow in charge of just about everything, recommended shelving the proposed mid-rise building and proceeding with the other two. Ayers agreed. Prospective lenders did not. They thought two big projects was one too many in those precarious times. The high-rise, like the mid-rise before it, was postponed. That left only the flagship. Dearborn Park could not tolerate a muddy, empty, two-acre tract at its strategic northeast corner indefinitely, precarious times or not.

Any construction at all was too risky for John Perkins, president of Continental Bank and a key figure in South Loop plans since 1971. He reluctantly concluded that Continental, Chicago's biggest bank and the favorite of City Hall, could not participate in a new loan. The bank already had a lot on its plate, Perkins told Kramer—much more, it would be revealed later, than was good for it.

First National Bank, under its new leadership and eager to replace Continental as Chicago's lead bank, stepped in to save the flagship. Its president, Richard L. Thomas, put together a $26.8-million loan in October at a floating prime rate for three years. His lending partners were First Federal Savings and Loan, whose president, E. Stanley Enlund, had played a major role in arranging previous Dearborn Park loans, and National Electrical Contractors Association Pension Benefit Trust, a longtime client of Draper & Kramer.

That solved only half of the financing problem, if a loan at 18.9 percent could be considered part of a solution. The 10 percent mortgage fund was gone, but 95 units from the first phase were still unsold in October—most of them those little studios. Phil Klutznick, back in Chicago and in charge of the executive committee, wanted all 95 sold before the flagship came on the market. He recommended renting them. Edward N. Cox, senior vice president of Baird & Warner and chief of the Dearborn Park sales team, suggested contract sales, or offering them to investors. But the committee wasn't ready to drop its requirement that buyers must live in their units. The scramble for mortgage money continued.

Ferd Kramer began another round of high-pressure visits to banks, savings and loans, and insurance companies. Frederick C. Ford, chief financial officer of Draper & Kramer, remembered his 80-year-old boss "beating the sidewalks for money" throughout the summer and fall of 1981. As in 1979, his argument was: Times are tough, but this is not just another development; the future of downtown Chicago is at stake; if this project is stalled now, forget about salvaging the South Loop; it's dead.

No one wanted to risk much money. But small amounts—$1 million here, $500,000 there—came dribbling in. By November Kramer had scraped together a mortgage package of $3.5 million at 12 percent interest over 29 years; that was 4.5 percentage points below the going rate. He did it, Kramer said later, "by hammering the banks and S&Ls over the head. Otherwise Dearborn Park would have failed."

It got its first park, too. The Chicago Park District finally implemented the landscape architects' designs for a formal, pedestrian-oriented space behind Dearborn Station. Half of the pedestrians turned out to have four legs. The park quickly became the evening gathering spot for Dearborn Park's many dogs and their owners. Work also began on the second park, the one with tennis courts, a jogging path, and a ball diamond.

Lest the year end on a happy note, Dearborn Park's general manager, Sheldon Kantoff, brought bad news to the executive committee's December meeting. The city was planning a subway link below the project's undeveloped south portion, near State Street. This could force a three-year delay in construction there, Kantoff said, during which Dearborn Park would have to pay a total of $350,000 in real estate taxes on the vacant property. And its building plans for the area might have to be changed. Phil Klutznick hit the roof. He already was fed up because Mayor Byrne had yet to give written confirmation that the city would provide infrastructure in the south half. Dearborn Park had recently fought and helped kill plans for a nearby sports stadium and an expressway connection running the length of its site a short distance to the west; now here was another threat to what was supposed to be a showcase, city-supported effort.

Ferd Kramer met with Byrne. She assured him she would do nothing to hurt Dearborn Park. She even had found money for the south infrastructure, she said. Planning would begin immediately. But by this time, the Dearborn Park leaders no longer had faith in any City Hall promise that came without a written commitment.

A few days later, Klutznick had another reason to be angry. He had a

130

"Beating
the
Sidewalks"
to Stay
Alive

phone call from George Dunne, president of the Cook County Board and chairman of the Public Building Commission, a city-county agency with bonding powers and the owner of Dearborn Station. The commission had bought a portion of the station in 1979 to use for a school and got the rest as a gift from Dearborn Park Corporation with the understanding that it would create a community center there, with space for restaurants, shops, and a supermarket. All that the commission had done, however, was tear down the station's waiting room and announce that it couldn't afford the $6-million renovation bill. Dearborn Park Corporation couldn't afford to fix up the station, either. Sales had slowed to about one a week, payments on its loans were getting harder to meet, and it had 220 new units coming on the market in a year. George Dunne told Klutznick the commission didn't know what to do with the station, so it was putting it up for sale.

Dearborn Park's founders had hoped that the station would be the new neighborhood's cherished landmark, a link to its past, a magnet not just for its residents, but also for the entire area. They wanted some say in what happened to it. At the moment it was an embarrassment, grimy and boarded up, its rear rudely amputated. An ugly chain-link fence was added to keep out vandals, but it wasn't working. The station was hurting sales and infuriating residents.

John Baird, active in salvaging the Printers Row buildings north of Dearborn Park, had finally engineered a deal with Treasure Island, Chicago's premier supermarket, to open a branch in a renovated station. Now that probably was dead. And Dearborn Park's leaders would have no way of assuring that future uses—assuming there were some—would be compatible with their new community. They wondered if the station

Topping-out of Dearborn Park's flagship building in June 1982, with Ferd Kramer inserting flag into last bucket of concrete. Others, *from left*, Sheldon Kantoff, Thomas G. Ayers, and E. Stanley Enlund. Courtesy Dearborn Park Corporation.

could be demolished. But that peripatetic preservationist Harry Weese had managed to get it on the National Register of Historic Places; trying to tear it down would raise a stink.

Four months later, on April 7, 1982, the Dearborn Park leaders got a surprise. Their own Stan Enlund and his First Federal Savings and Loan had bought the station for $1 million and a promise to spend $10 million restoring it. First Federal would move its headquarters into part of the 100,000 square feet of new office space, construct an addition at the rear, and build a parking garage for 50 cars. This was not the retail mall–community center that Dearborn Park leaders had hoped for, but it would solve a humiliating problem. The executive committee passed a resolution praising Enlund.

John Baird, though, was decidedly unhappy. He and architects Laurence Booth and Harry Weese and their other Printers Row partners had wanted the station but were outbid. Enlund, they thought, was paying twice what the wreck was worth. They were experienced in renovation and had plans for a bright and lively array of stores, restaurants, galleries, and community spaces that would be an ideal complement for Printers Row and Dearborn Park.

Baird's resentment looked more and more justified as months and then a year went by and the renovation did not begin. The Federal Savings and Loan Insurance Corporation (FSLIC), mired in sinking S&Ls throughout the country, delayed approval for First Fed's $10-million capital expenditure for the station. Twenty months after First Fed bought the station, it was obvious that the FSLIC was never going to say OK. By that time, First Fed's own financial problems precluded spending any money on a century-old curiosity. Ferd Kramer planted shrubbery around it to mask its sorry state.

Meanwhile, the financial problems accumulating in 1981 worsened with the new year. By the end of April, Dearborn Park still had 65 units left from its first phase—which meant only 30 sales in the previous six months; Sheldon Kantoff told the executive committee that holding them was costing $37,000 a month. By the end of the year, the corporation would not be able to meet the repayment schedule on its loans; it was facing a cash shortage of about $900,000.

On top of that, townhouse owners were complaining about leaning roof parapets and leaks and cracks in exterior concrete-brick walls. They hired a consulting firm, which uncovered numerous mistakes by contractors, including an absence of flashing—metal plates installed around windows, chimneys, and other joints to make them watertight—and inadequate spacing and location of masonry control joints. The contractors had gone out of business; there was no way to extract money from them. Dearborn Park's construction manager said the corporation had three choices: Repair the deficiencies;

132

"Beating
the
Sidewalks"
to Stay
Alive

make minor repairs and try to persuade homeowners to live with the other problems; or insist that the leaks and cracks were normal wear and tear, refuse to do any corrective work, and let the homeowners sue. Tom Ayers was adamant: The corporation represented the Chicago business community. It had promised good value and it must deliver. It must pay for adequate repairs. It did, at a cost of $620,000.

By the summer of 1982, it looked as if the corporation would not make it into another year. Ferd Kramer had an idea: Sell The Oaks, the fully occupied, rent-subsidized building for the elderly. It was worth $7 million; at 20 percent down, that would bring in $1.4 million. He talked to State Farm Insurance Company about buying it, but State Farm's legal department advised against it. The Dearborn Park executive committee told Kramer to proceed with syndication of the building. In August, he formed a limited partnership that acquired The Oaks for $7 million, with $1.4 million down, at 10 percent interest and a final payment at the end of 17 years. The Draper & Kramer Insurance Agency and Frederick Ford of Draper & Kramer became the general partners. The sale covered Dearborn Park's cash needs, keeping it afloat until the new flagship was ready for buyers.

Next, to get rid of those pesky studio condominiums, Kramer persuaded the executive committee to drop the requirement that owners must live in their units. The two-year stipulation already had expired on early buyers. A new marketing strategy was developed. Residents were invited to buy them and either rent them out or tear down a shared wall to enlarge their own apartments. Dearborn Park shareholders were urged to promote them among their employees. Residents were offered $1,000 finder's fees for referring buyers.

Kramer went to work on another scheme—selling the studios to shareholders at discounted prices of $42,000 to $52,000. They could then let Draper & Kramer lease the units, or they could use them for out-of-town business visitors or for their own pieds-à-terre. In two months, Kramer sold 17 studios. First National Bank bought three.

The troubles eased, but not for long. A mortgage fund of $25 million was needed to sell the flagship complex. Kramer considered it one of the best in design and construction in the city, but how many buyers would pay mortgage rates of 16 percent? Phil Klutznick wondered whether they should sell the whole thing to an investor.

A start-up mortgage fund arrived just in time for the grand opening, from the guardian angel of Dearborn Park finances during its second decade: First National Bank. Its president, Richard Thomas, offered $5 million at a fixed rate of 12 percent for 30 years or at 10 percent ballooning higher after 7 years.

With that commitment from First, Thomas and Ferd Kramer were able to persuade other institutions to make smaller commitments at the same rates. The Illinois Housing Development Authority helped out with $1.13 million at 10.55 percent with as little as 5 percent down for first-time home buyers with annual household incomes under $50,201.

Sales opened on April 9, 1983. Six weeks later, the results were depressing: Only 6 of the 220 units were sold. And 22 remained unsold from the earlier buildings. People were looking but not buying. Ed Cox, head of the sales team, proposed and received permission to cut prices by 10 percent—and, if necessary, 15 percent. Mortgage rates were lowered to a fixed-rate 11 percent, with Dearborn Park Corporation picking up the service charge of 1.5 points. Its advertising agency started a new campaign and created a name for the flagship complex: The Terraces. The price cuts, though, were a subsidy from the corporation. It was heading toward a deficit again soon after the sale of The Oaks had restored a fragile financial stability.

And when they looked south from their almost-empty Terraces, the Dearborn Park leaders saw 1.6 undeveloped acres north of Roosevelt Road, site of their shelved high-rise and mid-rise buildings, and 27 undeveloped acres south of Roosevelt. The city still had done nothing about installing streets and other infrastructure in the south neighborhood. But it had begun tearing up a strip for a subway tunnel. It was a thoroughly depressing sight. They had come through an extraordinary experience in reasonably good shape and had created a community of about 1,500 people, with several thousand more living in the renovated buildings to the north. Now they were tired—and getting on in years.

By the time they were trying to sell The Terraces, in the summer of 1983, the Dearborn Park leaders had been at it for a dozen years. Their numbers had dwindled to a hardy core. Tom Ayers was 68; Phil Klutznick, 76; Ferd Kramer, 82. They never missed a meeting. A number of the other founding directors had retired, moved away, or died. Some had simply grown weary of balancing all the 7:30 A.M. breakfasts and nonstop frustrations and worries with their demanding corporate jobs. Their key replacements on the executive committee in Dearborn Park's second decade included Ernest Collins, president of Seaway National Bank; Robert Carter, a vice president of Inland Steel; James J. Brice, senior partner of Arthur Andersen & Company; Claude M. Ireson, a vice president of Sears; and Richard Thomas of First National Bank. Several Draper & Kramer executives had active roles, including Ferd Kramer's sons, Anthony and Douglas, and his senior vice president, Fred Ford.

134

"Beating
the
Sidewalks"
to Stay
Alive

This leadership group was diverse; Collins, Carter, and Ford were black. Mary Ward Wolkonsky, founder and guiding spirit of Chicago's Bright New City forums, was another stalwart from the early days.

The three core leaders were immersed in other projects. Ferd Kramer had just built a Loop skyscraper with three stacked atriums, a first in office design, produced by architect Bruce Graham and Skidmore, Owings & Merrill. Kramer was losing his struggle to keep the Prairie Shores–Lake Meadows development racially integrated, now that federal authorities would no longer wink at his manipulation of waiting lists, but his management firm kept it attractive and well maintained. He had begun to turn his attention to Chicago's miserable high-rise public housing, working on ideas to replace it with safer, more livable, scattered-site developments.

Phil Klutznick was no longer active in the development company he had founded but was deeply involved in trying to bring peace to the Middle East. In the early 1980s, he shuttled back and forth to Israel, Egypt, Jordan, Syria, and Saudi Arabia as part of a four-member fact-finding mission organized by Seven Springs Center, a private foundation. Its report—and Klutznick in particular—were bitterly attacked by a number of U.S. Jewish organizations. Klutznick was accused of selling out to the Palestine Liberation Organization, an outrageous charge but one that did not deter him.

Tom Ayers had stepped down as chairman of Commonwealth Edison in 1980 but stayed on its board and took on a new civic crusade. Ayers, John Perkins, Bruce Graham, and other Dearborn Park shareholders and Chicago business leaders laid the groundwork for a Chicago World's Fair in 1992. It would celebrate the 500th anniversary of Christopher Columbus's voyage and the 100th anniversary (almost) of Chicago's Columbian Exposition, which got under way a year late in 1893. Their planning process was similar to the one that had created Dearborn Park: The business group, headed by Ayers, raised money from their corporations and hired Bruce Graham and his Skidmore team to prepare models and site plans. These were dazzling, implementing many of the lakefront recreational and cultural improvements advocated for years by civic groups. Mayor Jane Byrne, who loved a good Chicago party, was enthusiastic. So was Illinois Governor James R. Thompson.

On December 8, 1982, a delegation headed by Ayers won approval for the fair from the International Bureau of Expositions in Paris, which also approved a 1992 fair in Seville, Spain. Soon after, several Chicago community activists organized an anti–World's Fair coalition. Some of them were veterans of the anti–Chicago 21 campaign nine years earlier. This time, they were more sophisticated in their use of the news media and in focusing their complaints, which were a sharpened version of their 1973 cry: The planning was carried out in secret by an elite group with no community input; the fair would spend scarce public dollars frivolously, at the expense of poor neighborhoods.

Richard Thomas's role in Dearborn Park became especially significant as the takeovers and collapsing deals from the go-go early '80s took their toll on Chicago financial institutions. Continental Bank was shaken and nearly done in by big losses on risky energy-related loans; all of its top officers and managers left or were dismissed, including John Perkins, Dearborn Park's president during its early years. Late in 1983, New York's Citicorp bought the troubled First Federal Savings and Loan, taking Stan Enlund out of the picture. Six months after its acquisition of First Federal, the new Citicorp of Illinois announced that the vacant red eyesore it had inherited, Dearborn Station, was once again for sale.

Finances weren't the only cause for concern. Mayor Byrne had enraged Chicago's black community during 1982 by replacing several black members of the boards that ran the city school system and its public housing projects with whites; about 90 percent of the public housing population was black, as was 60 percent of the school population. Byrne's blunders fueled the same kind of revolt by black voters that had sunk her opponent Michael Bilandic in 1979. Their candidate was the most popular black politician in the city: U.S. Representative Harold Washington. With the help of a successful voter registration drive in the black community, his tough but engaging style, and a split in the white vote between Jane Byrne and Cook County State's Attorney Richard M. Daley, son of the late mayor, Washington narrowly won the Democratic nomination. Normally, that meant a lopsided victory in April. This time, with racial divisions raw and tense, the Democratic nominee won only 51.7 percent of the vote.

Richard L. Thomas, architect of Dearborn Park's financial rescue plan.

Chicago's first black mayor had campaigned on a platform of de-emphasizing big projects and focusing mayoral attention and city resources on needy neighborhoods. As in the case of Jane Byrne, the Dearborn Park leadership had no idea what to expect from him, nor did the committee to bring a World's Fair to Chicago.

By the summer of 1983, it was clear that further discounts—that is, further subsidies—were

136

"Beating
the
Sidewalks"
to Stay
Alive

needed to sell The Terraces. The executive committee authorized the sales staff to cut prices again.

Ferd Kramer helped things along by recruiting one of the most successful real estate salespeople in the Chicago area, Florence Jacobs. Her flamboyant jewelry, furs, long red fingernails, and red Mercedes-Benz sports car with its "SOLDOUT" license plates gave a new image to the gray Dearborn Park crew. She began a "walk to work" campaign, hired planes to fly over Bears, Cubs, and White Sox games trailing that message, and organized a high-pressure effort among employees of the Dearborn Park shareholder corporations.

Her work brought results. But these sales were subsidized, and Dearborn Park Corporation faced a loss of perhaps $3 million on The Terraces. In February 1984 it had to draw $585,000 from its construction and gap loans for operating expenses. Worse, the $26-million loan that built The Terraces was due in October, and the way things were going, Dearborn Park could not make the payments.

Richard Thomas gave the executive committee three choices. It could sell its vacant land; it could sell The Terraces; or it could try to get a new loan of about $7 million from its original investors, covering its looming shortfall. In the meantime, First Chicago would provide a gap loan to meet the October payments. There was some talk about selling all of Dearborn Park's remaining assets. Fred Ford's testing of that market produced one offer of $20 million—too low by about $10 million, as far as the leadership was concerned.

The executive committee decided to go with Thomas's suggestion of a new loan from shareholders. On February 14, a letter went to all of them from Tom Ayers, Phil Klutznick, and Ferd Kramer. It reviewed the early successes, when "sales proceeded at a phenomenal rate." It discussed inflation's terrible impact on subsequent years and the sizable price reductions. "It has not been easy to attract a large number of people to the development because many are not familiar with the South Loop," they wrote, "but those who now reside there, mostly professional people—lawyers, physicians, accountants, architects, educators—find it a fine area in which to live."

The future was bright, they said, particularly with the new construction and renovation in nearby areas and plans for a 1992 World's Fair on Near South Side lakefront and river sites. "Dearborn Park is at the 'front door' of the Fair, so to speak," the three wrote. "This property will escalate in value as it all becomes reality."

They asked the shareholders to put up half of their original investment, for a total of close to $7 million. The loan would mature in seven years with interest of 11 percent accruing and added to the principal. Unlike the original $14-million investment, with its understanding that the principal might never be repaid, let alone any interest, this time there was a firm commitment. Also, the lenders would receive 50 percent of net proceeds from the sale of land after repayment of the loan and accrued interest. First National Bank would be the agent for the loan without any charge to Dearborn Park.

Eighteen of the original 32 investors participated, contributing $3.6 million. Continental Bank was out, as was the Roman Catholic Archdiocese of Chicago. Others with financial problems or new ownership did not join, including Marshall Field Company, Harris Bankcorp, International Harvester Company, Montgomery Ward, and Peoples Gas. Citicorp and First National Bank invested $1.28 million each, and the National Electrical Contractors Association Pension Benefit Trust put in $783,333 to bring the total to $6.94 million.

Dearborn Park was on firmer financial ground, and its other problems also seemed closer to resolution. A development group from San Francisco and Cleveland bought Dearborn Station with a high bid of $1.2 million. This was more than twice what an independent appraiser had said it was worth, and once again local bidders who believed they had a better feel for the site lost out. The new owners made a fine choice for the renovation, though—Chicago architect (and Dearborn Park resident) Wilbert Hasbrouck. Six months after the purchase, and six years after sales began at Dearborn Park, work finally got under way on the 100-year-old depot and its 138-foot clock tower. There would be 28,000 square feet of offices, 69,000 square feet of retailing, a glass-enclosed, two-level arcade topped by a 120-foot-long skylight at the rear, and a 55-space parking lot.

Also in 1984, the Chicago Board of Education fulfilled a part of its seven-year-old promise to open a school in Dearborn Park. Kindergarten, first grade, and second grade opened in townhouses the Public Building Commission bought for the school system. Third grade was to be added in 1985. After that, presumably, the school board would buy land in Dearborn Park's undeveloped south area and build a full-fledged elementary school for the neighborhood and other renovating areas to the north and west. At least, that was the plan that Judith Hoch and her South Loop School Committee had been pushing for years.

Phil Klutznick, who was leaning more and more in favor of selling all of Dearborn Park's undeveloped property, persuaded the executive committee to test the market with its vacant 1.6 acres in the north neighborhood. Developer Jack McNeil, gambling that the early Dearborn Park residents were ready for something bigger, snapped it up for $700,000. He built 51 townhouses to replace the scrapped high-rise and mid-rise, with their combined 297 units. It was the first time the corporation had let someone else build on

137
"Beating
the
Sidewalks"
to Stay
Alive

"Beating
the
Sidewalks"
to Stay
Alive

Brick-and-stucco
townhouses
trimmed with pipe
rails, by developer
Jack McNeil, re-
placing scrapped
high-rise and mid-
rise buildings of
Dearborn Park's
northern neighbor-
hood. Architect:
Michael Realmuto.
Photo by Michael J.
Kardas.

its land, and the first major deviation from the Skidmore plans that had been carefully nurtured for eight years. And what a deviation. The Skidmore architects thought the yellowish stuccoed walls and busy array of colors, shapes, and heights looked cheap and spoiled their neat harmony of brick and lush greenery. Some architectural critics, though, welcomed the diversion. The authors of the popular book *Chicago on Foot: Walking Tours of Chicago's Architecture* enjoyed architect Michael Realmuto's "wild vernacular" of red brick on the first floors, cream stucco above, deep blue "streamlined pipe rails," and the "references to houses of the 19th century in oversized quoins, keystones and window lintels, and a hint of gabled roofs."

McNeil's biggest units had four levels, four bedrooms, and 2,000 square feet, selling for $184,900. He introduced private garages and fireplaces to Dearborn Park. By the time his townhouses went on the market, in mid-1985, inflation had eased and interest rates were falling. Talman Services Corporation, a Dearborn Park shareholder and participant in its loan funds, offered mortgages at 10 percent.

As McNeil had expected, many Dearborn Park residents had outgrown their homes—but didn't want to leave the conveniences and congeniality of the South Loop. Almost half of his townhouses sold in a few weeks, with most buyers coming from Dearborn Park and Printers Row. Some combined two units, demonstrating that the South Loop could now command prices of $250,000, perhaps higher.

Sales also had picked up at The Terraces and the remaining first-phase units. But there were two lawsuits from condominium associations unhappy with construction work; some of the townhouses at The Terraces had construction problems; there was renewed talk about a stadium just southwest of Dearborn Park; Mayor Washington's staff had done nothing about infrastructure in the south area; and Dearborn Park had to go back to First National Bank for $300,000 in operating cash and an extension of its last construction loan.

When Florence Jacobs and the sales team finally sold the last of the Dearborn Park condominiums in April 1986, and the joint Draper & Kramer–Baird & Warner marketing venture was dissolved, it was clear that Tom Ayers and Phil Klutznick and Ferd Kramer and the others had no desire to do it all over again in their south half. Nor did their shareholders, who had been remarkably patient, want to embark on another big venture. The success of Jack McNeil's townhouses proved they didn't have to. Other developers were sending out feelers about buying some of the south land.

In that sense, the Dearborn Park founders had accomplished their mission. They had demonstrated that the old railroad yards south of the Loop

140

"Beating
the
Sidewalks"
to Stay
Alive

could be transformed into a stable, multiracial, multi-ethnic neighborhood, and they had been a catalyst for other developers. By the end of 1986, some 2,000 people were living in Dearborn Park and another 5,000 in the residential developments, new and recycled, that had sprung up around it. Townhouses that sold for $100,000 in 1980 were going for $140,000 in 1986. Printers Row lofts were selling for $75,000 to $350,000.

The South Loop could now make it on its own. The subsidies the founders had poured in during their long struggle to get the north portion established would not be needed in the south. The corporation would put it up for sale—as soon as the city got around to installing the necessary streets, sidewalks, sewers, water connections, and parks that any prospective developer would expect.

When the Board of Education announced that it would pay the requested $601,840 for 1.3 acres for a Dearborn Park school and begin construction in mid-1986, it looked as though the most important missing piece of the new community finally would be in place.

The real agonies of the school struggle, though, were just beginning.

12

"Our Neighborhood Lost Its School"

MAUREEN MURPHY SCHUNEMAN TOOK HER 11-MONTH-OLD BABY BOY AND HER 3-YEAR-old daughter to a weedy field a block south of her home for a festive gathering the morning of July 30, 1986. About 100 Dearborn Park residents, most of them mothers with young children in tow, watched and cheered as George Muñoz, president of the Chicago Board of Education, and Manford Byrd Jr., the school superintendent, broke ground for a $5-million South Loop School.

Maureen had moved to Dearborn Park when it opened seven years earlier, a single woman buying her first home. Now, like many of the young newcomers she had met in that freshman year, she was married, had children, and was living in her second Dearborn Park residence—a two-story condominium with a little brick-walled garden in a mid-rise building. She was enthusiastic that July morning. This was assurance that the new neighborhood had a bright future, she told *Chicago Tribune* education writer Casey Banas.

"Chicago's only community without its own neighborhood school is about to get one," Banas wrote.

A mile south of the ground-breaking site, another group of mothers gathered, definitely not in a festive mood. They met in Jackie Russell's living room in a 22-story curving slab of poured concrete that bore the distinctive stamp of Chicago architect Bertrand Goldberg. Like his Marina City and River City creations, the Hilliard Homes buildings were striking, gigantic pieces of sculpture. But dramatic architecture did not make life better for the people who dwelled there. Behind the curved concrete walls, Hilliard was just another of the Chicago Housing Authority's ineptly managed, deplorably **141** maintained high-rise hells. As in the others, the residents were all poor, nearly all black, and isolated from surrounding communities by expressways, railroad tracks, or industrial districts. The absence of firm tenant-acceptance standards and controls left them vulnerable to gang violence and drug-driven crime.

Six years earlier, Jackie Russell and other Hilliard mothers had asked the Chicago Board of Education to replace the rusted, rat-infested mobile class-rooms across the street from Hilliard with a full-scale elementary school. Their children spent kindergarten and first and second grades in the mobiles and then transferred to the aging, crowded Haines School one-half mile away at the edge of the Chinatown neighborhood. The board never responded. Nor did it make repairs in the mobiles. In 1984, after the Hilliard mothers' protests caught the attention of new Mayor Harold Washington, the school board re-lented. But it agreed only to replacing the mobiles with a factory-built steel structure for the primary grades, not a full-scale elementary school.

A lemon-yellow, $1.2-million structure—built with prefabricated, modu-lar steel units assembled on the site—had been open for six months when ground was broken for South Loop School a mile away. It looked cheerful in-side and outside, but unmistakably low budget, with hand-me-down equip-ment and furnishings. The Hilliard mothers were angry. Sheila Garrett, who at the time had a second grader in the yellow steel school, recalled the hurt and bitterness. "Our kids were here before Dearborn Park was built," she said. "We should have been first to get a new school, but instead it went to the rich people. We felt we weren't being treated equal because we were poor."

By September, the spectacle of two sets of parents, one poor and one well-off, fighting over a small public school had achieved national notoriety. It was a tale of two vastly different cities, only a mile apart, separated not by race but by class. It laid bare the severe problem confronting public school systems in America's urban centers: how to give all children—poor and middle class, aca-demically gifted and disadvantaged—the educational resources they needed to fulfill their potential. No big-city school system had figured out a way to do that. In the South Loop, the problem was exposed in vivid microcosm that fall of 1986.

A few years later, the school, in effect, belonged to Hilliard Homes. Sheila Garrett's son was enrolled there. Maureen Schuneman's daughter was bused miles away.

It would have been appropriate if that first shovel on July 30 had been wielded by Judith Hoch. She had crusaded for this day since she, her hus-band, and their two babies moved into the brand-new Dearborn Park in 1980.

For four years, she concentrated on persuading Ruth B. Love, school superintendent at the time, to open primary grades in Dearborn Park townhouses bought and equipped for that purpose by the Public Building Commission.

Ruth Love responded that there weren't enough children in Dearborn Park and its vicinity. In 1981, her survey counted only 29 in the kindergarten-through-third-grade age bracket. Judy Hoch and her South Loop School Committee countered with a blizzard of letters to Love, Board of Education members, city officials, and shareholders of Dearborn Park Corporation citing school board resolutions from as far back as June 8, 1977, promising a school in Dearborn Park.

The question was, which should come first: more children in the South Loop to fill a school, as Ruth Love wanted, or a school to attract more families with children into the South Loop, as the parents wanted? Dearborn Park's founders had been warned of this dilemma back in their early planning days. Dorothy Rubel, executive director of the Metropolitan Housing and Planning Council, and Harold Jensen, head of Illinois Central Railroad's real estate division, had urged the group to take the initiative in creating a model school before the first families arrived. Don't trust the Chicago school system to do it for you, Rubel and Jensen said; you'll never budge that bureaucracy.

It looked as if they were right. But, prodded by Judy Hoch, a long list of political, business, and civic leaders wrote to Ruth Love and to school board members, demanding that they keep their promises and open a temporary school in the townhouses.

Cook County State's Attorney Richard M. Daley was one of those who contacted Ruth Love. "It is clear to me that in order for the South Loop area to become even more attractive for families, a quality public school must be made available for that neighborhood's children," he wrote. "As we both know, good schools are among the most essential elements of any community."

Alderman Fred Roti sent letters every few months. Barry C. Burkholder, chairman of Citicorp of Illinois, wrote to Love, as did Richard Thomas, president of First National Bank. Bette Cerf Hill, founder and president of the new South Loop Planning Board, sent demographic figures to bolster her claim that when residential units currently in planning stages were completed, there would be more than enough children to fill the townhouse classrooms.

On May 23, 1984, Judy Hoch made a presentation before the Board of Education at a meeting attended by scores of South Loop parents, business owners, and representatives of Dearborn Park Corporation. The next day Ruth Love sent her a brief letter: "I have recommended to the Board that a Dearborn Park School be opened in September, 1984 . . . ."

Kindergarten and first and second grades got started that year, with 32 children enrolled. Third grade was added in 1985, and fourth in 1986. By that time, construction of a new, 540-student elementary school, which in Chicago is kindergarten through eighth grade, already was under way in Dearborn Park's undeveloped south portion. Children from Printers Row and the new apartment buildings that had risen nearby also attended the townhouse school. Its boundaries, set by Board of Education officials, extended from 15th Street—the southern border of the Dearborn Park site—north to the Chicago River to include the small number of children who lived in the few high-rise residential towers in the northern part of the Loop.

The primary-grade children of Hilliard Homes were still in their rusting mobile classrooms when the Dearborn Park townhouse school opened. Their mothers asked if they could enroll there, but Board of Education officials said no, they didn't live in the attendance area.

In 1986, as construction began on the new South Loop School, 65 children were attending the townhouse classrooms; 42 were black, 13 were white, and 10 were Asian or Hispanic. Fourteen came from lower-income families who lived in nearby rent-subsidized apartments. Those figures indicated that South Loop School would need a larger percentage of white students to comply with the 1980 consent decree that settled a U.S. Department of Justice suit against the Chicago Board of Education. In that agreement, the board promised that any new neighborhood school would be "integrated" within three years of its opening, which under the plan's definition meant the student body had to be at least 30 percent minority *and* at least 30 percent white.

At the time the decree was signed, white enrollment in the Chicago school system was 14 percent and falling—in a city that was about 41 percent white. The townhouse school didn't reach 30 percent white, but enthusiastic South Loop parents who were helping to plan the new school were confident that its excellence would soon fill all 540 seats and comply with the 30 percent requirement.

Judy Hoch, Martha Clement, Kathryn Moery, Robert Grisham, Carmen Mugnolo, Jay Lawrence, and others on the school committee—black and white, from Dearborn Park and Printers Row and the growing community around them—worked with the school architect to accommodate a fine-arts curriculum. They wanted special offerings in music, art, dance, and theater to take advantage of the cultural amenities within an easy walk of the new school, and strong, challenging programs in science, mathematics, and reading.

Judy Hoch solicited donations from Dearborn Park Corporation, Citicorp, and a dozen or so other companies for musical instruments, computers, and other special equipment for the school. She asked for comfortable furniture for school volunteers from The Oaks, the Dearborn Park building for people 62 and older. Her committee raised money by selling handiwork at an arts fair on Dearborn Street. A choir from The Oaks sang at their fund-raisers. A tiny orchestra from the townhouse school performed.

"This school will flow into this community, and the community will flow into this school," an ecstatic Judy Hoch told reporters at the ground breaking.

When construction began on South Loop School, the Hilliard mothers petitioned for a boundary change that would include their buildings and Long Grove, a huge, nearly all black, subsidized development east of Hilliard. Long Grove children had been attending Drake School, a mile to the south; its achievement scores were lower than state norms but at or above citywide levels. Dearborn Park and Printers Row parents, black as well as white, adamantly opposed the boundary change. Combined, Hilliard and Long Grove had about 450 children of elementary-school age. The new, 540-seat school could not possibly accommodate Hilliard, Long Grove, and the growing South Loop community. Nor could it comply with the 30 percent white requirement of the desegregation decree. But the South Loop community could not yet fill the school by itself.

A 1987 survey by the South Loop Planning Board indicated that 500 children, newborn through age 13, lived in Dearborn Park, Printers Row, and surrounding South Loop buildings; 70 were babies born in the previous 12 months. Of the 250 school-age children, 60 percent were nonwhite. About 20 percent lived in rent-subsidized apartments or received some other form of public assistance. Based on these numbers, the neighborhood would have more than enough children to fill a 540-seat school in about eight years, when the south portion of Dearborn Park and other new and recycled residences on the drawing boards would be occupied. The demographics also suggested that the school would meet the requirements of the desegregation decree and have an economically diverse student body as well.

When that survey was conducted, 35 percent of the school-age South Loop children attended private institutions, mostly Roman Catholic. The rest were in Dearborn Park's townhouse school or were bused to 12 other locations throughout the city.

As the new building neared completion, School Superintendent Byrd came under increasing pressure from both Jackie Russell's Concerned Parents of Hilliard Homes and Judy Hoch's South Loop School Committee. It was an awful predicament, he told reporters, because both sets of parents had the same goal—quality education. But whatever the decision, he pledged that it "will not conflict with the desegregation decree" that all new schools must be at least 30 percent minority and 30 percent white.

Judy Hoch's group had two proposals for accomplishing that: Extend the attendance boundaries west instead of south, to take in the racially integrated, gentrifying Near West Side around the University of Illinois at Chicago; or extend the boundaries south to include Hilliard Homes and Long Grove but restrict enrollment from those two developments to students who test at grade level or above. Students from Dearborn Park and other South Loop locations would get in no matter what their test scores. For the Hilliard and Long Grove students who didn't meet the academic requirements, the South Loop group suggested beefed-up remedial programs at Haines School and early-learning programs at the Hilliard modular school.

The Hilliard mothers found this distinction offensive. The South Loop committee argued that it was sound urban planning, in the best interests of the entire city, to cater to groups like theirs. "Stress the importance of *quality* education in the South Loop," Judy Hoch advised in a memo to her cadre of letter-writers peppering public officials and the news media with mailings. "Stress the importance of neighborhoods like the South Loop to the city as a whole. We must be able to attract middle-class, tax-paying families to live in these new central city developments."

The Concerned Parents of Hilliard Homes sent school officials their own message, powerful and poignant. "I understand that you want to please the richer kids," said Jackie Russell. "But what about us? Our kids' math and reading scores continue to go down and down. Are you just writing us off?"

The South Loop parents lost this public-relations battle. News reports portrayed them as elite young professionals standing at the door of a public schoolhouse, determined to bar poor children—just as white Southern governors tried to bar blacks from state universities decades earlier. The yellow modular school at Hilliard Homes was made to seem worse than it was—a flimsy tin box, according to some newspaper accounts, set in the midst of junkyards. The junkyards part was true, and disgraceful; but the school itself was cheerful, lively, and orderly, inside and out. The Hilliard buildings mysteriously moved closer and closer to South Loop School. Jonathan Kozol, who has written passionately and powerfully of the plight of disadvantaged children in America's cities, must have drawn from these reports for his book *Savage Inequalities*, which placed South Loop School across the street from Hilliard Homes, when it was a mile away.

The situation was far more complex than a simple matter of affluent parents objecting to sharing a school with poor people. By the late 1980s, when the battle over South Loop School was raging, the horrors of the Chicago public school system had been dramatically documented by the city's newspapers and television stations. William J. Bennett, U.S. secretary of education under President Ronald Reagan, called Chicago schools the worst in the nation. In an acclaimed 1988 series of reports by the *Chicago Tribune*, Patrick Reardon and R. Bruce Dold wrote:

The Chicago Public School system is a case of institutionalized child neglect. . . . Two-thirds [of its students] live in poverty, and many come to school with a background of deprivation that would make learning difficult under the best of circumstances. . . . They encounter teachers from an ingrown, aging and protected work force of uneven ability, qualification and motivation. Pupils and teachers alike are trapped in a system inadequately administered by political appointees and career bureaucrats whose concern for comfort, survival and status quo strangle the system. . . . There is not enough money to go around, and the children always seem to have the last claim.

Achievement scores in schools with predominantly low-income student enrollment generally were abysmal—and most of the city's 595 schools were predominantly low income. Half of the 65 high schools placed in the bottom 1 percent of U.S. schools in American College Test scores. Out-of-control classrooms were rampant, especially in poor neighborhoods. The Chicago school system had total revenues from local, state, and federal sources of $4,000 a year for each student—almost $800 less per pupil than the suburban average. Yet its job was far more demanding than that of most suburban districts.

The result, as Reardon and Dold wrote in the *Tribune*, was years of "bright flight"—middle-class children, black and white, leaving the school system. In 1971, when the idea of Dearborn Park was born, public school enrollment in Chicago was 580,000; in 1986, when construction began on South Loop School, it was only 420,000. This rate of decline was nearly twice that of the overall city population. (By 1996, 83 percent of the student body was classified as low income, compared with 68 percent in 1987; enrollment was 423,000.)

In that setting, it was not surprising that middle-class parents who prized education were reluctant to send their children to a Chicago public school unless they could be assured that it would meet their expectations.

The Concerned Parents of Hilliard Homes didn't like the Chicago school system, either. But they couldn't afford to escape it by moving to the suburbs or paying private school tuition. Nor did they show much interest in trying to use the city's complicated magnet school network; they had heard it was impossible for children who were black, poor, and performing below grade level to get into one of these 46 special schools, with their superior teachers and resources. That wasn't true, but it was difficult. Acceptance was based on lotteries, but within limits: The school had to have enough white students to

meet desegregation guidelines, so it was easier for whites to get in. Some—
the "classical" and "scholastic" academies—limited enrollment to the acade-
mically gifted. And well-informed, middle-class parents tended to be more
familiar with the magnet system and its opportunities than parents living in
the city's enormous, isolated public housing projects.

The Hilliard parents felt they had to rely on a neighborhood school, and
they were convinced that a nice new building with nice new equipment was
the answer to their children's scholastic problems. It was not, as they learned
later, after they had won their battle with Dearborn Park residents.

Most news accounts continued to distill the struggle as a war of the rich
against the poor, but a few—in particular, *Newsweek* magazine and reports
by writers Dirk Johnson in *The New York Times* and John Kass in the *Chicago
Tribune*—identified the underlying issue: a war over inadequate resources.
Or, as *Newsweek* correspondent Tim Padgett put it, "Who's going to get what
little quality remains in public schools like Chicago's?"

The Chicago Panel on Public School Policy and Finance, a private, nonprofit group, was harsh on the Dearborn Park parents. Their assumption that
their children were smarter than poor children was "insulting," the panel's
Diana Lauber told Dirk Johnson of *The New York Times*. Besides, she said,
the higher-achieving Dearborn Park children could elevate the achievement
of the Hilliard children, and themselves benefit from the interaction.

Gary Orfield, an urbanologist at the University of Chicago who had devoted much of his career to promoting school integration, was more understanding. "You've got to sympathize with the kids in the projects," he told Dirk
Johnson. "But it's very important to retain the middle-income people, black
and white. If you have a very high proportion of kids from the projects, you'll
lose the middle-class kids. Then you've got another predominantly minority,
very poor school on the South Side. Unfortunately, we've already got hundreds of them."

The *Tribune's* John Kass wrote about the squeeze on city politicians.
They wanted to attract middle-class residents, whose tax revenues they sorely
needed. But when this goal clashed with the demands of minority groups,
who had demonstrated their power at the polls in recent city elections, they
went into hiding or backed off.

Many of the Dearborn Park parents were acutely uncomfortable with
their stance. They considered themselves social progressives; after all, they
had chosen to live in a racially and ethnically diverse neighborhood in the
center of the city. They didn't object to a certain number of Hilliard children,

they said—perhaps 20, 25 percent of the school's enrollment—but they didn't want them to dominate the classrooms and divert the school's resources to remedial programs.

Dearborn Park's black parents, in particular, were torn. "This hasn't been easy for anybody," Valerie Grisham, a systems marketing analyst, told Dirk Johnson. She recalled her childhood in a poor neighborhood. "I hear talk about how we're keeping ghetto kids out of the school. And I think, wow, that was me. I was a ghetto child."

Her husband, Robert, a communications company executive, told John Kass of the *Tribune* that his family "sacrificed to get me away from the West Side, and to a private school out of the ghetto. I didn't forget where I come from. I worked in lunchrooms to pay my tuition to high school and college. I just don't want to experiment with my children's education. It's either a quality school or we leave the city."

The Chicago Board of Education did not want to take sides in the war between the parents. Board president Muñoz, a Dearborn Park resident, asked the two groups to work out a compromise. But the South Loop committee would not budge from its position that children from Hilliard Homes, Long Grove, and Pilsen—a third, largely Hispanic neighborhood that also demanded access to the school—should be admitted only if they met certain academic requirements. And the Hilliard group would not settle for what they considered second-class treatment.

Tom Ayers, Ferd Kramer, and the rest of Dearborn Park Corporation's leaders were aghast at these developments. From the start, they considered a superior, racially integrated school essential to the community's success. Now, after years of wrangling, they were finally about to get their school—only it wouldn't really be theirs.

Well, that was the problem, said Sheila Garrett, new president of the Concerned Parents of Hilliard Homes. "They expect the Board of Education to build them their own private school." But with Harold Washington as mayor, she said, "they don't run things anymore."

Ferd Kramer asked James Brice, senior partner of Arthur Andersen & Company, a Dearborn Park board member and a friend of Mayor Washington's, to please go talk to him. The future of Dearborn Park and all that it could mean to the city was at stake. The mayor responded that it wouldn't be proper for him to intervene in school affairs, but several high-ranking members of his administration said that they—and Washington himself—sided with the Hilliard parents.

By June 1987, with opening day nine months away, it was obvious that the warring parents were never going to find middle ground. So the Board of Education imposed its own compromise. It was, as the *Chicago Tribune* said in an editorial, the most complicated attendance policy in the city:

All South Loop children would be accepted at the new school, beginning at kindergarten. Hilliard and Long Grove children would attend the modular school in kindergarten and first and second grades. After that, they had a choice of joining the South Loop children in the new school, without academic requirements, or remaining in Haines. Pilsen children would be admitted to South Loop School, chosen by lottery, to fill any available slots. Additional vacancies would be filled citywide, chosen to enhance integration.

The Hilliard parents were furious that their children had to stay in the modular school until third grade, and they threatened to sue the school board. But school system demographers insisted that limiting the Hilliard enrollment was the only way the new school could comply with the desegregation decree's 30 percent white requirement.

"There is no avoiding the preference the compromise gives to Dearborn Park," the *Tribune* said in the editorial. "Considerations of social class are always troubling. But so are the consequences when well-intentioned policies disrupt efforts of integrated neighborhoods to stay that way."

Judy Hoch was unhappy about the absence of academic admission standards but pleased that the board decided to keep the fine-arts curriculum and other programs usually found only in magnet schools. She enrolled her two children in the new school when it opened in February 1988. Her son had been attending fifth grade in Andrew Jackson Language Academy on the city's Near West Side—a high-achieving magnet school—and her daughter was in fourth grade in the Dearborn Park townhouse school. She urged other South Loop parents to do the same, but few did. Most kept their children where they were, despite the inconvenience of busing and, in some cases, the high tuition.

Robert and Valerie Grisham's two sons stayed in Skinner Classical Academy, another high-achieving public school on the Near West Side. Children were admitted to the rigorous Skinner only if they tested in the upper 20 percent nationally. The Grishams didn't see how the new school could match Skinner's academic excellence.

Tim and Noreen Donovan kept their two children in Franklin Magnet School on the Near Northwest Side. They were happy with Franklin. Besides, "We wanted them to go to an integrated school," Tim said, not one that would be nearly all black.

Maureen and Paul Schuneman applied to LaSalle Language Academy, a magnet school on the North Side, for their five-year-old daughter. By LaSalle's rules, only one-eighth of its student body could be white female. The other eighths: white male, black female, black male, Hispanic female, Hispanic male, Asian or other female, and Asian or other male. In addition, the school aimed for a 25 percent low-income student body. About 600 children applied for the 56 kindergarten slots available that year. Waiting to find out if little Amanda would be one of seven white girls admitted to LaSalle's kindergarten was like waiting for word from Harvard's admissions office. Amanda made it. "It's a very enriching culture," her mother said later of LaSalle. "The South Loop School could not be."

Still, the school did manage to have a somewhat diverse student body its first two years: 25 percent white, 70 percent black, 5 percent Asian or Hispanic. Only 18 of the 124 white students came from the South Loop. The rest were bused in from other parts of the city, attracted by the fine-arts program, enhanced offerings in the basics, and a Board of Education waiver that had given Principal Joan Fron permission to select a superior faculty. Yet this was a start, and if that smattering of South Loop parents was satisfied with the school, Judy Hoch felt, more would use it in the future.

That possibility faded as fighting continued after the school opened. Elections of its Local School Council, which has teacher, parental, and community-at-large representatives and considerable authority in the decentralized Chicago system, became fierce battlegrounds. Once, pushing and shoving erupted at a council meeting on a hot steamy night in a Hilliard community room when throngs of young blacks crowded in; South Loop residents feared it was a gang invasion and summoned police. Another time, after South Loop residents won control of the council, Hilliard parents charged that they couldn't get to the polling place because the Chicago Fire Department had sealed off their buildings. The Board of Education declared the election void. But the Fire Department said it had sealed off only one hallway in one building because of a gas leak, and for just 30 minutes. Sidley & Austin, Dearborn Park Corporation's law firm, represented the South Loop parents for no fee and eventually won a decision in U.S. District Court to reinstate the ousted representatives.

When Hilliard and Long Grove parents won control in a subsequent election, South Loop residents complained that black activists from outside the area had rounded up Hilliard residents and bused them to the polling station.

Even shrubs and flowers were ensnared in the bitterness. Dearborn Park Corporation, unhappy that the Board of Education had done nothing with the dirt around its new school, offered to donate $14,000 for landscaping design and installation. The school council, dominated by Hilliard residents, said it would accept the offer only if the corporation also landscaped the Hilliard modular school. Ferd Kramer, outraged, refused to do that. Eventually the council relented and let him spend the $14,000 to beautify the school.

Then, in the summer of 1990, any fragile hope for a successful union was shattered by a new school superintendent. Ted Kimbrough, eight months on the scene from California, announced that requiring primary-grade Hilliard children to attend the yellow modular school while their South Loop counterparts went to the new building was a form of segregation "reminiscent of the Jim Crow South." Beginning in September, he said, all kindergartners and first graders from the South Loop would be bused to the Hilliard Homes modular branch.

There was nothing wrong with the modular school. The continued protests from Hilliard parents who objected to using it were baseless. But, as Kimbrough must have known, the South Loop parents would erupt at the notion of busing their tiny children to a school in the shadow of a big public housing project. Too dangerous, they said—the gangs, the drugs, the violence. Of course, Hilliard parents had to live with this danger 24 hours a day.

Kimbrough's decision seemed calculated to drive South Loop parents away from the school. Ferd Kramer tried to get an appointment with him but failed. At a public meeting with angry South Loop residents, Kimbrough acknowledged that some parents might pull their children out of the school. "They have a right to do that," he said. "But I would hope that people would unite and live together." When someone in the audience said Dearborn Park parents might leave for the suburbs, Kimbrough responded: "Let them go."

James Compton, interim president of the Board of Education, head of the Chicago Urban League, and an architect of Dearborn Park's affirmative action plan during its construction stage, supported Kimbrough. "The children of Hilliard Homes have suffered a long ordeal of discrimination," he said. "The board was long overdue in corrective action."

When Kimbrough delivered his busing edict in 1990, the school had 114 whites in a student body of 636. Three years later, it had 31 whites and an enrollment of 568. In 1990, 66 percent of its students came from low-income families. Three years later, it was 86 percent. The flow of kindergartners and first graders from Dearborn Park and Printers Row into the school stopped cold. Older children from the South Loop also were withdrawing from the school; their parents blamed disruptive classrooms and an erosion of academic programs. They went instead to magnet schools or private schools. Francis Xavier Warde School, on the campus of Old St. Patrick's Catholic Church about two miles from Dearborn Park, became the neighborhood school for those who could afford the $3,900-a-year tuition and got on the waiting list early enough. With its promise of an elementary education "grounded in the Judeo-Christian tradition," Warde attracted Roman Catholics and non-Catholics in about equal numbers, and a student body that was 42 percent minority. Other families stretched their budgets to cover the $9,000- to $10,000-a-year tuition at the University of Chicago Laboratory School.

The remaining alternative was the suburbs; 1990 saw the beginning of a continuing exodus of families with three- and four-year-olds from Dearborn Park and Printers Row. Other young couples replaced them, only to leave when their children reached school age.

One of the saddest aspects of the South Loop School saga was that the new building, the handpicked faculty, and the special academic offerings did not improve the poor performance of its disadvantaged students. Perhaps it could have, if the Hilliard enrollment had been limited to 30 or 40 percent, the percentage of low-income students in many of Chicago's high-achieving magnet schools and in Francis Xavier Warde, which offered subsidies to poorer families. But five years after Kimbrough's busing edict, South Loop School was 90 percent low income and having a difficult time helping its needy students. Only seven of its students came from the South Loop neighborhood. Test scores continued well below statewide norms and below even the pathetic citywide norms. In the fall of 1995, eighth graders—who by then had spent five years in South Loop School—were as far below state- and citywide norms as they had been when they entered the school in the third grade. Achievement levels were below those at Haines, where Hilliard children had gone before the boundary change, and at Drake, where Long Grove children had attended. Hilliard students still had the option of enrolling at Haines, which moved into a stunning new building in 1994, but only a few dozen did—even though it was closer to their homes than South Loop School.

The Hilliard and Long Grove residents who controlled South Loop's Local School Council were dismayed by the lack of achievement. They discarded several principals before settling early in 1995 on Anthony Biegler, a white man who had been principal of a Roman Catholic elementary school. They used their council money—discretionary funds dispensed by the citywide Board of Education—to provide a full-day kindergarten at the yellow modular school, which had been enhanced by a generous neighbor, the Warshawsky & Company auto parts firm. Warshawsky cleared away the infamous junkyard facing the school, transformed it into a landscaped playground, and donated it to Hilliard Homes. With the rest of its discretionary money, the council hired a strong black male teacher to run a "detention room" at South Loop School, where disruptive students were sent to cool down. The council asked parents to dress their children in uniforms—white tops and blue skirts or pants. They told their new principal to concentrate on raising achievement levels in reading, writing, and math.

Their corrective measures were promising. In most categories, 1996 test scores inched above those of 1995. But frustrations remained. Several teachers complained that children frequently came to school poorly prepared and that too many parents ignored requests for meetings or failed to respond in other ways. "Kids are acting up constantly," one veteran teacher said. "I understand that they have many problems in their lives that we as a school are not prepared to resolve, but it makes teaching extremely difficult." In that way, South Loop School was no different than hundreds of other Chicago public schools—which is precisely what the residents of Dearborn Park and surrounding areas had predicted when the Board of Education extended the school's boundaries south to include Hilliard Homes.

Judy Hoch DeLeon, remarried since her school-crusading days, kept her children in South Loop and said they did all right. Her son qualified for the city's elite Whitney Young Magnet High School. Her daughter formed friendships with Long Grove girls, which pleased her mother greatly, and moved on to a Roman Catholic high school.

Other South Loop parents who kept their children in the school were not so happy with the results. Sandra Reberski's son graduated in 1993 with all A's. The school was too easy for him, his mother said, because the faculty had to spend so much time on children with learning problems and on disruptive students. After coasting through elementary school, adjusting to a more demanding Roman Catholic high school was difficult for him at first. But he and his parents liked the faculty and students at South Loop, where he was the only white boy on the basketball team and his parents attended every game. His younger sister, however, went to a Catholic elementary school because her parents wanted a more rigorous academic atmosphere.

Gail Inskip also sent an older son to South Loop but enrolled the younger in a Roman Catholic school. Of the older, she said, "He got A's and B's with his eyes closed. They taught at the lowest level. On the other hand, he has street smarts. He knows how to handle himself."

Ten years after the ground breaking of 1986, South Loop School belonged to Hilliard Homes and Long Grove and was beginning to serve their needs. But with this shift, it was not equipped to serve the middle-class children of Dearborn Park and Printers Row. Periodically, parents of preschoolers in those communities talked about sending their children to South Loop School as a bloc—no one would attempt it individually—and then working with the faculty to develop the programs they wanted. But busing them to the Hilliard modular school for kindergarten and first grade was an impenetrable barrier.

Ferd Kramer and other Dearborn Park founders thought the solution was a new, full-scale elementary school for Hilliard Homes and Long Grove, leaving the South Loop School to the South Loop children. "We don't want it," said Sheila Garrett, president of South Loop's Local School Council. "We have our school. They are welcome to use it."

Robert Grisham blamed the Board of Education for squandering the opportunity back in the early 1980s to create a school that would be economically as well as racially integrated. The board didn't think ahead, he said, and build a facility big enough with sufficient resources to serve both communities that had been clamoring for a new school.

To Stephen C. Carlson, an attorney who represented his Dearborn Park neighbors in their legal battles with the Board of Education, its failures were far more serious than a lack of foresight. As he saw it, "Our neighborhood lost its school to a handful of agitators who put political pressure on gutless school board members who did not give a damn about sound urban planning or rational educational policy or even feigning compliance with the desegregation decree." Carlson, who is white, sent his children to the University of Chicago Laboratory School. So did his neighbor, who is black.

"What the Board of Education got with all of its bungling and indecisiveness," said Judy Hock DeLeon, "was just another ghetto school."

Late in 1996, a series of changes converged to brighten the future of South Loop School. The impetus came the previous year from the Illinois General Assembly. Fed up with decades of steadily deteriorating Chicago schools and a succession of Chicago mayors who complained that they were powerless to improve the system, state lawmakers threw out the old Board of Education structure and shifted its authority to the city's mayor. For six years, that had been Richard M. Daley, whose father had helped shape Dearborn Park and who had supported its drive for a neighborhood school back in 1984 when he was Cook County's chief prosecutor. He also happened to be a new resident of the growing South Loop community, one who didn't mind telling his neighbors that he thought the Board of Education had failed middle-class parents.

Daley appointed his budget director, Paul G. Vallas, to the powerful new position of chief executive officer of city schools. After a year of ferreting out one scandal and incompetency after another in the school bureaucracy, Vallas turned his attention to the South Loop. The community now had about

500 children of elementary school age. So did Hilliard Homes and Long Grove. Vallas proposed replacing the Hilliard branch school with a new facility big enough to accommodate the lower grades of both communities. Upper grades would attend the existing South Loop School in Dearborn Park. He promised improved and accelerated academic programs, plus a variety of after-school activities open to all children in the area—whether or not they attended South Loop School.

Some South Loop parents were unhappy. They wanted their younger children in the Dearborn Park facility, not bused to a building near Hilliard Homes. But that area was changing fast. Expensive townhouses were rising across the street from the branch school; more were planned. The old fears about sending little tots to the vicinity were baseless.

Young families with toddlers and infants were filling Dearborn Park's new south neighborhood and other nearby developments. They were not burdened with bitter memories of the school wars. They were receptive, or at least not hostile, to the Vallas plan and to the prospect of helping to shape a new South Loop School. Two Dearborn Park residents campaigned for election to South Loop's Local School Council and won.

Other parents, veterans of the school struggles, intended to keep their children in magnet schools or private schools but welcomed the after-school enrichment programs at South Loop. "If those work out for my two older ones," said a mother of three, "I might enroll my four-year-old in the new school. I'll see. It's too early to tell what will happen."

And there was such a long way to go. Only a mile, by one reckoning, but a distance that the school system and the city it served had yet to bridge.

13

Winding Down, Closing Out

DURING THE SUMMER OF 1986, WHEN THE NORTH HALF OF DEARBORN PARK WAS SELLING out and construction of the new school was beginning, the project's success was attracting attention around the country. Planners and developers from other cities, professors and students and real estate financiers came to see this thriving new neighborhood built on the carcass of old rail yards. Nearly every big and mid-sized city had unused rail property and a shelf full of proposals for doing something with it. Here was something that actually went beyond the idealized drawings and scale models.

Mayor Harold Washington's staff took 450 people who were in Chicago for a meeting of the Urban Land Institute on a bus-and-walking tour of Dearborn Park. Architects, city officials, and railroad real estate managers came from Toronto, which had about 200 acres of obsolete rail yards near its downtown. The Dearborn Park staff showed off its community to urban planners from a half dozen European countries and to a delegation from China.

Elizabeth L. Hollander, Mayor Washington's planning commissioner, particularly enjoyed going to Dearborn Park with a delegation from the Wall Street firms that rate municipal credit. The more impressed they were with the city's health and vitality, the better Chicago's chance to get a good grade—and a low interest rate on its bonds.

"When they stood in the middle of Dearborn Park in the sunshine and looked over at Sears Tower—it was like a scene from central casting," Elizabeth Hollander recalled. "They were dazzled. A Chinese woman with her baby

157

in a stroller came by, and a black couple, some whites. And when they heard the prices, it blew their minds. Of course, they were from New York. But that middle-class families could live this close to downtown, with all those beautiful trees and walkways and greenery around them . . . ."

It is interesting that Mayor Washington's administration was so pleased to show off the half-finished Dearborn Park, because the Dearborn Park leaders were having a terrible time convincing the mayor and his staff to help them complete the project.

Mayor Byrne had assured them that she would find the money to provide streets, sidewalks, sewers, and water installations in Dearborn Park's undeveloped south portion. Engineering studies were under way, she said. But she left office in April 1983 without producing the confirmation or enabling city ordinance that Tom Ayers, Phil Klutznick, and Ferd Kramer had been pressing to get from her.

A few months later, the three began their quest for a commitment from Mayor Washington. Weary from their battles with inflation, struggling to sell the last of the units they had built in their northern 24 acres, they did not want to start all over again in the southern 27. Nor did their shareholders, who had not received a dime back from the $14 million they had invested 10 years earlier. They weren't complaining, but they had made it clear that it was time to pull out of the development business and sell the rest of the land. The trouble was, no one was likely to buy it unless the city provided the necessary infrastructure. This had cost $6.6 million for the north portion and was expected to total at least that much in the south.

At an introductory meeting with her staff and Ferd Kramer and Phil Klutznick, Liz Hollander said the Washington administration's priorities were somewhat different from previous ones'. Several other cabinet members and a few of her deputies opposed spending $6 million or so to help a downtown community of relatively well-off people. Dearborn Park was a big success, they said. Let the developers pay for the infrastructure. Federal aid to cities had plummeted; the city administration was working hard to balance its budget and at the same time do more for neighborhoods that were a lot needier than Dearborn Park.

Ayers and his crew, still struggling to pay off their construction loans and stay alive in a sick real estate market, were furious. But in their first meeting with the new mayor, they were impressed with his graciousness and jovial good humor. They came away thinking that he had said his staff would get to work promptly on the improvements Dearborn Park needed. That was late in 1983.

Thus began the infrastructure chronicles.

March 21, 1984. Sheldon Kantoff, Dearborn Park's general manager, has been regularly pestering Ira J. Bach, Mayor Washington's director of development, to find out when the work will start. Bach writes to Ferd Kramer, asking for a "firm commitment" that the development will proceed, and an estimate of the total dwelling units, before the city allocates any money. Kramer complies.

June 29, 1984. Liz Hollander writes to Ferd Kramer and Phil Klutznick, giving a possible scenario for the financing. Money for street construction and sewer design will come from the Illinois Department of Transportation. Sewer construction will come from city general obligation bonds. The city does not have the money for all the water work, so it will apply for a federal Urban Development Action Grant to cover part of the cost. Sewer work will begin first, probably in February 1985. All of this is contingent "on your commitment to commercial retail construction in the next phase, so as to provide the necessary employment generation." Also, "the city requires a detailed development proposal complete with project scheduling." Very organized, very businesslike, Kramer and Klutznick think. A far cry from Mayor Daley's handshake agreements.

Klutznick, whose memos and letters habitually misspell names, is upset because his is spelled "Klutznik" in Hollander's letter. In a note to Ferd Kramer, he writes: "You might tell her that the first rule of being a public servant is to spell a person's name accurately. I know she is not a foreigner where they leave out the *c*."

July 19, 1984. Ayers, Kramer, and Kimbal T. Goluska, the Skidmore, Owings & Merrill partner assigned to Dearborn Park, meet with Liz Hollander, Ira Bach, and three assistants. They tell the city people they want about 50,000 square feet of retail space in the south neighborhood. This is satisfactory to the city. Everyone agrees it is important to move promptly so the land can be sold and developed.

October 1, 1984. Anthony Licata, the Sidley & Austin lawyer representing Dearborn Park, completes a 40-page application for an Urban Development Action Grant.

October 10, 1984. The city tells Licata that the federal government has a new grant application form. Licata submits new documents.

October 22, 1984. The city asks Licata for a second revision of the grant application, to conform with additional federal regulations, and asks for additional supporting documents.

December 11, 1984. Lucille Dobbins, deputy city planning commissioner, tells Licata that the city will postpone its request for the federal money.

Among the reasons: The city has not been able to arrive at a firm estimate of the cost of water improvements, and federal officials are reluctant to finance any speculative commercial development—so Dearborn Park will need an anchor tenant or a supportive market study. Ayers and the others are disgusted; they have been trying for almost 10 years to sign up their preferred "anchor tenant"—namely, a supermarket.

January 11, 1985.   Ayers, Klutznick, and Kramer meet again with Liz Hollander and other members of the Washington administration. Klutznick delivers an angry lecture to the city officials and threatens to call a press conference denouncing the 15-month delay in securing an infrastructure agreement. Instead, he goes back to his office and writes a four-page, single-spaced letter to Hollander, laying out, in rather formal, stuffy language, the history and goals of Dearborn Park, its problems and triumphs, the sacrifices of its founders, and the importance of completing the project. He attaches a list of the 32 Chicago corporations that invested in the effort and the names of the prestigious executives who sit on Dearborn Park's board, noting how eminent they are. This is not the way to impress the populous-minded Washington administration, or extract money from it.

February 4, 1985.   Liz Hollander sends Ferd Kramer a memo from her assistant in charge of federal grant requests, who complains that Dearborn Park staff members seem to be reneging on their agreement to provide all the information the feds want. She tells Kramer she will investigate other possible sources of funds, including a new city bond issue and federal Community Development Block Grants. But the latter, she warns, require some low-income housing.

March 20, 1985.   Phil Klutznick writes to Ferd Kramer, wondering whether they should forget about developing their southern acres for now and wait to see if the latest version of the 1992 Chicago World's Fair—to be situated near Dearborn Park—might suggest other uses for the land. But prospects for the fair are flagging; neighborhood activists influential with the Washington administration have stepped up their opposition and ridicule studies that show a payoff in jobs and tax revenue. (Three months later, the fair is dead, killed by the mayor's indecisiveness, the backers' failure to articulate its public benefits, and the refusal of Democratic leaders in the Illinois House of Representatives to endorse any tax-supported financing plans.)

July 10, 1985.   Frederick Ford, vice president of Draper & Kramer, meets with city planning officials and reports back that they are prepared to make a commitment on the south infrastructure.

July 26, 1985.   Ferd Kramer writes a "Dear Commissioner Hollander" letter to Liz, whom he knows well and worked with when she was executive director of the Metropolitan Housing and Planning Council. It states that "as you are aware," the city back in the days of the Chicago 21 Plan agreed "to install, at its expense, the infrastructure necessary to create the residential areas to be developed under the guidance of Dearborn Park." And, "We have agreed with the City that the City will proceed promptly to commence construction of the infrastructure for the South Neighborhood." He asks her to sign it and return it to him, and she does.

November 6, 1985. Ferd Kramer tells the Dearborn Park executive committee that city officials indicate infrastructure work will start before the end of 1985.

December 11, 1985. Ferd Kramer tells the executive committee that city officials indicate infrastructure work will start in mid-1986.

June 16, 1986. Ferd Kramer writes to Liz Hollander, again summarizing Dearborn Park Corporation's history and goals, repeating its commitment to assure that the south neighborhood is developed for residential use. She has requested this because some of her associates in the Washington administration, which is fond of lengthy collegial debates as a prelude to decision making, are balking at city payment of infrastructure costs for wealthy developers.

September 5, 1986. Midyear has come and gone; no infrastructure work has begun. Nearly three years have passed since the first meeting between Mayor Washington and Dearborn Park leaders. Tom Ayers, Ferd Kramer, and Phil Klutznick meet again with Harold Washington, Liz Hollander, and other city officials. They tell the mayor about Richard J. Daley's promises of city help, and what the business leadership has endured to get this far. When they leave, they think they have a commitment from Washington to start the work promptly. But in Liz Hollander's opinion, the mayor was noncommittal; she thinks—no doubt, with good reason—that the executives did not know how to make their case. What Washington wanted to hear was what a city investment in Dearborn Park would do for Chicago as a whole and for its new emphasis on neighborhoods, not what Daley had promised 10 years ago. The Dearborn Park leaders are accustomed to getting their own way, she thinks; they simply don't acknowledge the city's financial predicament and the demands on its scarce dollars.

September 19, 1986. Ferd Kramer sends a Western Union Mailgram to Liz Hollander: "I HAVE BEEN TRYING TO REACH YOU SINCE OUR MEETING WITH THE MAYOR WITH NO RESULTS. THE CITY'S FAILURE TO PROVIDE THE INFRASTRUCTURE FOR PHASE II OF DEARBORN PARK IS PREVENTING ALL POSSIBILITY OF PROVIDING MORE MIDDLE INCOME HOUSING FOR THIS AREA."

October 20, 1986. A breakthrough! Phil Klutznick corners Harold Washington at an evening reception. The talkative, intellectual Klutznick and the equally talkative, intellectual mayor have a rewarding exchange on the condition of urban America in general and Dearborn Park in particular. In a memo to Ferd Kramer and Tom Ayers, Klutznick writes that the mayor "appeared to be surprised" that nothing was happening with the infrastructure. Klutznick then telephones Liz Hollander; he is delighted to hear, he reports in a note to Ferd Kramer, that "she is putting together a new bond issue and she thinks she can get the whole problem solved if we will wait one more week. I said of course we can wait a week, but not much longer. . . . I shall call her if I do not hear from her."

December 8, 1986. Five weeks pass and nothing happens. Ferd Kramer and Phil Klutznick meet again with Mayor Washington and Commissioner Hollander. They ask for a firm commitment, which they thought they had the last time they met with him. Klutznick again threatens a press conference. This time, he says, he means it.

January 7, 1987. The mayor finally gives an unequivocal "yes" to Dearborn Park infrastructure. It is left to Liz Hollander to find a way to pay for it with the least possible damage to the city budget. In a letter to Ferd Kramer, she writes that the city will allocate $1.8 million of its state highway bonds for streets, lights, and sidewalks; $1.7 million from city bonds for sewers; and $535,000 from the city's water fund for water service. In addition, the city will spend $2.9 million of its federal highway money for rebuilding peripheral streets.

The work finally got under way about three and a half years after the Dearborn Park group first met with Harold Washington. Once started, it proceeded efficiently and was finished in less than 18 months—a speedier job than earlier city administrations had done in the north half. Work on a subway tunnel cutting under a corner of the south neighborhood also was completed in the summer of 1988. By that time, Chicago had another new chief executive; Alderman Eugene Sawyer was elected acting mayor by the City Council after Harold Washington's sudden death from a heart attack on November 25, 1987.

With the long infrastructure ordeal resolved, Ferd Kramer devoted his energies to persuading the Chicago Park District to accept Dearborn Park's gifts of two park sites—1.1 and 2.2 acres—in the south neighborhood. Jesse Madison, the district's executive director, said thanks, but no thanks; he did not have the money to develop them.

The 86-year-old Kramer began his customary round of calls, letters, meetings, and presentations to get what he wanted for Dearborn Park. It took a year and a half, but he eventually won approval from business executive

William Bartholomay, president of the Park District board. Skidmore's landscape architects produced the designs with the Park District, but another year elapsed before work started.

The Dearborn Park staff sent brochures throughout the country offering the south land for sale and development of middle-income housing. The only real interest, however, came from Chicago developers already familiar with the project. And, judging from the offers it was getting during the summer of 1987, it was obvious that Dearborn Park Corporation would not be able to repay all of the $14 million invested by its shareholders in the mid-1970s, let alone any dividends. It had a legal obligation, though, to repay the $7-million shareholders' loan of 1984, plus 11 percent interest and 50 percent of the net proceeds of land sales after repayment of the loan, its accrued interest, and any outstanding debts.

The south land would have to sell at $24 a square foot to repay the $14 million, without any earnings, and the $7 million, with interest. That price was out of the question. The corporation was asking $20 a square foot, but the bids were in the $14-to-$15 range. Several developers wanted the entire site, but their offers were too low or their payment schedules were too lengthy to be considered.

The search for suitable buyers lasted about a year. One bidder who had taken an option on one-third of the land let it expire when he realized that his planned emphasis on high-rise buildings was wrong for the current real estate market. Another major bidder died: Jack McNeil, who had built the last townhouses in the north area. Still another ran into financial problems and had to drop out.

Any lingering desire to mirror the north area in the south was fast disappearing. Prospective bidders who wanted to build high-rise and mid-rise condominiums or rental apartments couldn't get financing. Townhouses were the hottest things on the market in the late 1980s—the only hot thing, in fact. Developers liked them as much as buyers did; they could be built and sold a few at a time, cutting the costly overhead (and anxiety) involved in filling big buildings.

Hopes for a retail component also faded. Ferd Kramer's son Anthony, a Draper & Kramer vice president, had pursued supermarket chains, but they concluded that the South Loop did not have enough residents to support a large store. And they were not interested in operating a smaller one. An independent grocery about one-sixth the size of modern supermarkets opened in Two East Eighth, the new apartment building kitty-corner from Dearborn Park; residents used that or drove to supermarkets elsewhere in the city.

The retail experiences of Dearborn Station and Printers Row, at the front door of Dearborn Park, were hardly encouraging. Renovation of the station was completed early in 1987, nine years after city and Board of Education officials promised to transform it into a school and community center. It looked splendid, but its out-of-town owners had a terrible time finding tenants for the festive retail galleria they envisioned. In 1990 it was sold again, this time to a Chicago brokerage group headed by Sam Roti, a grandnephew of Alderman Fred Roti. After trying unsuccessfully to sell it, Roti bought the station himself. He loved the building, he told reporters, and didn't want some future owner to tarnish it.

Roti was counting on the commercial real estate market to revive, and to some extent it did. First Chicago Corporation opened a branch bank in the station. A real estate firm arrived. A yoga center. An attractive Mexican restaurant. A music school and a ballet school flourished. Law firms and a clinic affiliated with Northwestern Memorial Hospital settled into the beautifully remodeled interior. But retail life was scant: The galleria had only a food shop, a coffee bar, and a beauty salon.

On Printers Row, just north of Dearborn Park, several retail businesses were struggling, though restaurants and two bookstores thrived. Dearborn Park's leaders, always a cautious lot, decided to forget about retail or other commercial space in their south acres.

When the south land finally was sold, it was to developers who planned to concentrate on townhouses. About one-third of the available 960,000 square feet went to Ogden Partners, a firm formed by Mark Ordower, who had built townhouses on Chicago's Near North Side, and architect Laurence Booth, who had designed the mid-rise buildings in Dearborn Park's north neighborhood and was a major factor in the creation of Printers Row. Their payments of $14 and $15 a square foot would stretch over 20 months. Daniel E. McLean and his MCL Development Companies, the largest builder of luxury residences in Chicago, ventured south for the first time and bought the other two-thirds. This sale also would be stretched over 20 months; some portions went for $23 a square foot.

A third developer entered later. Ogden Partners sold part of its land to McLean, who sold part of his original purchase to George H. Thrush Development Company. Thrush was noted for attractive low-cost housing, built with the assistance of nonprofit corporations and city subsidies, as well as upscale townhouses and single-family homes.

On average, the land sold for $17.30 a square foot, bringing in about $16.6 million to Dearborn Park Corporation. But before anything could be built, the city had to approve changes in the Dearborn Park Planned Unit Development ordinance passed by the Chicago City Council in 1977. It specified a south half much like the north, with a mix of high-rises, mid-rises, town-houses, and parks, plus a retail segment of about 50,000 square feet. It also specified that Dearborn Park Corporation would develop the entire site. Planning Commissioner Hollander, who Dearborn Park leaders thought had given them a tough time in the infrastructure struggles, pulled them out of a jam. She offered to kill the retail component and approve other changes administratively, without going to the City Council, so long as several conditions were met: Parks must be provided as promised in the ordinance, density limits must not be exceeded, and Dearborn Park Corporation must approve design and construction plans.

Kim Goluska, the Skidmore representative on Dearborn Park's executive committee, became, in effect, a combination planning commissioner–zoning commissioner for the south neighborhood. He worked with developers on site plans and reviewed all architectural plans. Once these had his approval, they went to Ferd Kramer for a final OK. It was a smooth arrangement, though there were a few disputes—dialogues, Goluska called them—when developers wanted to use cheaper materials and landscaping than they had specified (or than Goluska, a Dearborn Park resident, thought Dearborn Park should have). Occasionally a developer tried an end run around Goluska and went directly to Kramer, but he consistently turned them away. Goluska thought the friction was to be expected; in Dearborn Park's second half, unlike the first, developers had to make money.

The street patterns in the south were similar to those in the north. The only entrance-exit was at 14th and State streets, just as the only entrance-exit in the north was at 9th and State streets. Neither area had a street that cut through, whether north-south or east-west. Pedestrians had two additional routes in and out, a sidewalk in the north to Polk Street and one in the south to State.

The question of whether to connect the two neighborhoods with a street was left open as work began on the south. The city was assembling a package of federal funds to rebuild the crumbling, dangerous Roosevelt Road, the elevated thoroughfare that separated Dearborn Park's north and south areas. It would remain elevated over the railroad tracks west of the community but hit grade level at State Street, Dearborn Park's eastern border. City officials decided to give residents a choice in a year or so, when plans would be prepared: Did they want an underpass for auto traffic between the two areas, or one for pedestrians only?

Acting Mayor Eugene Sawyer shoveled the first dirt at the ground breaking of Dearborn Park II late in 1988. Next to him, also with a shovel, dressed in her customary bright red, was Florence Jacobs, the salesperson who pushed the north neighborhood to a successful close and would be in charge of sales for both MCL Development Companies and Ogden Partners in the south neighborhood.

Six months later, on April 4, 1989, Chicago had another new mayor: Richard M. Daley coasted to victory over two opponents—one black, one white—by margins that would have made his father proud. By that time, the South Loop had about 9,500 residents in the 4,000 dwelling units of Dearborn Park, Printers Row, and adjacent high-rise developments and residential conversions of commercial buildings. A survey by the Burnham Park Planning Board—née South Loop Planning Board—indicated that 54 percent were white, 40 percent black, and 6 percent Hispanic or Asian.

Two major projects, also on unused rail yards, were set to rise nearby. One-half mile beyond Dearborn Park's south border, business leaders in the Chinatown neighborhood were about to enliven and expand their community with Chinatown Square, a 32-acre development with a colorful retail mall, plaza, restaurants, and professional offices, plus 450 townhouses, mid-rise condominiums, and rental apartments for the elderly. It was designed by Harry Weese & Associates; Weese had been the inspiration and lead architect of Printers Row.

One-half mile east of Dearborn Park's south neighborhood, near the lakefront, Forest City Enterprises of Cleveland and the Chicago-based Fogelson Properties bought a 72-acre site from Illinois Central and Gulf Railroad and talked about a $3.5-billion, mixed-use complex of townhouses, office towers, shops, and hotels. The first stage of this new Central Station development—subsequent ones were left for a distant, hazy future—would be 300 homes by Dan McLean, major developer of Dearborn Park's south portion. The plans were under review in City Hall. The mayor himself, it turned out later, was among the many South Side residents intrigued by the prospect of life in a grand townhouse in a brand-new South Side lakefront community.

By the time the first townhouses in Dearborn Park II were ready for sale, late in 1989, scores of veteran Dearborn Park I and Printers Row residents were eager to move up and spread out. They wanted private garages, more storage space, bigger bathrooms and kitchens, and master-bedroom suites. It looked as if this new development, with its roomier, more elegantly appointed dwellings, couldn't miss. There were, however, a few concerns.

Mortgage rates for new residential construction were still slightly above 10 percent, where they had been stuck for four years. Also, Dearborn Park II stretched south into untested territory. Much of the surrounding land was vacant fields, a bit of light industry, a huge empty warehouse, a few run-down transient hotels. Would buyers be willing to venture beyond the security of

Dearborn Park I and Printers Row? Then, too, the struggles over South Loop School, which sat in the south area, were getting heavy coverage in newspapers and on television. Word was spreading that only a dozen or so families from Dearborn Park were willing to use the school.

"When we started building, and we had a lot of money on the line, I was really afraid," said architect Paul Hansen, Larry Booth's partner. "I was extraordinarily afraid that people would see what was going on at that school, and they would just not buy those houses."

He didn't have to worry. The developers built 486 homes in Dearborn II over the next six years, and they sold about as fast as contractors could produce them. One of the buyers was Paul Hansen.

The south neighborhood turned out to be a mix of architectural styles and housing types. It was either a hodgepodge or an appealing variety, depending on one's penchant for cohesiveness. Townhouses and free-standing homes were stately or quaint, elegant or pared down, angular or edging on fussy. In general, residences were bigger and costlier than in Dearborn Park I, but priced 10 to 18 percent below comparable new homes in the Lincoln Park area and other fashionable neighborhoods on Chicago's North Side.

With all those townhouses, Dearborn II did not have as much open space as Dearborn I, but it was also less dense—486 units on 27 acres, compared with 1,210 on 24 acres in the north. Indoor parking was more abundant in the south; most units had attached garages. Yet cars, parked or moving, were more prominent on the streets there.

Each of the three developers offered a range of prices and designs. George Thrush's red-brick Federal Square townhouses started at $135,300 for a 1,250-square-foot, three-story unit with attached garage aimed at first-time buyers to $379,000 for a 3,000-square-foot townhouse with a glass-enclosed atrium.

In Ogden Partners' charming Metropolitan Mews, prices ranged from $179,000 to $260,000. In their Newgate Square, the largest units had 2,600 square feet, a penthouse, a two-car garage, and a big kitchen with a deck; they sold for $329,000. Their Rowhouses, copper trimmed and built around a center green, were $219,000 to $339,000.

Some of Dan McLean's Prairie Manor Homes, with their elegant limestone and beveled glass and hints of Frank Lloyd Wright, hit 5,100 square feet and $720,000. McLean's angular Prairie Town Homes combined rust-brick ground floors with upper floors of beige brick and insets of teal and dark brown.

The big surprise, and a big hit with buyers, were McLean's 36 detached, single-family Chicago Homes, tall and narrow, with the high front porches

and brightly painted frame exteriors of Chicago houses a century earlier. Half
of them also were a dramatic departure for Dearborn Park: Their front
porches and gated front yards opened onto State Street. The security of
Dearborn Park was now so well established that a developer felt confident
enough to turn the houses outward rather than inward. At $299,900 plus ex-
tras, the buyers loved them.

One of 36 Chicago
Homes in Dear-
born Park's south-
ern neighborhood.
Photo by Wayne
Wille.

The bigger homes in Dearborn II filled quickly with émigrés from Dearborn I. Barbara Schleck and her husband, Gary M. Ropski, had lived in a mid-rise condominium for nearly 10 years when they bought one of the new single-family homes designed by Larry Booth and Paul Hansen. They had looked elsewhere, but realized that something comparable in other parts of the city either cost more (if new) or involved high maintenance (if old). The Lincoln Park area had wonderful homes but was too congested, with "no real sense of community." And they were too accustomed to walking to work and to Loop theaters and concert halls to put up with suburban commuting.

Patricia and Stephen Carlson, both attorneys, and their three children had outgrown their white townhouse in Dearborn I. They bought a big house in beautiful Lake Bluff, not far from the North Shore suburb where Stephen grew up. But before they moved, "we realized it was the biggest mistake of our lives," Patricia said. "The commute would have been at least an hour. We would have been so far away from everything. We paid $600 to get out of the deal." Instead, they bought one of McLean's Prairie Manor Homes. It was across a park from South Loop School, but their children went to the University of Chicago Laboratory School and Francis Xavier Warde.

According to McLean's calculations, his buyers were "a third from the suburbs, 25 percent African American, 5 percent Asian, 5 percent Hispanic, and almost equally spread between the 25-to-55 age group." He estimated that one-third had children living in the home. By the time the south area was fully occupied, Dearborn Park overall was roughly 58 percent white, 30 percent black, and 12 percent Asian or Hispanic. The children in the south, like those in the north, attended outlying public magnet schools or private schools.

The 12 households in Barbara Schleck's and Gary Ropski's cluster were typical of the bigger Dearborn II units: Of the 24 adults, 3 were black, 2 were Asian, and 1 was Hispanic. The others were of Italian, Jewish, Irish, Polish, and German descent. There were lawyers, physicians, accountants, a journalist, a restaurant owner, and a dealer in musical instruments. Five households included children; none attended South Loop School. The others had no children, were empty nesters, or had children from earlier marriages living elsewhere.

George Thrush reported that about half of the buyers in his more moderately priced Federal Square were single—particularly women, who felt safe living alone in Dearborn Park.

The good public response to the south neighborhood depressed real estate values in the north, at least for several years. The Carlsons' three-bedroom townhouse, for example, was on the market for a year. They managed to sell it without a loss, but not everyone could afford that year's wait. As a result, Dearborn Park gained more economic diversity. Smaller condominiums and townhouses became good bargains, affordable to moderate-income families. Many owners who moved to the south neighborhood leased their old units. In the high-rise and mid-rise buildings of Dearborn I, the number of rental units ranged from 15 to 23 percent by the mid-1990s.

Twenty years after it was formed, Dearborn Park Corporation's job was finished. On April 29, 1994, the shareholders voted to dissolve it. A few things didn't turn out the way they had hoped, Ferd Kramer told them. He was disappointed that The Oaks, the rent-subsidized building for the elderly, was now about 90 percent minority—as he had predicted years before when federal regulations prohibited him from juggling waiting lists to favor whites. Mainly, though, he was saddened about the school. The hope for the future, he said, was that the Board of Education would build a new school near the public housing project, and Dearborn Park would have the neighborhood school its founders had envisioned.

Tom Ayers, who had chaired the project since its inception, recounted its financial struggles and thanked the corporations that had stood by it. All in all, he said, it had fulfilled its purpose: Dearborn Park was a superior, beautiful, racially integrated community, a catalyst for development throughout the South Loop.

All that was left was for Frederick Ford of Draper & Kramer to work out a repayment plan for shareholders. For each $100 share, they would get $41 back.

For a company that had invested $250,000 in 1974 and $125,000 in the 1984 loan, this was the return: $102,500 on the 1974 shares; the full $125,000 on the loan, and $128,388 in interest on the loan and land-sale proceeds. That totaled $355,888, or $19,112 less than the $375,000 the company had given to Dearborn Park Corporation. A final distribution of Dearborn Park's contingency fund would likely result in a small second payout, Ford told the investors.

One investor noted that if his company had put its $250,000 into a fund that paid 5 percent interest over 20 years, it would have grown to $660,000 instead of dwindling to $102,500. But he wasn't complaining, and neither did the other shareholders. "We weren't in this to make money," he said. "When you look at what Dearborn Park has accomplished for the city, it was well worth our $250,000."

14

"How Could I Ever Leave This Place?"

DEARBORN PARK'S FIRST RESIDENTS COMPARED THEMSELVES TO PIONEERS ON THE prairies, looking out over windswept fields as birds swooped up from the riverbank. Of course, if they turned their heads a bit they saw Sears Tower and the First National Bank Building, not the farmhouse down the road. Yet a shared sense of discovery infused their lives; they reveled in the excitement and pride of building something new, together. And they wondered what their raw little settlement would be like in the future, assuming it had a future.

Sixteen years later, no one in Dearborn Park felt like an adventurer or a pioneer. Homeowners were more likely to be worried about escalating property taxes—a by-product of their neighborhood's success—than the challenges of creating a community out of nothing. They had an urbane assortment of high-rise neighbors to the north, clusters of grand townhouses and a restoration effort creating a Prairie Avenue Historic District spreading from the east, and lively Chinatown moving up fast from the south. A $50-million residential project called Millennium began construction late in 1996 and proposed to close much of the gap between Chinatown and Dearborn Park by the start of the next century. Three dozen discarded buildings that once had darkened the landscape—north, south, east, and west—had been transformed into sophisticated residences. "It's loft-o-mania," marveled Larry Booth, an architect in both halves of Dearborn Park and a prime mania motivator. And, to the great joy of South Loop residents, Dominick's Finer Foods announced plans to build a 74,000-square-foot supermarket on Roosevelt Road one-half mile west of Dearborn Park.

The South Loop, two words that marketing advisers once said should never be uttered publicly, had become "The South Loop! Hotspot stop for buyers!" in real estate advertisements. Two-bedroom condominiums were available for as little as $110,000 in Dearborn Park's older, north portion. The 5,100-square-foot, five-bedroom Prairie Manor Homes in its south section went for $725,000. The newest "soft lofts"—finished apartments with gleaming kitchens and baths, rather than the rustic expanses of the early Printers Row versions—sold for $90,000 for a one-bedroom unit or $130,000 for a two-bedroom in one of the latest conversions, a formerly dismal building in the formerly dismal area just west of Printers Row near the elevated rapid transit tracks. In the ex–Standard Oil Building on South Michigan Avenue, across the street from the lakefront's Grant Park, an elegant three-bedroom unit cost $356,000.

In just three weekends, with nothing more to show than floor plans on the walls of a sales trailer, a developer sold two-thirds of the 69 units created out of a long-vacant hospital building across the street from the new Central Station townhomes.

By early 1997, the South Loop had about 14,500 residents in 7,000 dwelling units—townhouses, free-standing homes, high-rise rental apartments, high-rise and mid-rise condominiums, and converted office buildings, warehouses, printing plants, and the hospital.

One of the new South Loop residents was the mayor of Chicago, Richard M. Daley, who with his wife, Maggie, bought a $450,000 Central Station townhouse in 1994. His reasons for leaving the blue-collar Bridgeport neighborhood on the Southwest Side—where he, like his father and his father's parents and three other Chicago mayors had been born and reared— were similar to those of hundreds of other new residents of the South Loop. Two of the three Daley children were in college. The family's housing needs had changed. And Central Station had the latest attractions in homes: state-of-the-art kitchens, big master-bedroom-and-bath suites, and the privacy and security of sheltered courtyards.

Central Station had something else that was important to Daley. It was south of Madison Street, Chicago's dividing line. Developer Dan McLean guessed that most of his Central Station buyers, and probably most of those who bought his Dearborn Park homes, were "diehard South Siders." Whether they had lived in the city or in one of its southern suburbs, whether they were black or white, newly rising in their careers or newly retired, when the time came to look for something fresher and classier, they could not abide a North Side address. Where all of these people would have gone if there had been no South Loop residential renaissance was a mystery.

In Dearborn Park, people watched this growth around them with parental pride. They had started it all. And they had created something more remarkable than thousands of new lofts and townhouses: a genuine neighborhood.

After its first year on the market, the partially completed Dearborn Park was 67 percent white, 28 percent black, and 5 percent Asian or Hispanic. Sixteen years later, the composition had shifted only slightly: about 58 percent white, 30 percent black, 12 percent Asian or Hispanic (more Asian than Hispanic). In other ways, though, the population had changed significantly. Early on, 60 percent of the residents were single adults without children; by the time the roomier townhouses in the southern section were completed, that group had shrunk to about 40 percent. About 35 percent of the households were couples with no children in the home, and 25 percent were couples or single parents living with children.

Dearborn Park was aging in more ways than one. In 1980, nearly 70 percent of those who did not live in The Oaks (for people 62 and older) were in their late 20s to middle 40s; only about 12 percent were over 55. Sixteen years later, the percentage over 55 had almost doubled. A growing number were retired. It was a natural transition. Most had moved in when they worked in the Loop and decided that the conveniences and security were ideal for their retirement years; others arrived after they retired, and for the same reasons. Working couples whose children were no longer living at home also streamed in. David K. and Marilyn Robson were typical: Both were suburban born and had raised their three children in the suburbs. But as soon as the youngest graduated from high school, they left for the city. "There's so much energy and excitement here," Marilyn Robson said. She missed gardening and cross-country skiing but liked walking to work, to concerts in Orchestra Hall and Grant Park, to restaurants and theaters.

Some of the new residents got to know Dearborn Park through relatives who lived there, and they were dazzled. Extended families were forming. One couple combined three white townhouses in Dearborn I into one residence and bought the townhouse next door for a parent. Catherine Mugnolo's sister was the first in her family to move into Dearborn Park. Her mother followed, in a separate condominium. Next, Catherine and her husband, Carmen, arrived. And then another sister. (Dearborn Park became the Mugnolos' professional address, too. In 1993 they opened a gourmet Italian restaurant on Printers Row, Trattoria Catarina.) In 1979, Kathryn Moery's parents were among the first buyers of a Dearborn I townhouse; the following year, Kathryn and her husband, John, and their two children left their western suburb and bought one nearby. Greg and Terri Buseman and their two small daughters lived just a short stroll down a Dearborn II sidewalk from Greg's sister, Carol, and her husband, Gerald J. Roper, president and chief executive officer of the Chicagoland Chamber of Commerce.

The Mugnolos and the Busemans were representative of another growing Dearborn Park faction: people who were in their third Dearborn Park dwelling. "I often think, if I won the lottery, where would I move?" said Sharon Thomas Parrott, another three-time buyer. Her friend Lynda Young, in her second Dearborn Park home, cut in: "To another house down the street?"

"That is exactly my answer," said Sharon Parrott. "I would go and buy a bigger house in Dearborn Park."

"You start to be so rooted," said Terri Buseman. "When we had our second child, I was so touched by the way everybody would come and take my first one for the day and then bring her home with two presents, one for her and one for my younger one. Everybody was calling up and asking, 'What can we do for you?' And I'm thinking, how could I ever leave this place?"

Dearborn Park's many sets of grown siblings and in-laws and three-generational families and households that ventured no farther than a half mile or so when they moved were more typical of a small town in early 20th-century America than a 1990s metropolitan community, city or suburban. Its residents thought so, too; when they described it, they talked about "a real-life Mayberry, R.F.D." or "a throwback to the old Chicago neighborhood" or "an old-fashioned village." One phrase they avoided: "like a suburb."

"The suburbs are so lonely," was a frequently heard complaint. "In the suburbs, people walk into their houses and lock their doors and forget they have neighbors," said former suburbanite Kathryn Moery. "In the suburbs," said Catherine Mugnolo, "you become dead."

They basked in their small-town atmosphere, but they prided themselves on being city people. They relished downtown Chicago's theaters, concerts, museums, lakefront, restaurants, and magnificent architecture. Suburban-born Carol Sullivan bought a small condominium in Dearborn I soon after it opened because she had wanted to live in the city "the minute I saw Marshall Field's windows as a child." She married a police officer who lived in a condominium across the street, and later they bought a townhouse in Dearborn II.

Lynda and Lawrence Young also had lived in the suburbs, but their first city address was in the trendy Lincoln Park area on Chicago's North Side. They found Dearborn Park better suited to life with their three children. Lincoln Park was lively and exhilarating, but too congested, too transient, too impersonal, less safe. In Dearborn Park, said Lynda Young, "We've all been thrust upon each other and live on sort of an island. Here we are, all together. When I was pregnant with my third and had problems, one of my friends here rushed me to the doctor. And when Eric was born, people came over and watched my kids while they had chicken pox. I thought, would I have been able to get this much help from my neighbors anywhere else? Would they have been home? I had a list of at least five people I could call. Would I have known that many people elsewhere who would have done that for me?"

Sharon Parrott recalled the reaction of a cousin from Midtown Manhattan. "She said, 'It's incredible—your grass, your trees, the kids here. It's

"Your grass, your trees, the kids— it's Sesame Street." Marisol Meleán Berkowitz, *at left*, with Brendan, 14 months, and Terri Buseman with Victoria, 4. Photo by Wayne Wille.

Sesame Street.' All of these things that you think of as very American-apple-pie are happening in the central city."

Yet there were things missing in Dearborn Park that set it apart from small towns and old, tightly knit city neighborhoods. There were no poor people. Blue-collar workers were as scarce as empty parking spaces on the street, which meant they were virtually nonexistent. (Residents eager to trumpet their community's diversity announced that a city bus driver had moved into a Dearborn I condominium building, a city parks maintenance worker into another.) No odd neighborhood characters sat on porch stoops or roamed about; people had different skin colors, but they dressed and talked and acted alike and held similar jobs. There were no little Ma-and-Pa storefronts tucked among the residences. Nor were there any of the small changes—an addition here, a remodeling job there, a new color on somebody's house— that add piquancy to other communities. In Dearborn Park, no one even dared paint a door or window trim a different color; that would violate a townhouse association rule.

This tranquil conformity opened Dearborn Park to ridicule by academic and media critics. They called it sterile, a pseudosuburb. "Starched and contradictory: prim, leafy, laid-back, walled-in," wrote urban affairs specialist (and Dearborn Park resident) M. W. Newman in the *Chicago Tribune* in 1995, as the last buyers were moving into Dearborn II. "It deliberately keeps the pressure-cooked city at bay. It is turned in on itself, behind brick walls, railings, gates and discreet dead ends. Its patios and sheltered courtyards, swimming pools and secluded doorways are genial and open to the skies— but closed in at ground level. All that, of course, may be standard procedure in today's security-driven America. But it hardly is the open hand and the diverse way of life that cities supposedly promote." Yet, "the people who live there seem to love it."

Those "discreet dead ends" and "sheltered courtyards" might have offended urban-planning purists, but they created Dearborn Park's sense of security. Without them, the whole effort might have failed back in 1979 and 1980, when the tiny new neighborhood was surrounded by abandoned buildings, abandoned rail yards, mean bars, and weird porn shops. All of Dearborn Park's dwellings opened onto interior streets or courtyards except for the strip in the newer, southern portion, where some front porches and patios faced State Street. And with only two exit-entrance streets for autos and only four exit-entrance sidewalks, it was no wonder that residents joked about "no drive-by shootings here," or "a mugger couldn't find his way out." But given Dearborn Park's proximity to the downtown, any street that cut through would have been clogged with traffic, chopping up the community and creating a hazard for children.

Residents and civic groups that watch such things rated Dearborn Park as Chicago's safest neighborhood. A major reason, according to Commander Ronald C. Jablon, in charge of the Chicago police district that included Dearborn Park, was the "restricted auto access and cul-de-sacs." He also credited other factors: a private security service hired by the condominium associations of Dearborn I that patrolled the area by car; the Chicago Police Department's use of foot-patrol officers in city neighborhoods; the police headquarters building on State Street; the city's community-policing program, which held frequent meetings between residents and neighborhood-based officers. And, as Jablon said, the perception of security bred security. People in the South Loop felt safe enough to walk at night, which made it safe for them to walk at night.

"Well, look at what we've got," said Samuel F. Falcona, a Dearborn I resident who moved there with his wife, Kathleen, and young son from a Printers Row loft. "We've got no vehicular access from the west, none from the south, none from the north. The only way you can drive in is from 9th Street or 14th Street, and we've got a security guard at 9th. We've got a White Hen store that is open 24 hours a day with a coffee bar where police sit and fill out reports. If they're not there, they're in our cul-de-sac filling out reports."

The White Hen Pantry in a Dearborn I high-rise building assumed mythic proportions. Stories circulated of residents who yelled when accosted by muggers or purse snatchers, only to be rescued almost instantly as their cries were relayed to the White Hen and police officers poured out to corner the astonished culprit. Some of the stories actually were true.

Late one night in 1982, a woman parked her car near her Dearborn I building and was walking to the entrance when a man grabbed her. According to a security service's report, "He told her he had a gun and not to scream. In the process of the struggle she bit his finger and began to scream. . . . Two security officers came running. . . . The policemen having coffee in the White Hen immediately got in pursuit of the subject. The subject climbed over a fence and was apprehended by Chicago police on the other side. The arrest was made within five minutes of the incident."

One night, there was a ruckus outside one of the Dearborn I townhouses. Something was thrown at a window. The officers of the White Hen brigade zoomed up, sirens blaring. They found several sailors from Great Lakes Naval Training Station north of Chicago who had overcelebrated a weekend in the city. They were lost and looking for a railroad station.

Panhandlers sometimes tried their luck around the high-rise buildings and the park behind Dearborn Station. The area's community organization—South Loop Neighbors Association—advised residents to "Say No to Panhandlers" and direct them instead to GracePlace community center on Printers Row or Pacific Garden Mission nearby on State Street, a venerable institution serving the down-and-out.

Sightseers occasionally wandered through, too. Richard Boulton discovered Dearborn Park on a noontime walk from his downtown office, and was so taken by the "clean, strong, Bauhaus overtones" of the white Dearborn I townhouses that he brought his wife, Dorothy, for a look and they bought one. During the 1994 World Cup soccer games in Soldier Field, two men from Iceland wandered past Gary Ropski's and Barbara Schleck's house in Dearborn II. "They had been walking south from the downtown, through the hustle and bustle of a big city on a summer evening," Gary Ropski said. "Then they got to this quiet little village and were astonished at its serenity, so close to the downtown. They couldn't believe that a big American city had this island of peaceful living. I told them, 'But this is Chicago; this is what Chicago is really like.'"

Well, not all parts of Chicago. An incident in the fall of 1996 made it distressingly clear that violence could come lapping at the shore of that "island of peaceful living" at any time. A 17-year-old girl was shot and killed as she left a movie-theater complex in the beautifully renovated Burnham Park Plaza apartment building just a few minutes' walk from Dearborn Park—and from the Chicago Police Department headquarters. Police officials blamed warring gangs from public housing developments two miles to the west, where the girl lived. South Loop residents and business owners, angry and shaken, blamed the theater management's booking policies, which often featured brutal action-adventure films that attracted a violence-prone young crowd. A crime-fighting tenants organization in the public housing development agreed, and demanded that the theater complex shut down. A theater spokesman dismissed the killing as "a very isolated incident" unlikely to happen again, but in Dearborn Park people wondered whether the pressure-cooked city that M. W. Newman wrote about in the *Tribune* was on the verge of discovering their serene hideaway.

When city officials found the money to rebuild the elevated Roosevelt Road that separated Dearborn I from Dearborn II and asked residents for advice, a series of meetings produced a clear consensus. They wanted a connecting underpass just for pedestrians; Dearborn II already had too much auto traffic, as far as they were concerned. The result was a tidy, brick-faced foot tunnel lit by a rosy glow from its lamps. Concrete panels under the rest of the 1,500-foot-long bridge formed a wall between the two parts of Dearborn Park, as residents had requested. They worried about the security implications and the aesthetics of a long, dim stretch under an open viaduct.

The bridge itself turned out to be a whimsical beauty. Diane Legge Kemp and her associates at DLK Architecture decorated it with obelisks and sculptures that represented the area's famed lakefront museums and the University of Illinois at Chicago. They also had an imaginative eye on the future. The viaduct's concrete panels were removable. A gallery of shops and self-storage units could be created under the span, moving west to a plaza, a community and sports center, and a walk along the river. The design won an award from the Chicago Chapter of the American Institute of Architects in 1996.

The two parts of Dearborn Park did not resemble each other, but residents sounded alike when they described their surroundings. "People really are connected to each other," said Ruth Wuorenma, a single woman who lived in a Dearborn I townhouse and commuted to a suburban job in housing development. "You can always strike up a conversation just by going outside. I don't have a dog, but I know who walks what dogs at what time. If you run first thing in the morning, there are the Chinese men from The Oaks walking in the jogging track or exercising in the park."

From her townhouse in Dearborn II, Catherine Mugnolo had a similar observation: "We're all very connected. We don't have backyards, so we're forced to go in the parks. We're forced to know one another and know one another's children. This really helps us contract in a very good way as a community. If we see each other's children, we take care of them."

Joseph Spingola, who like the Mugnolos moved to Dearborn II from Dearborn I, detected a difference in the communality. He missed the central meeting place of the White Hen Pantry in Dearborn I, where he and a group of friends gathered every Saturday morning for coffee. He missed knowing who was home and who was not. "In the townhomes [of Dearborn I], you saw their cars parked outside," he said. "You saw who was driving in. Everybody watched out for everybody else. Now everybody's got a garage."

South Loop School was intended to be a unifying element for the residents of Dearborn Park, and in a perverse sort of way it was. Parents of young children talked about it constantly, wondering if anything could be done to make it serve their needs and desires. And then they talked about tuition payments and about possible moves to the suburbs. Linda Middleton and Matthew Franciskovic didn't know what would happen when their older child, a three-year-old, was ready for school. "I know of no one in Dearborn Park who goes to South Loop," Linda said. "It's not race; you wouldn't live here if you were a white supremacist. The parents here want their kids to be pushed in school. They want them to have really good programs. Look at our park before lunch—you'll see a zillion little kids. Where will they be in two, three years? We will move to a suburb, or Carter will go to a private school. But we would love to stay here."

Greg and Terri Buseman paid $3,900 a year to send their older daughter to Francis Xavier Warde School and planned to enroll the younger one, too. Lynda and Larry Young were delighted that their two older children won lottery slots in Andrew Jackson Language Academy, a magnet school. They contemplated sending their youngest to South Loop School, but only if improvement plans materialized.

Martin S. Jaffe, an associate professor of urban planning at the University of Illinois at Chicago, followed the route of hundreds of Dearborn Park parents before him. He left—reluctantly. The Jaffe family moved to a North Shore suburb after 10 years in Dearborn Park to escape tuition costs of $18,000 a year for two children at the University of Chicago Laboratory School. He loved the Dearborn Park ambience and lifestyle, Martin Jaffe said, "but I was not willing to sacrifice my children's education."

So many families moved away when their children started school that Dearborn Park had few teenagers. Childhood friendships were ruptured. "At one time Johnny had 13 friends his age," said Kathryn Moery of her 15-year-old. "He has one left. All of the others went to the suburbs."

Every weekday morning, a good portion of the "zillion" toddlers and their mothers—or nannies—that Linda Middleton worried about appeared in the play lots of Dearborn I and the big South Park of Dearborn II. They were one of the community's most populous segments. Another was the dog walkers. Kim Goluska, the architectural overseer of Dearborn II, enjoyed watching them from the bay window of his Dearborn I high-rise. "Every night about 10 the park starts filling up," he said. "All the dogs know each other, and they have their party. And all the owners know each other. They're standing 10, 15 feet away, in clusters. It's a whole social event."

Women living alone—retired or employed—were a growing faction. They appreciated the security and the convenience of walking nearly everywhere they wanted to go. They sold their cars; taking cabs or riding public transportation was cheaper than maintaining a car. Subsets formed and met for casual suppers or in small groups for concerts and plays: working women who were single mothers; women who worked in housing development and real estate law; retired women who volunteered as ushers or in ticket offices of theaters and saw free performances; women who sang in a chorus sponsored by Merit Music Program, a school in Dearborn Station that was a popular resource for South Loop residents of all ages (its youngest band featured 18-month- to 3-year-olds).

Among the retired women, Eunice Napolillo appeared to be the champion volunteer with a five-day-a-week schedule that included the Harold Washington Library Center a half mile away, the Newberry Library north of the Loop, Northwestern Memorial Hospital, and the American Cancer Society. Jeanne Barry, who moved into Dearborn Park with her husband when it opened in 1979 and stayed after she retired and her husband died, swam daily at the Chicago Hilton & Towers a short walk from her building, enjoyed museum memberships and theater subscriptions, and took sailing lessons on Lake Michigan.

A group of residents, spearheaded by Carmen Mugnolo and Joseph Spingola, an attorney and chairman of the Chicago Zoning Board of Appeals, revived the dormant South Loop Neighbors Association. They made certain its views were relayed to City Hall, where Spingola and association activists had good connections.

One of Dearborn Park's oldest residents had no time for volunteer activities. Ferd Kramer, at 95, still walked to his Draper & Kramer office in the Loop and played tennis with fellow real estate elder statesman John Baird.

The taller of the two high-rise buildings, the one with an abundance of small condominiums, developed a character distinct from the rest of Dearborn Park. Many residents were young singles, living away from home for the first time. The building also became a haven for divorced men; the lakefront's cultural and recreational attractions were ideal for weekend visits from their children. It was popular, too, with people living alone who traveled on business and liked the security and the services. Frank Readus, curriculum development specialist for the U.S. Postal Service, usually saw his one-bedroom apartment on the 18th floor only on weekends. To unwind after a hectic round of airports, he simply sat and enjoyed his view of Lake Michigan and the South Side of Chicago where he grew up. Or he visited Buddy Guy's Legends, a blues spot a few blocks away.

A young woman who was raised in the Chinatown neighborhood south of Dearborn Park said her parents permitted her to leave their home and live alone only after they investigated Dearborn Park and concluded that people would watch out for her. Another young woman, raised on Chicago's Southwest Side, said her parents were shocked when she told them she wanted a place of her own. "They're from the old country," she said. "They expected me to live at home until I got married, and if I never got married, then I'd be there until I was carried out to the cemetery." Her parents relented after they visited the building and talked to older women living there.

Singles, however, frequently left Dearborn Park for livelier, gentrifying areas northwest of the Loop or the lofts of neighboring Printers Row, if they could afford them.

Jeanne Barry enjoyed the mix in her high-rise building: "Chinese, Filipino, Korean, a lot of black people, some Hispanics. It's just a wonderful amalgam, and works wonderfully well." Dearborn Park residents often cited racial diversity as one of the community's major attractions. Whites seemed more apt to enthuse about how well it worked than blacks, however.

Lynda Young told of her four-year-old daughter, Emily, who described a new friend in detail. When Lynda met the little girl, she discovered to her delight that she was black—and Emily had not noticed. Catherine and Carmen Mugnolo left Dearborn Park temporarily for "a very nice large home with a yard" in suburban Elmwood Park. A few years later they came back with their two children. "Our daughter is Brazilian," Catherine said, "and I wouldn't want her to feel that she's different. I want her to be with children from diverse cultures, and Dearborn Park really meets that."

Linda Middleton was proud of the diversity among owners of the 72 Prairie Town Homes where she lived; one-half were white, one-third black, the rest Asian or Hispanic. African-American families lived in four of the five townhouses across her cul-de-sac. The fifth family was Chinese American.

Ruth Wuorenma recalled the "endearing images" of her 80-year-old father, visiting from his white suburb, sitting on a bench and enjoying conversations with "a Chinese gentleman or an African-American gentleman."

Dearborn Park's black residents appreciated the amicable racial mix too, but a few saw nuances that apparently escaped notice by whites. Sharon Thomas Parrott thought the smooth course of racial integration was hardly surprising. "There is a socioeconomic sameness here," she said. "Dearborn Park is a white community that black people live in." Hyde Park, the area around the University of Chicago where she previously lived, is "a black community that white people live in. I'm not saying this as a negative. But I think the flavor of Dearborn Park is not African American. It is white. I happen to be comfortable. But it is just a different feel than Hyde Park."

A few black residents were not entirely sunny about race relations. "Well, people are friendly, yes, but there really is not a lot of socializing," said a woman who moved with her husband from the suburb of Evanston to a Dearborn II townhouse. Another woman said she herself had many good friends among white residents, but she noticed that some whites looked with disapproval at teenage black boys having noisy fun in a Dearborn Park swimming pool. Someone, she said, told her that an older white man was overheard using the word "nigger" in referring to them.

Another black woman spoke with sadness about the controversy over South Loop School. "That was the first time I saw the community move away from what I always thought we represented—diversity," she said. "It was like they were really frightened to think that their kids would be going to school

Aubrey Thompson's fourth-floor "backyard" in Prairie Town Home, ideal for summertime entertaining and hailing friends. Photo by Wayne Wille.

with kids from Hilliard Homes. In my limited discussions with parents about it, I thought, the school can only get better if you allow your kids to attend. But I guess it's different if it's your own, if you're a parent, which I am not."

Black and white parents alike cringed when they heard their children refer to "project kids" at South Loop School. Several black teachers at the school resented what they maintained were false reports of students stealing mail from Dearborn Park mailboxes, banging on doors, jumping on parked cars. "They say they love integration," said one teacher of Dearborn Park's white residents, "but they come here with their attitudes." Stephen Carlson, a white homeowner who lived across a park from the school, thought some of the complaints might be justified. "But that could happen up in Lake Forest, too," he said, referring to the tony suburb where he grew up.

Robert Grisham was one of several African-American residents who mentioned a telling omission. Dearborn Park had tennis courts, jogging paths, and softball diamonds. There was organized volleyball and football in its parks. But there was not a single basketball net, and there were residents who would fight to keep them out. "They're afraid basketball would attract the wrong element," Robert Grisham said, choosing his words with elegant sarcasm. "Tennis would not."

Other complaints about life in Dearborn Park were more mundane. Rising property taxes. The profusion of big dogs in the park behind Dearborn Station, scaring small children. Walking past Pacific Garden Mission on State Street, with its clients clustered around its doors. (Others scoffed and said the shelter was a benign neighbor; they routinely gave the mission clothing or left-over food from parties.) There were complaints of people not cleaning up after their dogs. Of having to drive to get to a good supermarket. Of too many cars driving too fast in Dearborn II. Of the lack of parking spaces in Dearborn I. Even Ferd Kramer griped about the parking, for which he could thank his old friend Phil Klutznick, who insisted on sacrificing parking spaces to cut costs.

And everyone wondered about the bushy fields to the west, between Dearborn Park and the Chicago River. When the South Loop venture began, this was considered the prime land for development. Whatever happened there would profoundly affect Dearborn Park. There were questions, too, about whether and where to build low-income housing for families. Whether and where to develop a retail strip. How to maintain the community's precious sense of security. And, of course, the future of South Loop School. "Dearborn Park," said longtime resident Barbara Schleck, "is still very much a work in progress."

15

"Dearborn Park Was the Key"

WHEN TOM AYERS AND HIS COLLEAGUES WERE MAKING THE ROUNDS OF CORPORATE boardrooms, soliciting capital from Chicago businesses to build the housing that became Dearborn Park, they talked about three goals. They wanted a stronger downtown, securing investors' property. They wanted a catalyst for further development, bolstering the city's tax base. And they wanted to staunch the flow of middle-class families to the suburbs.

Dearborn Park delivered on the first two. With 14,500 people living in the South Loop and thousands more moving into new and renovated buildings to the west and northwest, downtown Chicago no longer emptied out at night. It was lively and it was safe. Its streets were brightened with new stores, restaurants, coffee shops, delis, and carryout establishments, all going strong after dark. Bonnie Lindstrom, a professor of urban sociology at the South Loop's Roosevelt University, told the *Chicago Tribune* that the Loop had become "far more like a European downtown, where people live and work in the same place."

The great State Street retail corridor, however, did not survive the 1980s. Five of its seven department stores folded as shoppers flocked to glitzy new vertical malls on North Michigan Avenue. But the best of the State Street seven, the Marshall Field's and Carson Pirie Scott stores, underwent magnificent renovations in the early 1990s. State Street remade itself as smaller shops and well-known discount stores filled retail spaces in the north portion and educational institutions moved into the south half, near Dearborn Park and Printers Row. With Roosevelt University, Columbia College, and the School of the Art Institute on Michigan Avenue and the museums on the lakefront, the South Loop developed an impressive educational cluster that enhanced the growing residential community.

After years in which more structures were abandoned than built, the South Loop blossomed with $1.4 billion in new construction and renovation in less than two decades. Most of that investment occurred after 1983, when it was clear that Dearborn Park would be a success (and when interest rates began a descent to single digits).

The growth brought a bonanza to the city in sales, utilities, and real estate taxes. In real estate taxes alone, the 1995 levy in the tract that covered Dearborn Park and the surrounding one-fourth mile was $34 million; this was almost double the 1983 figure—converted to 1995 dollars—even though the tax rate itself fell by 9 percent during those years. For the decade before 1983, the tax levy in that area—again, converted to 1995 dollars—was virtually flat.

The 51 acres of Dearborn Park generated about $90,000 in real estate tax revenue in 1976, before construction began (about $242,000 in 1995 dollars). In 1995, homeowners in the not-quite-completed Dearborn Park paid $5.1 million in real estate taxes. The city would reap a handsome return on the $18 million it spent on internal and peripheral streets, sewers, parks, and other improvements to make Dearborn Park livable. Chicago's public school system and its finance authority got 49 percent of the new real estate tax money.

The Loop was healthier and Chicago's tax base was stronger, and it was Dearborn Park that provided the impetus. "Dearborn Park was the key," said Miles Berger, former chairman of the Chicago Plan Commission and managing partner of Heitman Financial, Ltd., one of the nation's largest real estate advisory and mortgage-banking firms. "It showed that you could do a development on the Near South Side and succeed. That was critical."

Even its most enthusiastic admirers, however, would have to acknowledge that Dearborn Park did not deliver on its third goal. It did not attract 120,000 residents to the South Loop within 20 years of its initial fund-raising, as its founders prophesied it would in their 1974 booklet to potential investors. And of course it did not stop the flow out of the city. Those goals never were realistic; after a few years, no one mentioned them. The city was still losing people, though the numbers and the rate had lessened. During the 1970s, Chicago's population declined by 350,000, or nearly 11 percent. During the 1980s, it dropped by 186,000, or 6 percent.

Dearborn Park's founders hoped for a child-centered community. But without a neighborhood school that had parents' confidence, only about 25 percent of Dearborn Park households had children living in the home. And they were a revolving group that often moved out when the children reached school age.

In income and profession, residents of Dearborn Park and the surrounding South Loop were not much different from residents of the upscale apartment towers north of the Loop, though the founders had talked about a more broadly based crowd. A 1993 survey by the Burnham Park Planning Board (formerly the South Loop Planning Board, soon to become the Near South Planning Board) reported that 72 percent of employed residents were in professional or management jobs.

Dearborn Park turned out to be smaller and costlier and to have fewer children than its founders intended. But they did achieve another important goal. Dearborn Park and the South Loop overall were racially diverse from the week the first occupants arrived, and they remained that way.

The people who fought Dearborn Park in its planning stage argued that a new, upscale South Loop community would creep into old neighborhoods to the west and northwest, driving up housing prices and driving out low-income residents. The dreaded gentrification did occur, but it would be ridiculous to blame Dearborn Park. Affluent rehabbers began to colonize old city neighborhoods and aging industrial districts throughout the near-downtown belt and beyond in the mid-1980s, but not because of Dearborn Park. Fixing up old buildings in areas close to central business districts had become a fad in cities around the country, as sociologist Morris Janowitz had predicted in Chicago 21's early days. Wim Wiewel, dean of the College of Urban Planning and Public Affairs at the University of Illinois at Chicago, worked closely with gentrifying neighborhoods and concluded that Dearborn Park may, in fact, have delayed the process. "Chicago was fortunate to have a lot of vacant land close to downtown to accommodate housing," he said. "The pressures might have been stronger if that had still been railroad land." The number of affordable housing units lost through gentrification was smaller, according to Wiewel, than the number lost through decay and abandonment. But gentrification was a problem for lower-income families, and it underscored the need for renovation and construction of affordable housing.

Next to Dearborn Park's $250 million in new residences, the most significant private investment in the South Loop was the $150-million renovation of the Chicago Hilton & Towers, one-quarter mile east on Michigan Avenue. It was completed in 1986. Eight years earlier, Hilton Hotel Corporation had been on the verge of leaving the area. The business community's confidence in the South Loop, as demonstrated by its investment in Dearborn Park, prompted Hilton to stay; Hilton, in turn, bolstered Dearborn Park with its lavish restoration. A 2,200-room hotel sitting dark and empty would have devastated hopes for residential growth. The elegant new Hilton (with its refurbished rooms enlarged, reducing the total to 1,600) and its restaurants, health club, and shops became part of the community. One Dearborn Park resident remarked that seeing the lights on at the Hilton when he returned home, no matter what time of night, was "the equivalent of a porch light for the community."

The southward expansion of the city's financial district also was of inestimable value. Robert Wislow, chairman of U.S. Equities Realty, assembled land west of Dearborn Station, where the old LaSalle Street Station had stood. Beginning in 1982, he built One Financial Place, a 40-story tower anchored on the north by new quarters for the Chicago Board Options Exchange and on the south by the new Midwest Stock Exchange straddling Congress Parkway. While Wislow was creating his $170-million office-and-trading complex, its neighbor to the north, the Chicago Board of Trade, expanded with a 24-story, $45-million postmodern addition. Together, they assured that Chicago would remain the world capital of futures trading. Only a dozen years earlier, LaSalle Street's biggest bank, Continental, had wondered whether it was secure in that ominous landscape.

In 1984, work began on a $34-million renovation of the empty Sears store on South State Street. It became One Congress Center, a computer-oriented office building. In 1990, the new $60-million Northern Trust Operations Center, housing the bank's computer operations, opened about one-half mile west of Dearborn Park.

The growth of the South Loop's financial district was a major factor in the addition of about 15,000 downtown jobs during the 1980s, swelling the Loop-area workforce to 542,000—or one of every six jobs in the six-county metropolitan region. It also provided hundreds of homeowners for nearby Dearborn Park and Printers Row.

Usually in urban renewal efforts, public investment stimulates private investment. In the South Loop, it was the other way around. The impetus came from the business community, with city government slowly—and at times reluctantly—joining in. But as the private investment grew and it was obvious that something remarkable was happening in the South Loop, City Hall became an increasingly helpful partner. Its contributions soared under Mayor Richard M. Daley, South Loop resident. One of the most important moves, however, came under the administration of Mayor Harold Washington. In 1986 the city picked a seedy stretch of South State Street just north of Printers Row as the site of its new central library, overruling jittery civic leaders who wanted a more presentable North Loop location. The $145-million Harold Washington Library Center, the nation's largest municipal library, rose where the city's last burlesque house and several pawnshops once did business. It fit neatly into the emerging educational community in the South Loop. DePaul University bought the handsome but vacant Goldblatt's store kitty-corner across State Street and transformed it, at a cost of $65 million, into its downtown campus, with a lively Chicago Music Mart on the concourse and street levels and city offices above. Columbia College, a rapidly growing institution nearby on Michigan Avenue that specialized in film, theater, and communications arts, expanded into several other South Loop locations and then bought the old Lakeside Press Building on Printers Row for a dormitory. Overnight, Dearborn Street had an infusion of young life—and new customers.

By the mid-1990s, the area had received two other major injections of public money. One stemmed from the Daley administration's decision to use tax-increment financing (TIF) to help clean up and develop remaining patches of blight and vacant land. The second removed the traffic-choked highway that separated the Field Museum of Natural History from its lakefront partners, the John G. Shedd Aquarium and the Adler Planetarium.

Late in 1990, the City Council approved Daley's request to sell TIF bonds to pay for infrastructure and other improvements in the 72-acre Central Station project east of Dearborn Park. Four years later, the TIF district was expanded to cover 250 acres stretching two miles from north to south. With this designation, the city was able to sell 20-year bonds to help finance land acquisition, demolition, site preparation and improvements, and infrastructure in a largely vacant area pockmarked with abandoned and deteriorating buildings. Under Illinois law, TIF bonds are repaid with the new real estate tax revenue generated by redevelopment. Their use is controversial, because local government and schools do not benefit from the increased tax base until the bonds are repaid. But, theoretically at least, TIF is limited to blighted areas that would not improve without this aid.

For Central Station, the city agreed to issue $40 million in TIF bonds over 22 years to help create a mixed-use complex of hotels, stores, office buildings, institutional facilities, and residences. The first half of the $70-million Chinatown Square development south of Dearborn Park benefited from $6 million in TIF bonds, plus $9.3 million in low-interest development loans obtained through the city.

In 1993, the equalized assessed valuation of the entire TIF area—the figure used in Cook County to determine real estate tax liability—was $128 million. By 2005, according to city planners and their advisers, the equalized assessed valuation in the TIF area would be $530 million, assuming the various projects proceeded as planned.

Late in 1996, the city finished a $90-million relocation of Lake Shore Drive's northbound lanes, moving them from the east to the west of Soldier Field to create a graceful campus around the trio of famous museums and clear the way for 10 acres of new parkland along the lakefront. The relocation, financed by Metropolitan Pier and Exposition Authority bonds as part of a $1-billion expansion of the McCormick Place convention complex, had been sought for years by the museums and civic groups and had been recommended in the 1973 Chicago 21 Plan.

Daley wanted to enhance the new museum campus by implementing another Chicago 21 lakefront proposal. When the city's 50-year contract with the Chicago Park District and the Federal Aviation Administration to operate Merrill C. Meigs Field expired in the fall of 1996, Daley closed the airstrip and unveiled plans for a water-oriented park on the site. Meigs occupied Northerly Island, a 90-acre, 4,500-foot-long landfill peninsula running south from the Adler Planetarium. Northerly was big enough for all the elements envisioned by Teng & Associates, the planning firm hired by the city: fishing ponds, snorkeling lagoons, prairies, bird sanctuaries, beaches, picnic areas, children's playgrounds and learning centers, a lakefront promenade. This "new kind of park" would be a major attraction for tourists as well as Chicago-area families, wrote Blair Kamin, the architecture critic of the *Chicago Tribune*. It would shield them from the rush of traffic while "vividly revealing the secrets of earth, water and sky (which, not coincidentally, are the respective subjects of the Field, Shedd and Adler)."

Meigs had lost nearly 45 percent of its business in the previous 15 years. By 1996, it was used mainly by state officials flying back and forth to Springfield, the Illinois capital, and by several dozen operators of private aircraft. But that was enough to prompt Governor Jim Edgar and the Illinois General Assembly to pass legislation seizing Northerly Island from the city. The state relented only after Daley agreed to keep Meigs open until 2002.

Fortunately, the self-interest of state politicians did not conflict with other public improvements proposed for Chicago's South Loop. As Dearborn II neared completion, the city spent $10.5 million on a new subway station and an elevated transit station at Roosevelt Road and State Street, $42 million to build a new Roosevelt Road viaduct, $15 million to extend Roosevelt to Lake Shore Drive, $10 million to create a stunning gateway to the lakefront's Grant Park at Congress Parkway's plaza, $3 million to make the park's spectacular Buckingham Memorial Fountain even more beautiful, and $25 million to rip up the cold, uninviting State Street Mall and restore the great street's charming visual character with Beaux-Arts lampposts, lacy ironwork framing subway portals, and planters filled with honey locust, ash, and pear trees. The new old-fashioned look inspired plans to convert several historic but nearly empty State Street commercial buildings into apartments. The residential reuse phenomenon that began 20 years earlier in Printers Row was marching right into the heart of Chicago's downtown.

Thus, in the space of a decade, the new South Loop acquired an important connection to the lakefront via Roosevelt Road, enhanced access to the lakefront museums, two new transit stations, and elegant public places. Dismal South State Street was liberated with the disappearance of the crumbling Roosevelt Road viaduct and adorned with plantings. More flowers and greenery were lavished on the area around the developing Central Station community.

With the additional millions available through tax-increment bonds, residents and businesses expected a continued blossoming of the Near South Side. It was an astounding transformation of an area that 20 years earlier had been a forsaken expanse of abandoned buildings and unused rail yards.

Dearborn Park strengthened downtown Chicago and became a safe and comfortable neighborhood in the heart of the city. But even after it was fully occupied and continuing to seed growth, there was unfinished business that dimmed its success.

The school. The sight of South Loop School sitting in the midst of the community but unused by its residents was so unsettling that it was difficult to comprehend how this situation could continue year after year. Dearborn Park parents felt betrayed by the Board of Education, and they had been. But how could anyone not be moved by the knowledge that the children of Hilliard Homes arrived at that school every day on their buses only to see the children of Dearborn Park leaving every day on *their* buses because the Hilliard children were arriving? The board's decision to change the boundaries to include Hilliard, when the elementary school it had been using was closer and about to be rebuilt, was done as much to punish the parents of Dearborn Park as it was to please the parents of Hilliard Homes. Once the decision was made, however, reversing it became a political impossibility.

The problem could have been averted if Dearborn Park Corporation had paid attention to advice it got in its planning stages. But in those days its leaders were too distracted with staying financially viable and too trusting of mayoral and school board promises. They should have gone back to the business

community to raise $4 million or $5 million to build a school, and then contract with one of the educational institutions in the area—the University of
Illinois at Chicago, Roosevelt University, the University of Chicago—to operate it in cooperation with the Board of Education as a model for the city.
And this model school should have been big enough to accommodate low-
income children from surrounding areas as one-third or so of its student
body, selected at random from applications, as Chicago's magnet schools do.

Another, more ambitious alternative was proposed by Evans Clinchy, the
Boston-based educational consultant hired in the early 1970s by Dearborn
Park's planning arm. Clinchy recommended formation of a new school district consisting of a Dearborn Park school and three or four schools in surrounding communities. Each school would have a distinct educational philosophy or specialty. Parents within this new district could apply to any of the
schools on a first-come, first-served basis. With the expansion of Chinatown,
the growth of Central Station, and the diverse community around the University of Illinois at Chicago, such a school district would have a broad racial,
ethnic, and economic mix. Busing would be needed for most students, but
the distances would not be great.

That plan could still be implemented. Mayor Daley suggested as much in
a meeting with South Loop residents late in 1995, soon after the state government gave him greater authority over city schools. The old Board of Education
didn't care about the middle class, he said, adding: "When this [South Loop
School] was built, it was built for Dearborn Park. But they lied to you. They
changed the boundaries." The challenge now, he told applauding residents,
was to create schools that middle-class families would use. What is wrong, he
asked, with a school that is 70 percent middle class and 30 percent poor?
Nothing, of course, as far as his audience was concerned. The difficulty was
arriving at that point in a fair and politically feasible manner.

Clinchy's plan could do that. So, in a narrower fashion, could the proposal from Daley's school chiefs to build a new facility replacing the little
Hilliard branch and to improve academic offerings for all grades. For the first
time, South Loop School would serve all children in its attendance area,
those who benefit from accelerated programs as well as those who require remedial education. Although it was often overlooked, both Hilliard Homes
and Dearborn Park have children in each category.

Nor should it be forgotten that both communities, and school officials as
well, were victims of a malignant condition they did nothing to cause. The
city's decision in the 1950s and 1960s to stuff massive concentrations of poor
people into isolated high-rise housing projects was surely the most disgraceful in its history. As long as those concentrations exist, there will be class seg-

regation in city schools. And as long as the school system fails to provide appropriate early education for every child who needs it, the gulf between disadvantaged and affluent will remain deep and destructive.

The riverfront.   A second disappointment in the Dearborn Park venture was the failure to develop land along the Chicago River. Architect Bruce Graham, a principal designer of the 1973 Chicago 21 Plan, was convinced that the city missed a great opportunity by not acquiring that land and making it available to Dearborn Park Corporation. "I don't think that [architect Bertrand] Goldberg's big River City is right for the riverfront," he said. "It should be more open, like the lakefront. A green belt." The first Mayor Daley could have obtained state permission to create a nonprofit corporation empowered to issue bonds, buy land, and package it for development, had he wanted to do that. But he was basically conservative, preferring to deal with market-oriented private developers rather than a quasi-public development agency. Dearborn Park's success as a catalyst bore out his beliefs. But the catalytic effect didn't work in the 80 acres of railroad land between the new community and the river, where it should have been strongest. The area seemed jinxed. The River City financial partners had an option on much of that land but failed to exercise it after their first phase went into default. Another big proposal, this one involving a hotel and office towers, was scrapped during the late 1980s after a spate of new hotels and office towers opened elsewhere in the downtown area and glutted the market. Shortly after that, plans for a mixed-use development with 2,500 units of housing and a commercial strip evaporated when the insurance company that was to be its chief backer suffered setbacks.

Early in 1992, a consortium of hotel and casino interests expressed a desire to build a $2-billion entertainment and casino resort along the riverfront. The second Mayor Daley tried for four years to get the necessary approval from the state government but was rebuffed. The casino plans did not die; other potential developers watched and waited, and the riverfront remained vacant.

That land west of Dearborn Park, desirable as it seemed, had a serious drawback. Metra, a regional agency that controlled the Chicago area's passenger rail system, continued to run trains on one small line that bisected the length of the property. Neither developers nor Chicago's business and government leaders could persuade Metra, dominated by suburban Republicans, to shift the little rail line—it served only about 15,000 riders daily—to the west side of the river, where it would join other lines coming into the city. The second Daley suggested that noise and dirt from the Metra operation could be lessened with berms or by depressing the tracks. Still, the area would be left with a broad, impenetrable gulch. Like the South Loop School situation, the Metra decision was a monument to the lack of coordinated planning among local government bodies.

The South Loop Neighbors Association favored low-density residential development compatible with their community atmosphere for most of the land to the west. But the real estate interests that bought it from the railroads with big plans in mind had paid too much for it to settle for another Dearborn Park or two.

Whatever happens there, the riverfront itself should be reserved for public walkways and parks, and for recreational and entertainment purposes, as the 1973 Chicago 21 Plan proposed. Mary Ward Wolkonsky, one of the original Dearborn Park board members, for years urged the board to promote development of a riverfront cultural-amusement-entertainment complex patterned after Tivoli Gardens in Copenhagen. (Tivoli has a casino, so her concept could be compatible with the 1992 casino plan.) It was a splendid proposal but too frivolous for her fellow board members, absorbed as they were in cash shortfalls and infrastructure delays and killer interest rates.

A Tivoli-type development along the river would make the area a destination point for people throughout the city and its suburbs, and for out-of-town tourists, too. That might alter the tranquility that many Dearborn Park residents prize, but it would be healthy for the city as a whole and good for its tax base—just as a middle-class community in the South Loop has been.

Low-cost housing. Dearborn Park's founders talked about economic diversity when they were promoting the project during its planning stage. Except for Philip Klutznick, however, they never seriously considered building subsidized housing for low- and moderate-income families. They didn't want the hassles and the delays and the regulations that came with those subsidies, and they were afraid that adding a low-income element would discourage potential buyers who already would be taking a risk by investing in an area with such an unsavory image. But the fully occupied Dearborn Park and the South Loop in general was no longer a fragile investment risk. By the mid-1990s, it was an established community with enough strength and dynamism to absorb housing for lower-income families.

Vacant land in the tax-increment district east and south of Dearborn Park is suitable for affordable housing, but with several qualifiers: It should be for sale, not rental; it should be low-rise; and it should be interspersed with other development. Two-flats and three-flats, discarded by early Dearborn Park planners, would be a particularly welcome addition.

The only housing in the South Loop available to lower-income families by the mid-1990s were 150 rent-subsidized apartments in high-rise buildings; those will disappear if the federal subsidies are not renewed. One-time subsidies that reduce sales prices make better financial sense than ongoing subsidies for renters, and they promote neighborhood stability. High-rise rental housing does not.

As 1997 began, the only forthcoming low-cost projects in the area were specifically not for families. One was a 96-unit rental building for older people, similar to The Oaks in Dearborn Park. The other two were city-subsidized "SROs"—single-room-occupancy buildings—to be constructed on vacant land southeast of Dearborn Park. They were replacements for decrepit skid-row hotels in the vicinity.

Advocates for the homeless and for more low-cost housing wanted the city to require that 20 percent of all residential units created in the tax-increment district be priced for low- or moderate-income people. The city responded by requiring a one-for-one replacement of low-cost housing demolished in the area, or a minimum of 300 units, whichever is greater. That did not satisfy the protesters, who periodically gathered near Mayor Daley's Central Station townhouse chanting from the song "Open the Door, Richard."

One possible mechanism for constructing affordable housing in the South Loop is New Homes for Chicago, an initiative of the Daley administration. Subsidies to developers in 1996 ranged from $20,000 to $40,000 for a single-family house, with the larger subsidies reserved for families earning 40 to 50 percent of the city's median family income. For them, sales prices were capped at $65,000. For moderate-income families, the cap was $99,000. George Thrush, one of the developers of Dearborn Park's south portion, used New Homes for Chicago to build three-bedroom, two-story houses reminiscent of old Chicago bungalows in a largely Hispanic neighborhood on the city's Northwest Side. They would fit in well in the tax-increment district. TIF bonds could help with site acquisition and preparation.

Robert Lucas, a veteran community and civil rights activist who fought Dearborn Park during its planning phase, concluded that his criticism was justified. "I predicted it would not be balanced development," he said, "and it's not. It's all middle- and upper-class."

James Compton, president of the Chicago Urban League and an architect of Dearborn Park's precedent-setting affirmative action program for contractors, agreed. "Dearborn Park has certainly been an asset to the city," he said. "But the South Loop appears to be developing in a manner that, I suppose, was predictable. There is no appreciable mix along economic and class lines.

"It is still a challenge for this city to incorporate lower-middle-income and low-income people into developments of this kind. I don't think great effort was put into trying to address that aspect of Dearborn Park. Oh, there is some affordable housing for seniors, but seniors don't tend to be threatening to the lifestyles of others. Dearborn Park continues the existing patterns of cordoning off poor and low-income people. It's a form of apartheid. There are racial as well as class connotations, because African Americans and Hispanics tend to be the two groups outside the economic mainstream."

One other shortcoming in Dearborn Park and the surrounding area is more easily correctable. Shops will arrive, but only after more residential growth. Placement of a retail component will have to reflect more thoughtful planning than went into the renovation of Dearborn Station, which turned its back on Dearborn Park instead of inviting the community in. Its central gallery opens only to the north. It is no surprise that stores and restaurants have not flourished in the station, despite the beauty of the interior renovation.

Architect Diane Legge Kemp's idea for shops under the rebuilt Roosevelt Road viaduct is a promising version of architect Harry Weese's proposal of 20 years ago to save the Dearborn Station sheds and create a festive marketplace there. The shops could flow into a zone of larger stores along Roosevelt to the east, creating a continuous retail strip to connect Dearborn Park with Central Station and any future housing to the west.

These residential enclaves would not easily knit together as a single South Loop or Near South Side neighborhood. Just as towers-in-a-park were the fashion of the 1950s and 1960s, groups of rowhouses or free-standing houses facing each other in insular compounds were the style of choice in the 1980s and 1990s. Urban planners did not like them, but buyers did. Pastora San Juan Cafferty, historian and urban specialist at the University of Chicago, thought that was understandable; they fulfilled a natural desire for private space and security in a dense urban environment.

As Dearborn Park Corporation was preparing to sell its south area, Philip Klutznick wondered whether it should have tried to do more. He had read an article in *The New York Times* about the New York City Housing Partnership, a nonprofit corporation formed by David Rockefeller that put together private and public assistance for construction and rehabilitation of affordable housing. The idea of an ongoing effort appealed to him. "I am afraid we are making too little plans," he wrote to Tom Ayers and Ferd Kramer.

There surely were enough vacant and blighted tracts on Chicago's South Side and West Side that could have benefited from Dearborn Park Corporation's influence in city government and the business community, its persistence, and its real estate savvy. But one of the main reasons for its success set it apart from the New York organization and from similar initiatives in other cities. It was not just an overseer of public and private funds; it was directly involved. Its shareholders' dollars were at stake, and the Dearborn Park leadership felt this responsibility keenly. The city itself was also an important motivator; corny as it may sound, Dearborn Park's founders loved Chicago.

Their emphasis on financial viability led them to a design that emphasized security and marketability rather than social idealism or architectural brilliance. "There were other ways to have done Dearborn Park, probably much more imaginative," said Kim Goluska, an architectural planner for the project and Dearborn Park resident. "But would they have succeeded? Dearborn Park was simple enough, unpretentious enough, easily assimilated enough, that it worked."

Two other factors made it work. The site was vacant; no one had to contend with the prolonged, painful, and difficult business of relocation. And the original Daley administration agreed with Dearborn Park's goal of market-responsive, racially integrated, middle-class housing; city officials did not try to impose other aims—housing for poor people, for example, or a more open site plan, or a commercial-industrial component, or some sort of community review. None of the five subsequent Chicago mayors tried to force a change in policy. This approach was not politically correct, even for the mid-1970s, but it did avoid pitfalls that sank other big public-private projects.

In the heart of Chicago's North Loop, an entire block between the Richard J. Daley Civic Center and the Marshall Field store sat empty because the city's renewal plan for the area was more responsive to what urban planners and architects envisioned than to what the market could support.

On Chicago's Near South Side, two miles from Dearborn Park, the South Commons development was conceived as a model community that would be integrated economically as well as racially. It failed at both. It ignored the fact, distasteful though it is, that a thorough blending of economic groups in a brand-new community built close to a big public housing project and a high-crime district carried too much risk. Better first to develop a strong middle-class core that is comfortable and secure, and then introduce subsidized housing for families—preferably in for-sale, low-rise units.

In Minneapolis, plans for Cedar-Riverside, a new community of 12,500 apartments and substantial retail and office space in a run-down area near the downtown, turned into "a can of worms to the max," in the words of one Minneapolis city planner. It was overly ambitious, gobbling up every government subsidy available. A U.S. District Court halted construction for three years during the 1970s while community objections were resolved. In the

1980s, much of the property went into foreclosure. It was eventually helped to a successful (and considerably smaller) conclusion by the Minneapolis Community Development Agency, an arm of city government.

Still, when looking at the empty fields west of Dearborn Park and the ad hoc development that popped up elsewhere in the vicinity, it is tempting to wish that Dearborn Park Corporation had evolved into an ongoing entity with a broader mission. The city became an enthusiastic partner in making the area attractive to investors with new financing mechanisms and with transportation and road improvements, but its role was largely reactive. There was no cohesive, overarching vision of what the area should be. A casino-entertainment complex on the river? A domed stadium adjacent to the latest McCormick Place expansion? A spot for light industry? Shopping, when the time was right? And housing, of course, a great deal more housing. But who knows where, or when, or what kind.

Milwaukee offered one model of continuing business involvement in downtown growth that would be useful for Chicago. In 1973, a year before Dearborn Park Corporation was born, the city's business leaders created the Milwaukee Redevelopment Corporation, a nonprofit body that worked with community and government agencies to initiate and implement projects that would not be undertaken by private developers acting on their own. It recruited investors, acted as a general partner on some projects, and granted low-interest loans.

Among its accomplishments: the multilevel Grand Avenue mall (with The Rouse Company); Milwaukee Center, a hotel-office-theater complex; Yankee Hill, a 350-unit luxury high-rise development; and East Pointe Commons, 600 units of upscale housing that mixed rental and for-sale townhouses, multifamily buildings, and a retail center.

Carl Bufalini, an economic development specialist who worked on the Dearborn Park staff as a young man, looked back on those days as a last hurrah for the old Chicago, "where you had a strong mayor, strong unions, a strong business community acting together. It was probably the last major effort the business community did together."

He may be right about the togetherness aspect; but individually, Chicago banks were more involved in neighborhood development during the 1990s than in the Dearborn Park days. In 1994, Continental Bank pledged $1 billion in loans to city neighborhoods. In 1995, First Chicago Corporation, parent of First National Bank, announced plans to lend at least $2 billion over six years in low- and moderate-income Chicago neighborhoods. Harris Bankcorp and a number of smaller financial institutions also were working with nonprofit groups such as Neighborhood Housing Services on block-by-block renewal efforts.

But the business community had changed. The ties that bound the old corporate clique that invested in Dearborn Park had loosened. Continental Bank was acquired by the California-based BankAmerica Corporation in 1994. Harris Bankcorp was acquired by Bank of Montreal in 1984. First Chicago merged with Detroit's NBD Bancorp in 1996 and became FirstChicago NBD Bank Corporation. Marshall Field Company and Carson Pirie Scott were acquired by non-Chicago corporations. Sears moved its operations to a Chicago suburb.

Corporate executives of the 1990s were too busy fighting takeovers and appeasing Wall Street to have time for the long lunches and after-work cocktails that solidified the relationships that led to Chicago 21 and Dearborn Park. They were more likely to eat lunch at their desks than at the Chicago Club. And they were on the move. A staff member of one prominent civic group complained that the rapid turnover among corporate leaders robbed his board of its memory. "Our trustees have civic pride," he said, "but so many of them know nothing of Chicago's history, compared to executives of the 1970s. They may not know each other all that well. I don't think one of them could say today, 'We need $15 million,' and go out and get it."

John Perkins, president of Chicago's biggest bank during Dearborn Park's formative years and a major participant in its financing package, said flatly, "The banks could not participate today, no way. The profit centers would say, we're lean and tough, we don't waste money on frills. That's a great project, but we're worried about the price of our stock. We can't justify that." Neither, probably, could the utility companies, under tight scrutiny by consumer groups.

Richard Thomas, retired chairman of First Chicago Corporation and one of Dearborn Park's financial saviors during the precarious early 1980s, noted that the business community united for several projects in the post–Dearborn Park era. It pledged $100 million for capital improvements for the city's two main musical treasures, the Chicago Symphony Orchestra and Lyric Opera of Chicago. Their boards still brought the area's corporate chiefs together, even if the dining clubs and the Central Area Committee no longer did. Businesses also were involved in projects to improve Chicago's schools, individually and through the Civic Committee of the Commercial Club of Chicago. Hiring young people who could read and write directly involved their self-interest, as did the blight in the South Loop 20 years earlier.

The cozy old relationship among local political leaders and the business community had faded. A feisty third element had intruded: community activists. The news media, which once could generally be counted on to support the political-business axis, listened to them and gave them generous coverage. The change could be pinpointed to the collapse of plans for a 1992 Chicago World's Fair, when a strong community coalition forged in the fight against Chicago 21 led the opposition, aided by a sympathetic Mayor Washington.

The new climate was just one reason the business community would not undertake another Dearborn Park, in Richard Thomas's view. It was discussed from time to time but "always came unstuck on the question of which neighborhood. What was unique about this particular neighborhood that would warrant the business community getting involved the way it did in Dearborn Park? In addition, we discovered that the politics of local neighborhoods are very difficult. Who do you work with? Who will your partners be? In areas where there are a lot of people living, there are no easy answers.

"What made Dearborn Park appealing was the availability and the immediacy to the business district. And it's much easier to do a project where there's nobody there."

Ferd Kramer discovered that in 1988, when at age 87 he proposed demolishing four vacant, decrepit, high-rise public housing buildings along the South Side lakefront and building in their place a racially and economically mixed community of townhouses and mid-rise buildings. He had the strong support of Robert Lucas, his onetime foe in the Chicago 21 days, but the area's entrenched political and public housing interests called the plan a landgrab and sank it.

Chicago's legendary business connections had frayed, but some ties remained and worked in the old way. Charles H. Shaw, a developer of quality housing for a broad income range, sat on the board of Chicago's Rush–Presbyterian St. Luke's Medical Center with Edward A. Brennan, chairman of Sears, Roebuck and Company. One day in 1989 after a Rush board meeting, Brennan asked Shaw to take a ride with him. They drove to the old Sears headquarters on Chicago's West Side, 55 acres with five million square feet of buildings sitting empty in the midst of one of the most ravaged, pitiful neighborhoods in any American city. The upshot was that Shaw created plans for Homan Square, with 600 units of mixed-income housing—low-rise, two-thirds of it owner-occupied—plus one million square feet of renovated commercial and light-industry space and facilities for recreation, a medical clinic, and social services.

Sears donated the property and $30 million for site preparation, carrying costs, and other predevelopment expenses. The city contributed low-interest loans and subsidies through its New Homes for Chicago program and converted one old Sears building into a training facility for Police Department undercover officers. Another city agency prepared to offer job training and assist new entrepreneurs.

Shaw, like Tom Ayers two decades earlier, made the rounds of corporations and individuals "with my beggar's hat on all the time" for help. The challenge was at least as great as the one that drove Dearborn Park; he aimed to re-create the community as it existed half a century ago, when people walked to their jobs and raised their families in the security of houses they owned.

One leader of the old Dearborn Park group did not agree that its success couldn't be repeated. Tom Ayers, who chaired the effort from start to finish, argued passionately that the business leadership would respond, if properly motivated, because the self-interest and the love for Chicago was still there, even if their corporations were run by people in Minneapolis or San Francisco or Montreal or Tokyo instead of hometown Chicago.

"Tom Ayers," said Pastora San Juan Cafferty, "is an eternal optimist. He never gives up." And that was another reason behind the success of Dearborn Park.

APPENDIX 1

Original Chicago 21 Corporation Board of Directors

(January 1974)

Chairman: Thomas G. Ayers, Chairman and President, Commonwealth Edison Company

President: John H. Perkins, President, Continental Illinois National Bank

Vice President: Warren G. Skoning, Vice President, Real Estate, Sears, Roebuck and Company

Treasurer: Harvey Kapnick, Chairman, Arthur Andersen & Company

Chairman of the Executive Committee: Philip M. Klutznick, Chairman of the Executive Committee, Urban Investment and Development Company

A. Robert Abboud, Vice-Chairman, First National Bank of Chicago

Joseph A. Burnham, President, Marshall Field Company

John Cardinal Cody, Archbishop, Archdiocese of Chicago

James C. Downs Jr., Chairman of the Board, Real Estate Research Corporation

Robert M. Drevs, Chairman, Peoples Gas, Light & Coke Company

E. Stanley Enlund, Chairman of the Board, First Federal Savings and Loan Association of Chicago

Robert C. Gunness, President, Standard Oil Company (Indiana)

William E. Hartmann, Partner, Skidmore, Owings & Merrill

Ben W. Heineman, President, Northwest Industries, Inc.

George E. Johnson, President, Johnson Products Company, Inc.

Ferd Kramer, Chairman, Draper & Kramer

William A. Lee, President, Chicago Federation of Labor and Industrial Union Council

Louis Martin, President, Sengstacke Newspapers; Editorial Director, *Chicago Defender*

Patrick L. O'Malley, Chairman of the Board, Automatic Canteen Company of
America

Carey M. Preston, President, Chicago Urban League; Vice President, Chicago
Board of Education

Mary Ward, Chairman, Bright New City

Charles F. Willson, Vice President and Director of Area Development, Continental
Illinois National Bank

APPENDIX 2

Chicago 21 Corporation (Limited Dividend) Investors

Investor	Investment
Commonwealth Edison Company	$1,000,000
Continental Illinois National Bank	1,000,000
First Federal Savings and Loan Association of Chicago	1,000,000
First National Bank of Chicago	1,000,000
Illinois Bell Telephone Company	1,000,000
Peoples Gas, Light & Coke Company	1,000,000
Sears, Roebuck and Company	1,000,000
Standard Oil Company (Indiana)	1,000,000
Marshall Field Company	600,000
Marcor, Inc.	500,000
Arthur Andersen & Company	300,000
Illinois Central Industries	300,000
Urban Investment and Development Company	300,000
American National Bank and Trust Company of Chicago	250,000
Carson Pirie Scott & Company	250,000
Chicago Title & Trust Company	250,000
Chicago Tribune	250,000
Harris Bankcorp, Inc.	250,000
Inland Steel Company	250,000
International Harvester Company	250,000
Material Service Corporation	250,000
Nortrust Corporation	250,000
Talman Federal Savings and Loan Association of Chicago	250,000

United States Gypsum Company	250,000
Archdiocese of Chicago	200,000
Fleetwood Realty Company	200,000
Johnson Products Company, Inc.	200,000
Ernst & Ernst	150,000
Skidmore, Owings & Merrill	150,000
Draper & Kramer	100,000
Northwest Industries, Inc.	100,000
Wieboldt Industries, Inc.	100,000
Total	$13,950,000

ACKNOWLEDGMENTS

THE BUILDING OF DEARBORN PARK, FROM ITS CONCEPTION TO ITS COMPLETION, stretched over 25 years. The people who created it left meticulous records of those years in the form of minutes of shareholders meetings, board of directors meetings, executive committee meetings, memoranda, personal notes and letters, consultants' reports, and financial statements. I am grateful to Thomas G. Ayers, Philip M. Klutznick, Ferd Kramer, Richard L. Thomas, Kimbal T. Goluska, Frederick C. Ford, Frank Livingston, William N. Larson, Carl B. Bufalini, Norman Elkin, and Glenn Steinberg for giving me permission to use their papers and documents. The book draws heavily on them. Their reminiscences also were invaluable, as were those of dozens of others involved in reviving Chicago's South Loop—architects, city planners, attorneys, community organizers, and developers; and those of the civic leaders, scholars, architects, and planners who observed the process. I am especially grateful to the people of Dearborn Park and Printers Row who spent many hours talking to me about life in the new South Loop. And a loving thank-you to my best friend and favorite traveling companion, Wayne Wille, who edited this manuscript with his usual intelligence and precision.

Unless otherwise indicated, the quotations in this book came from my interviews with these people, as did much of the background information:

Thomas G. Ayers, retired Chairman, Commonwealth Edison Company
Matthew Baio, Chicago Police Department Beat Officer, Dearborn Park
John W. Baird, Chairman, Baird & Warner, Inc.

Miles L. Berger, Vice-Chairman of the Board and Managing Partner, Heitman Financial, Ltd.; former Chairman, Chicago Plan Commission

Laurence Booth, Partner, Booth/Hansen & Associates

Carl B. Bufalini, Executive Director, North Business & Industrial Council

Pastora San Juan Cafferty, Professor, School of Social Services Administration, University of Chicago

Thomas Cokins, Executive Director, Chicago Central Area Committee

James W. Compton, President, Chicago Urban League

Hon. Richard M. Daley, Mayor, City of Chicago

Norman Elkin, former Vice President, Urban Investment and Development Company

Michael Foley, Owner, Printers Row Restaurant

Frederick C. Ford, Vice President of Board, Draper & Kramer

Sheila Garrett, President, Local School Council, South Loop School; President, Concerned Parents of Hilliard Homes

Bertrand Goldberg, Bertrand Goldberg Associates, Inc.

Kimbal T. Goluska, President, The Chicago Consultants Group, Inc.

Bruce J. Graham, Graham & Graham

Jack Guthman, Partner, Shefsky & Froelich, Ltd.

Richard Halpern, retired President, Schal Bovis, Inc.

Paul Hansen, Partner, Booth/Hansen & Associates

Dennis Harder, Development and Planning, Joseph Freed & Associates

Marilyn Hasbrouck, Owner, Prairie Avenue Bookshop

Wilbert Hasbrouck, Partner, Hasbrouck Peterson Zimoch Sirirattumrong

William E. Hartmann, retired Partner, Skidmore, Owings & Merrill

Bette Cerf Hill, President Emeritus, Near South Planning Board

Judith Hoch DeLeon, former Chairman, South Loop School Committee

Elizabeth L. Hollander, Executive Director, Egan Urban Center, DePaul University

Roletha Houston, Manager, The Oaks

Thomas Hynes, Assessor, Cook County, Illinois

Martin S. Jaffe, Associate Professor of Urban Planning and Policy, University of Illinois at Chicago

Valerie Jarrett, former Commissioner of Planning and Development, City of Chicago

Sheldon L. Kantoff, Vice President, Field Properties Management, Parliament Enterprises, Ltd.

Philip M. Klutznick, Chairman, Klutznick Enterprises

Thomas J. Klutznick, President, Thomas J. Klutznick Company

Ferd Kramer, Chairman Emeritus, Draper & Kramer

William N. Larson, Associate Partner, Skidmore, Owings & Merrill

Frank Livingston, Director of Marketing, Draper & Kramer

Greg Longhini, Assistant to the Commissioner, Department of Planning and Development, City of Chicago

Donald G. Lubin, Chairman, Sonnenschein Nath & Rosenthal

Robert L. Lucas, Executive Director, Kenwood Oakland Community Organization

Barbara Lynne, President & Executive Director, Near South Planning Board

Marcia Maras, Chief Deputy Assessor, Cook County, Illinois

James L. Marovitz, Partner, Sidley & Austin

William Martin, Urban Planner, Chicago Central Area Committee

Daniel E. McLean, President, MCL Development Companies

Kenneth Mescher, Finance Director, Tribune Properties, Inc.

Bernard Nath, Partner, Sonnenschein Nath & Rosenthal

Lawrence Okrent, President, Okrent Associates, Inc.

Charles J. Orlebeke, Professor of Urban Planning and Policy, University of Illinois at Chicago

John H. Perkins, retired President, Continental Illinois National Bank

John C. Pettigrew, Principal, Trkla, Pettigrew, Allen & Payne, Inc.

Carey M. Preston, Sales Associate, Rose Nayer Realty

Gerald J. Roper, President and Chief Executive Officer, Chicagoland Chamber of Commerce

Ulrich Sandmeyer, Owner, Sandmeyer's Bookstore

Charles H. Shaw, Chairman, The Shaw Company

Marsha Smith, former Assistant Principal, South Loop School

Joseph Spingola, Chairman, Chicago Zoning Board of Appeals

Glenn Steinberg, Urban Planner and former Pre-Development Coordinator, Urban Investment and Development Company

Doreen Thomas, Manager, Blackie's

Richard L. Thomas, retired Chairman, First Chicago Corporation

Arnold Weber, Chancellor, Northwestern University; President, Civic Committee of the Commercial Club of Chicago

Daniel Weinbach, Principal, Daniel Weinbach & Partners, Ltd.

Bill White, Owner, Kasey's Tavern

Wim Wiewel, Dean, College of Urban Planning and Public Affairs, University of Illinois at Chicago

Charles F. Willson, former Director of Area Development, Continental Illinois National Bank

Craig Wolf, Department of Transportation, City of Chicago
Shirley Woodard, Teacher, South Loop School and Faculty Representative,
    Local School Council, South Loop School

South Loop Residents:

Jeanne Barry

Dorothy Boulton

Richard Boulton

Greg Buseman

Terri Buseman

Patricia Carlson

Stephen C. Carlson

Noreen Donovan

Timothy A. Donovan

Joseph Ebster

Theresa Ebster

Kathleen Falcona

Samuel F. Falcona

Sue Ann Fishbein

Matthew Franciskovic

Noelle Gaffney

Jeannette Goluska

Robert Grisham

Valerie Grisham

Genell Harris

Gail Inskip

Vera Klement

Dennis McClendon

Linda Middleton

Amy Moery

John A. Moery

Kathryn Moery

Catherine Mugnolo

Sharon Thomas Parrott

Ruth Pomaranc

Frank Readus

Sandra Reberski

David K. Robson

Marilyn Robson

Carol Roper

Gary M. Ropski

Mary Schaafsma

Barbara Schleck

Maureen Schuneman

Susan Sidun

Carol Sullivan

Aubrey Thompson

Susan Weed

Ruth Wuorenma

Lawrence Young

Lynda Young

NOTES

The following are abbreviations of frequently used sources.

TA	Thomas G. Ayers	CDN	*Chicago Daily News*
PK	Philip M. Klutznick	CS-T	*Chicago Sun-Times*
FK	Ferd Kramer	CT	*Chicago Tribune*
JP	John H. Perkins	NYT	*The New York Times*
CW	Charles F. Willson		

Page

1. "It Is the Borderland of Hell"

5   "our biggest concern": "Downtown or Ghosttown: What's with the Loop?" *CDN*, Dec. 1, 1973.
     "I'll tell you what's wrong": Ibid.

9   "dirtiest, vilest, most-rickety": Duis and Holt, "The South Loop Legacy," *Chicago*. p. 238.
     "beastly sensuality": *CT*, Apr. 1957.
     "attracted houses of prostitution": Duis and Holt, *Chicago*. p. 240.
     "Vice has thrown off its masks": Ibid.

10   "flophouses, taverns, stumbling": Cafferty and McCready, "The Process of Economic Development in Chicago: The Heritage of Involvement."

2. "The First Step . . . a Meeting with the Mayor"

12   "The huge scale": Real Estate Research Corp., "The South Loop Area," Jan. 20, 1971.
     "tremendous cooperative effort": Ibid.

13   "the economic and social": Downs letter to TA, Mar. 16, 1971.

14   Downs was absolutely right: PK memo to TA, Dec. 1, 1971.

15   Klutznick volunteered: Ibid.

16   "Such an endeavor": Graham letter to Daley, Feb. 17, 1972.

213

17   With the help of his staff: PK to TA, et al., May 18, 1972.
18   "to determine a workable basis": PK letter to Hill, May 24, 1972.
      "As you know": PK memo to JP, Oct. 27, 1972.
19   "it would be an attractive transaction": Ibid.
22   Ten superblocks: "Plan Told to Rejuvenate Downtown," *CT*, Nov. 10, 1972.
23   They met with John Hanifin: PK memo to TA, et al., July 25, 1972.
      They met next: PK memo to TA, et al., Aug. 23, 1972.
      "South Loop Scenario": Draft plan by Urban Investment and Development Co.,
          Sept. 6, 1972.
24   He reported that: Downs letter to PK, et al., Oct. 9, 1972.
25   discussed his theories: "Plan Told to Rejuvenate Downtown," *CT*, Nov. 10, 1972.

3. Papa Bear Searches for a Den

26   They hadn't yet heard: JP memo to CW and PK, Jan. 23, 1973.
27   A few days later: Downs letter to JP, Feb. 6, 1973.
28   Next, Phil Klutznick met: PK memo to TA, et al., Mar. 14, 1973.
      news reports of the luncheon: "Domed Chicago Arena Near Downtown Loop Is Under
          Discussion," *The Wall Street Journal*, Mar. 21, 1973; "New Huddle on Sports
          Stadium Here," *CDN*, Mar. 21, 1973.
      Later, at a meeting: PK letter to Allen Hartman and TA, et al., Apr. 16, 1973.
29   "apologized profusely": PK memo to TA and JP, Mar. 12, 1973.
      The mayor surprised him: JP memo to CW, Apr. 17, 1973.
30   "He has in mind": JP memo to PK, Apr. 17, 1973.
      "100,000 residents in futuristic": "New Downtown Plan!" *CS-T*, May 15, 1973.
      "signals a renaissance": "New Plan for Central City Unveiled," *CT*, June 15, 1973.
      "pledge the creation": Ibid.
      Downtown, said Hartmann: "Vast Housing in Downtown Plan," *CS-T*, June 15, 1974.
      "may well be the most": "How 'New Chicago' Plan Grew," *CDN*, June 14, 1973.
      A lot of plans were gathering: Editorial, "An Uplift for Downtown," *CDN*, June 16, 1973.
31   "He told me": PK memo to TA and JP, May 12, 1973.
32   "What kind of priest are you?": "Father Dubi: A Man of Action," *CDN*, May 2, 1973.
33   "that unthinking people": PK memo to TA, et al., Mar. 12, 1973.
      "My dear Dick": PK letter to Daley, Nov. 5, 1973.
      "Dear Mr. Klutznick": Daley letter to PK, Dec. 9, 1973.
35   "produce acceptable operating profits": Duke, "Feasibility Study of a Domed Stadium in
          Chicago."

4. "A Small Town Establishment"

39   She noted that most: Cafferty and McCready, "The Process of Economic Development
          in Chicago: The Heritage of Involvement."
41   "The undersigned subscriber": "Chicago 21 Corporation (Limited Dividend) Subscrip-
          tion Agreement."
42   The plan described: CW, "South Loop New Town: A Proposal," Sept. 1973.
      Illinois Bell was slower: CW memo to TA, et al., Oct. 22, 1974.
44   "I am enthusiastic": Cardinal Cody letter to TA, Nov. 29, 1973.
45   Phil Klutznick attended: William Larson memo to William Hartmann and Graham,
          Jan. 30, 1974.

47 "most exciting": "Form Private Corporation for S. Loop 'Superplan,'" *CS-T*, Apr. 5, 1974.
    "if the heart of the city": "Firm Is Formed to Build S. Loop," *CT*, Apr. 5, 1974.

5. "An Awful Lot of Aggravation"

49 "The new community": Miller, "South Loop New Town," *Inland Architect*, p. 14.
    The *Chicago Tribune* published: Editorial, "Chicago 21 is Under Way," *CT*, Apr. 6, 1974.
    but the *Chicago Sun-Times*: Editorial, "Planning for Supercity," *CS-T*, Apr. 10, 1974.
    Given the scarcity: TRUST, "Impact of a South Loop New Town," June 1, 1976.

50 Phil Klutznick's immediate reaction: PK letter to Howard M. Landau, Sept. 5, 1974.
    Klutznick complained to James Hoge: PK letter to Hoge and Dedmon, Apr. 16, 1974.
    "One is compelled to ask": PK letter to FK, June 11, 1976.

51 "Fortress Loop": "Case of Corporate Myopia," *CS-T*, Jan. 26, 1975.
    Phil Klutznick shot back: PK letter to Babcock, Jan. 29, 1975.

52 "It is supposed to be": Miller, "South Loop New Town," *Inland Architect*, p. 14.
    It would be 10 times: Rubel, "Position Paper on Chicago 21 Plan," Aug. 19, 1974.

53 "I believe the stadium": Halas letter to Daley, Apr. 15, 1974.
    "I told him that in light": PK memo to TA, et al., June 26, 1974.

54 Goldberg wrote to Tom Ayers: Goldberg letter to TA, May 13, 1974.

55 John Perkins sounded out Lew Hill: JP memo to CW and PK, May 22, 1974.
    "We are working with City officials": TA letter to Goldberg, May 29, 1974.
    "I told him there were some people": PK memo to TA and JP, June 5, 1974.

56 "less than scintillating": Minutes, Executive Committee Meeting, Chicago 21 Corp.,
        Nov. 12, 1974.

57 Hill passed along: JP memo to PK, Nov. 21, 1974.
    "I do think we need": PK memo to JP, Nov. 29, 1974.
    George Halas was also fed up: "Bears Plan Move to Arlington Heights Stadium," *CT*,
        Apr. 12, 1975.
    Daley was livid: "Daley Says He'll Disown Bears If They Make Move," *CT*, Apr. 16, 1975.

58 "the best working meeting": PK memo to TA, et al., May 1, 1975.
    "There is just a slight": Halas letter to Lubin, July 26, 1975.

6. Ferd and Phil, Together Again

63 "meet a social need": PK memo to TA, et al., July 7, 1976.

64 "Refer to the development": Emily Edwards letter to PK, July 26, 1974.
    A marketing survey: Survey by Leo Shapiro & Associates, July 30, 1974.

66 The city's South Loop guidelines: City of Chicago, Dept. of Development and Planning,
        "South Loop New Town."

68 Traffic and security consultants: Dearborn Park Corp., "Developer Response to Environ-
        mental Security Report."
    "Whether or not": CW memo to JP, Jan. 19, 1976.

69 Willson also liked: Ibid.
    "if at all possible": CW memo to PK, Jan. 30, 1976.
    "an American tipping point": Chicago Economic Development Corp., "Dearborn Park
        Residential Market Study."

70 "We have now been involved": FK letter, unsent, to Bufalini, June 15, 1976.

71 He dazzled Chicago 21 shareholders: Hannon, "Results of Cooperative Planning."

71 Offer a choice to parents: Educational Planning Associates, "Community School
Downtown."

72 "felt somehow there was": JP memo to PK, Feb. 17, 1976.
"too much input from experts": PK memo to TA, et al., Dec. 9, 1976.

73 "a large degree of pro bono": Minutes, Annual Meeting, Board of Directors and shareholders, Chicago 21 Corp., Dec. 16, 1976.

7. "I Am at My Wit's End"

76 "I have your unsigned": PK letter to George Darrell, Jan. 11, 1977.
"If this decision is not": FK letter to TA, Jan. 31, 1977.
"the numerous occasions": FK letter to PK, Jan. 31, 1977.

77 "My dear Ferd": PK letter to FK, Feb. 14, 1977.

80 "managed integration": PK memo with letter to Raymond Wieboldt, Mar. 31, 1977.
"this corporation will take": "Affirmative Action Policy Statement," Dearborn Park Corp.
Executive Committee Resolution, Apr. 6, 1977.

81 The futuristic city heralded: "Reveal Details of South Loop Housing Plan," *CDN*,
May 2, 1977.

82 "I don't understand": "Dearborn Park Foes Lose Round 1," *CDN*, June 24, 1977.
"Anyone who listens": Ibid.
"the first step": Ibid.

83 "350,000 white and black": Dearborn Park Corp., "Application of Dearborn Park Corporation for a Planned Unit Development."
Most of it was a careful: Emmons, "Dearborn Park/South Loop New Town."

84 "currently contains no plans": "Break Ground for Dearborn," *Chicago Defender*,
July 14, 1977.
"the most modern and revolutionary": "Plan Unit Rejects River City Proposal," *CDN*,
Aug. 11, 1977.
Lew Hill said city guidelines: Hill, "Report to the Chicago Plan Commission."

85 it might be timely: PK letter to Raymond Wieboldt, July 19, 1977.
Late in November: Michael H. Bailey letter to JP, Nov. 30, 1977; Steven G. Nystrom
letter to A. Robert Abboud, Nov. 19, 1977.

8. A Fresh Start, and Fresh Snow

89 "The brick color": Graham letter to FK, Apr. 17, 1979.

91 "The following statements concern": Hill letter to Guthman, Mar. 2, 1978.

92 "in no way are we": JP letter to Abboud, Apr. 19, 1978.

93 A committee resolution told Carter: Minutes, Executive Committee, Dearborn Park
Corp., Mar. 14, 1978.
"Blacks 'shut out'": "Blacks 'Shut Out' in Dearborn Project," *Chicago Defender*,
Apr. 20, 1978.
"What is the obligation": Editorial, "Dearborn Park Project," *Chicago Defender*,
May 10, 1978.

95 A letter from: Material Service letter to Kantoff, July 10, 1978.

96 Kramer and Baird proposed: FK and Baird letter to Robert Merriam at Urban Investment, Aug. 23, 1976.
"Frankly, the more": PK memo to Merriam, Aug. 27, 1976.

96   the two made downward: FK and Baird letter to Edward Lawrence at Urban, Sept. 12, 1977.
      In a three-page: PK memo to Wieboldt, Sept. 20, 1977.

9. Neighbors Across a Mud Sea

103   "not exactly esthetically": "Dearborn Park Sales Soar Despite Housing Doldrums," *CT*,
      Nov. 1, 1979.
104   An urgent message: Wolak memo to FK, Aug. 3, 1979.
106   "There were rats": "South Loop 'Pioneers' Conquer a Hostile Land," *CT*, Mar. 9, 1982.
      "I thought, this is": "Dearborn Park: Satisfaction Blossoms Behind Grim Facade," *Crain's
      Chicago Business*, May 11, 1981.
110   A year after: Ury survey, Sept. 24, 1981.
112   "Since the project is located": Project Reference File, Urban Land Institute; Vol. 10,
      No. 18, Oct. 1980.
      "a patchwork": "New Town Downtown: At Last It's on the Way," *CDN*, Apr. 30, 1977.

10. "The Whole Street Was Just Empty"

121   "There I was": "Long-Dormant S. Loop Set to Bloom," *Crain's Chicago Business*,
      Jan. 3, 1983.
125   By 1989 all four: Edward Hinsberger, U.S. Dept. of Housing and Urban Development,
      letter to author, May 17, 1996.

11. "Beating the Sidewalks" to Stay Alive

131   a consulting firm, which uncovered: Report by Wiss, Janney, Elstner & Assoc.,
      June 15, 1982.
136   It reviewed the early: TA, PK, and FK letter to shareholders, Feb. 14, 1984.
139   "wild vernacular": Bach and Wolfson, *Chicago on Foot*, pp. 116–117.

12. "Our Neighborhood Lost Its School"

141   "Chicago's only community": "S. Loop's Yuppies Toast Their Latest 'In' Thing: Neighbor-
      hood School," *CT*, July 31, 1986.
143   Ruth Love responded: Love letter to Hoch, June 28, 1982.
      "It is clear to me": Daley letter to Love, Apr. 5, 1983.
      "I have recommended": Love letter to Hoch, May 24, 1984.
145   "This school will flow": "S. Loop's Yuppies Toast Their Latest 'In' Thing: Neighborhood
      School," *CT*, July 31, 1986.
      It was an awful predicament: "New School Becoming a Source of Class Conflict," *CT*,
      May 3, 1987.
146   "Stress the importance": Hoch, "South Loop Parents Position Paper," May 27, 1987.
      "I understand that you want": "Urban Class Problem Stirs Chicago Debate," *NYT*,
      Mar. 25, 1987.
      which placed South Loop School: Kozol, *Savage Inequalities*, p. 62.
147   "The Chicago Public School system": *Chicago Schools: "Worst in America"*, booklet
      reprinting *CT* series, May 1988, p. 35.
148   "Who's going to get": Padgett, "War Between the Classes," *Newsweek*, May 1, 1989, p. 64.
      Their assumption that their: "A City's Unwelcome Lesson About Schools and Class,"
      NYT, Apr. 2, 1989.

148 "You've got to sympathize": "Urban Class Problem Stirs Chicago Debate," *NYT*,
        Mar. 25, 1987.
    They wanted to attract: "New School Becoming a Source of Class Conflict," *CT*,
        May 3, 1987.
149 "This hasn't been easy": "Urban Class Problem Stirs Chicago Debate," *NYT*, Mar. 25, 1987.
    "sacrificed to get me away": "New School Becoming a Source of Class Conflict," *CT*,
        May 3, 1987.
    "They expect the Board": "No Agreement on Who Gets to Attend New S. Loop School,"
        CT, May 14, 1987.
150 the most complicated: Editorial, "Dearborn Dispute Ends Uneasily," *CT*, June 3, 1987.
152 "reminiscent of the Jim Crow": "Unity Slated for Split School," *CT*, June 21, 1990.
    "They have a right": "One School, Different Worlds," *CT*, Aug. 13, 1990.
    "The children of Hilliard": Ibid.

13. Winding Down, Closing Out
159 "You might tell her": PK note to FK, July 2, 1996.
162 "appeared to be surprised": PK memo to FK and TA, Oct. 29, 1986.
    "she is putting together": PK note to FK, Oct. 31, 1986.

14. "How Could I Ever Leave This Place?"
176 "Starched and contradictory": "A Model for Tomorrow's City?" *CT*, Aug. 13, 1995.
177 "restricted auto access": Jablon letter to author, Dec. 1, 1994.
    "He told her": Hawk Detective and Investigating Service, Report of Incident,
        Oct. 27, 1982.

15. "Dearborn Park Was the Key"
185 "far more like": "Loop Means Business, Shopping—and Now Residents," *CT*,
        Sept. 13, 1995.
186 with $1.4 billion: Center for Urban Affairs and Policy Research, "Downtown Develop-
        ment, Chicago 1979–1984"; "1985–1986." City of Chicago, Department of Planning,
        "Downtown Development, Chicago 1987–1990"; "1989–1992."
    In real estate taxes alone: Data compiled for author by Cook County Assessor Thomas
        C. Hynes and Cook County Chief Deputy Assessor Marcia Maras, Oct. 16, 1995.
188 the addition of about: "Loop Still Has Pull Even as City Jobs Slip," *CT*, Apr. 12, 1995.
189 In 1993, the equalized: Trkla, Pettigrew, Allen & Payne, "Near South Redevelopment
        Project Area."
190 "new kind of park": "A Plan for the People," *CT*, Sept. 9, 1996.
192 Another, more ambitious alternative: Educational Planning Associates, "Community
        School Downtown."
    "When this . . . was built": Daley talk to South Loop Neighbors Association meeting,
        Oct. 10, 1995.
196 "I am afraid": PK letter to TA and FK, Jan. 30, 1984.
197 "a can of worms": James Sutherland, Minneapolis Community Development Agency,
        interview with author, Oct. 16, 1995.
198 Milwaukee offered one model: "Milwaukee, the City That Works—with Developers,"
        CT, Nov. 15, 1987; Rabinowitz, "Highway to Housing," *Urban Land*, pp. 32–33.

SELECTED BIBLIOGRAPHY

Reports

Cafferty, Pastora San Juan, and William C. McCready. "The Process of Economic Development in Chicago: The Heritage of Involvement." May 1981. Report prepared for publication in *American Cities: Seven Case Studies*. Committee for Economic Development,Washington, D.C., 1982.

Center for Urban Affairs and Policy Research, Northwestern University. "Downtown Development. Chicago 1979–1984." 1983.

Center for Urban Affairs and Policy Research, Northwestern University; and City of Chicago Department of Planning."Downtown Development. Chicago 1985–1986." 1985.

Chicago Board of Education. "1993 School Report Card." South Loop School, City of Chicago School District 299. 1994.

Chicago Central Area Committee and City of Chicago Department of Development and Planning. "The Chicago 21 Plan." Sept. 1973.

Chicago Economic Development Corporation. "Dearborn Park Residential Market Study." Oct. 1976.

Chicago Panel on School Policy. "Chicago Public Schools Data Book, School Year 1992–1993." July 1994.

———. "Chicago Public School Data Book, School Year 1993–1994." 1995.

Chicago Public Schools, Department of Research, Evaluation and Planning. "Racial/Ethnic Survey: Students. As of September 28, 1990." Dec. 1990.

———. "Racial/Ethnic Survey: Students. As of September 30, 1991." Dec. 1991.

———. "Racial/Ethnic Survey: Students. As of September 30, 1992." Dec. 1992.

———. "Racial/Ethnic Survey: Students. As of October 29, 1993." Mar. 1994.

219

Chicago 21 Corporation. "South Loop New Town." 1974.

City of Chicago, Department of Development and Planning. "South Loop New Town: Guidelines for Development." Aug. 19, 1975.

City of Chicago, Department of Planning. "Downtown Development. Chicago 1987–1990." 1989.

———. "Downtown Development. Chicago 1989–1992." 1991.

Dearborn Park Corporation. "Application of Dearborn Park Corporation for a Planned Unit Development." Submitted to Chicago Plan Commission. June 23, 1977.

———. "Dearborn Park Plan." Dec. 16, 1976.

———. "Dearborn Park Pro-Forma." Dec. 16, 1976.

———. "Developer Response to Environmental Security Report for South Loop New Town." Submitted to City of Chicago Department of Development and Planning, 1977.

Duke, Keith E. "Feasibility Study of a Domed Stadium in Chicago." Stanford Research Institute, Menlo Park, Calif. Sept. 1973.

Educational Planning Associates, Inc. "Community School Downtown: A Community Education System for South Loop New Town." Boston. 1974.

Emmons, David. "Dearborn Park/South Loop New Town: A Project in the Chicago 21 Plan." Preliminary report by Citizens Information Service of Illinois. Jan. 1977.

Hannon, Joseph P., General Superintendent of Schools, City of Chicago. "Results of Cooperative Planning: The Educational Development of South Loop." Discussion draft, not for release. Mar. 31, 1976.

Hill, Lewis W., Commissioner of Development and Planning, City of Chicago. "Report to the Chicago Plan Commission." Aug. 11, 1977.

Real Estate Research Corporation. "Agreement for Consulting Services Concerning the South Loop Area of Chicago." Mar. 16, 1971.

———. "The South Loop Area." Jan. 20, 1971.

Rubel, Dorothy, former Executive Director, Metropolitan Housing and Planning Council, Chicago. "Position Paper on Chicago 21 Plan." Aug. 19, 1974.

Trkla, Pettigrew, Allen & Payne. "Near South Redevelopment Project Area. Tax Increment Financing Redevelopment Project and Plan." May 1994.

ULI-The Urban Land Institute. Project Reference File. Vol. 10, No. 18. 4th Quarter 1980.

U.S. Department of Housing and Urban Development. "Transmittal of Fiscal Year (FY) 1996 Public Housing/Section 8 Income Limits." Notice PDR-95–05. Dec. 14, 1995.

Books

Bach, Ira J., and Susan Wolfson. *Chicago on Foot: Walking Tours of Chicago's Architecture*, 5th ed. Chicago: Chicago Review Press, 1994.

———. *A Guide to Chicago's Train Stations, Present and Past*. Athens, Ohio: Ohio University Press; Swallow Press, 1986.

Berger, Miles L. *They Built Chicago: Entrepreneurs Who Shaped a Great City's Architecture*. Chicago: Bonus Books, 1992.

Byrne, Jane. *My Chicago*. New York: W. W. Norton & Co., 1992.

Chicago Tribune. Chicago Schools: "Worst in America". Chicago: *Chicago Tribune*, 1988. Reprint of newspaper series.

Holt, Glen E., and Dominic A. Pacyga. *Chicago: A Historical Guide to the Neighborhoods. The Loop and South Side*. Chicago: Chicago Historical Society, 1979.

Klutznick, Philip M., with Sydney Hyman. *Angles of Vision: A Memoir of My Lives*. Chicago: Ivan R. Dee, 1991.

Kozol, Jonathan. *Savage Inequalities. Children in America's Schools*. New York: Crown Publishers, 1991. Reprint, New York: HarperCollins Publishers, 1992.

Royko, Mike. *Boss: Richard J. Daley of Chicago*. New York: E. P. Dutton & Co. 1971.

Schulze, Franz, and Kevin Harrington, editors. *Chicago's Famous Buildings*, 4th ed. Chicago: The University of Chicago Press, 1993.

Sinkevitch, Alice, editor. *AIA Guide to Chicago*. New York: Harcourt Brace & Co., 1993.

Suttles, Gerald D. *The Man-Made City: The Land-Use Confidence Game in Chicago*. Chicago: The University of Chicago Press, 1990.

Wendt, Lloyd, and Herman Kogan. *Lords of the Levee: The Story of Bathhouse John and Hinky Dink*. New York: Garden City Publishing Co., 1944.

Magazine Articles

Carlson, Cynthia J., and Robert J. Duffy. "Cincinnati Takes Stock of Its Vacant Land." *Planning*, Mar. 1985.

Duis, Perry R., and Glen E. Holt. "The South Loop Legacy." *Chicago*, Sept. 1978.

Engelen, Rodney E. "Cedar-Riverside: A Case Study." *Practicing Planner*, Apr. 1976.

Miller, Nory. "Dearborn Park: What's in a Name—and What Isn't." *Inland Architect*, June 1977.

———. "South Loop New Town: Can It Make It?" *Inland Architect*, Oct. 1974.

Neil, Andrew. "The City That Survives." *The Economist*, Mar. 29, 1980.

Padgett, Tim. "War Between the Classes." *Newsweek*, May 1, 1989.

Rabinowitz, Harvey. "Highway to Housing: Milwaukee's East Pointe Commons." *Urban Land*, June 1994.

Newspapers

Various issues of *Chicago Daily News*, *Chicago Defender*, *Chicago Sun-Times*, *Chicago Tribune*, *Crain's Chicago Business*, *Near West Gazette*, *The New York Times*, and *The Wall Street Journal*.

Other Materials

Correspondence, memoranda, and other materials of Ferd Kramer.

Correspondence, memoranda, and other materials of Philip M. Klutznick.

Correspondence, memoranda, and other materials of Thomas G. Ayers.

Correspondence, memoranda, sales brochures, and other materials of Chicago 21 Corporation/Dearborn Park Corporation.

Files of Judith Hoch DeLeon.

Letter from Edward Hinsberger, Director, Multifamily Housing Division, Illinois State Office, U.S. Department of Housing and Urban Development, May 17, 1996.

Letter from Ronald C. Jablon, District Commander, First District, Chicago Police Department, Dec. 1, 1994.

Minutes of Chicago 21 Corporation, 1974–1977.

Minutes of Dearborn Park Corporation and of the Executive Committee, 1977–1994.

News releases of Dearborn Park Corporation and the City of Chicago Department of Housing.

Reports by the Near South Planning Board.

Reports from the 1990 United States Census.

INDEX

LOIS WILLE was born in Chicago and attended the Medill School of Journalism at Northwestern University. She reported urban issues for the *Chicago Daily News,* where her series of articles on health care for indigent women won the Pulitzer Prize for public service in 1963. She was awarded the Pulitzer Prize for editorial writing in 1989, when she was editorial page editor of the *Chicago Tribune.* She is the author of *Forever Open, Clear and Free: The Struggle for Chicago's Lakefront.* She and her husband, Wayne, lived for many years on Chicago's Near South Side and Near West Side. They now reside in Radford, Virginia.